ON A HINGE OF HISTORY

IVAN L. HEAD

ON A HINGE OF HISTORY

The Mutual Vulnerability of South and North

Published in association with the
International Development Research Centre

UNIVERSITY OF TORONTO PRESS
Toronto Buffalo London

© International Development Research Centre 1991
Toronto Buffalo London
Printed in Canada
First printed in cloth 1991
Reprinted in paper 1992

ISBN 0-8020-2766-0
ISBN 0-8020-7364-6 pb

Printed on acid-free paper

Canadian Cataloguing in Publication Data

Head, Ivan, 1930–
On a hinge of history

Includes index.
ISBN 0-8020-2766-0 cl
ISBN 08020-7364-6 pb

1. North and south. 2. International economic
relations – History. 3. Canada – Relations –
Developing countries. 4. Developing countries –
Relations – Canada. 5. World politics. I. Title.

HC59.7.H42 1991   337   C91-093533-5

Back cover photo: Ebenezer George
Cover design: Elaine Cohen

For Ann

Whereas it has long been known and declared that the poor
have no right to the property of the rich, I wish it also to be known
and declared that the rich have no right to the
property of the poor.

John Ruskin
Unto This Last
Essay iii

Contents

VII
Time Past / Time Now 191

Acknowledgments

In 1988, the Board of Governors of the International Development Research Centre gave approval to a series of studies linked together by the unifying theme of global disequilibria and the resulting mutuality of vulnerability of societies in both the industrialized and the developing regions of the world. Leading Canadian scholars in several relevant disciplines were invited to join the investigation. Each pursued independent research which was shared and evaluated periodically in seminar sessions. This volume is the first published result of that activity. Several others are expected to follow shortly, each dedicated to a specific sector.

The participants in this process are entitled to much of the credit for whatever value is found in this volume, though final responsibility for errors rests with me. I am grateful to them for their shared belief in the importance of this thesis of holism and for the enthusiastic support and advice they offered to me throughout the exercise. Without their professional competence, their fresh insights, and their broad experience, this essay would not have been possible. From the Canadian academic community there were involved: Daniel Birch, University of British Columbia; Robert Cox, York University; Arthur Hanson, Dalhousie University; Albert Legault, Laval University; Paul Lin, Vancouver; John Loxley, University of Manitoba; Jorge Nef, University of Guelph; Alan Simmons, York University; Alan Thomas, Ontario Institute for Studies in Education; and Alastair Taylor, Queen's University (emeritus). From IDRC, valuable contributions were made by Bev Chataway, David Nostbakken, Alan Rix, and Claire Thompson, all of whom either commented on successive texts or verified sources and citations. I am particularly grateful for the contributions throughout the life of the project made by IDRC colleagues Paz Buttedahl in her capacity of project manager, and Edward Israel as research intern. The immense contribution and extraordinary patience of Ann Carson who was responsible for all secretarial work deserve the kind of praise that only other authors are able fully to appreciate. Finally the enthusiasm and encouragement of Ian Montagnes of the University of Toronto Press is much appreciated.

Of the following material, portions of chapter I are drawn from my article 'South–North Dangers,' published in the Summer 1989 issue of *Foreign Affairs*.

Ivan L. Head
Ottawa, December 1990

Preface

Ancient Chinese cartographers employed five cardinal points on their maps: North, East, South, West, and the position where the observer stood. The first four were always relative to the fifth.

Notwithstanding this wise cartographic principle, men and women have all too often failed to account for their bias as observers as they gazed about them. In the age before the printing press, one's knowledge was limited to one's immediate environs; terrain and events more distant than a day's ride were generally unknown and certainly regarded as not proximate. Today, our television culture prompts us to assume that we are aware of all activities everywhere, that our knowledge is adequate, relevant, and balanced; to those events not telecast we are indifferent, for by definition they must be without merit.

In these circumstances, there is as much peril in twentieth-century arrogance as there was in fifteenth-century ignorance. Each leads the observer to assume an objectivity that is illusory. Each encourages vulnerability to the unknown and the unexpected.

This book seeks to penetrate one of history's most enduring illusions, one that arises out of ignorance and arrogance: the belief that the societies of the North (the industrialized countries) are intrinsically superior to the societies of the South (the 'developing' countries); that the North is inherently invulnerable to events in the South. It does so from the perspective, but not exclusively so, of Canada. The book will not be attractive to those who argue that privilege is a justifiable consequence of hard work and self-discipline. Nor will it enchant those who predict either that orderliness in international relations inevitably must prevail, or that history and beyond is a normative product of self-interest.

For half a century we in the North have been so preoccupied with our perception of menace from the Soviet Union and its communist allies that we have failed to notice the profound changes that have taken place all around us. Our dedication to military security, our desire for ever more comfortable lifestyles, our indifference to the immensely increased populations in the South, have in that period combined to threaten our environmental and social stability. These issues, much more than the possibility of nuclear war, now challenge the survival of the human species. Fortunately, the easing of East–West tensions and the release of energies and resources that that promises give to us the opportunity to shift our attention to these problems that may be of greater dimension, but that are nevertheless possible to solve, or at least to reduce. These problems arise in largest part from poverty that can be eased, and from an inequitable distribution of resources and political power that can be made more balanced, just as it should – and must – be balanced within Canada between those of aboriginal origin and those not.

In the final analysis, then, this is a book about ethics: ethics as an inherent human characteristic, as a contributor to the primacy of human dignity; ethics as the obligation of one generation to the next; ethics as a survival tool. It is not a doomsday message, however. It is offered, rather, as an end-of-millennium benediction.

ON A HINGE OF HISTORY

Introduction

Four of every five persons on this planet dwell today in one or other of the 'developing' countries, those hundred or so states whose economies are immature or unbalanced and whose inhabitants, for the most part, exist in conditions of wretched poverty and − much more ominous for the rest of us − share a desperate absence of hope for improvement. These are the countries of the 'South,' distant from the industrialized states of the 'North.'

Distant, tropical, *different*, those countries, nevertheless, have been linked to Canada for centuries. This linkage has not been in a colonial relationship, as it was with many of them during Europe's imperial period. Nor has it been of a kind approaching the episodic and involuntary inflow of values and interests imposed upon them by the military might of succeeding United States administrations. And it has not at all been like the ideological evangelism of the Soviet Union and its disciples who exported Kalishnokovs and communism with equal grimness.

The Canadian linkages with the countries of the South have been much less dramatic than any of these models, and certainly less threatening. They have been so lacking in visibility as to have escaped the awareness of most observers, Canadians included. That the links exist and the benefits from them flow in both directions is nevertheless part of the Canadian fabric. Much more important, the interdependencies that have been created are a microcosm of the vulnerabilities that now beset all nations in both North and South as they face one another.

The Canadian Pacific Railway was built by labourers brought from China for the purpose. The great timber industry, which began the industrialization of central Canada, was stimulated by a demand for forest products to build the sailing ships that projected and protected Britain's far-flung empire. Canada's first offshore experiences as capital exporter and technology vendor were in South America, where power plants, transmission lines, and public utilities were installed by Canadian engineers in the early years of this century. Long before that, the economy of Atlantic Canada depended on a triangular trade with New England and the islands of the Caribbean. Missionaries from Quebec have been extending 'salvation' and social services to parts of sub-Saharan Africa since long before Confederation. In the north of that continent, the British Expeditionary Force en route to Khartoum to relieve General 'Chinese' Gordon relied on Canadian voyageurs to navigate the heavy transport barges through the hazardous rapids of the Upper Nile.

In the past half-century, human contacts have multiplied by many millions. Tens of thousands of Canadian servicemen were exposed to action in North Africa, the Pacific, and Asia during the Second World War, in Korea thereafter, and in subsequent peacekeeping missions in the Middle East, Indo-China, the Congo, Kashmir, Cyprus, Central America, and Namibia. Many hundreds more were sent to the Persian Gulf. Canadian geologists, oil-drillers, and pipeliners are as at home in Indonesia, Libya, or Mexico as they are on Canada's frontier. Canada's airlines fly regularly into airports regarded as exotic only two decades ago, carrying Canadian tourists by the tens of thousands each year. The face of Canada itself has changed remarkably: some 4.5 per cent of all Canadians (and two-thirds of current immigrants) were born in developing countries. Communities that until relevantly recently had seldom seen persons of other than European origin are now burgeoning with residents from the Caribbean, Latin America, or Asia.

Canadian business has long understood the importance of these regions to Canada. Aluminum smelters in Quebec and British Columbia depend on bauxite from Jamaica and Guyana. The telecommunications and aerospace industries have installed or contributed to communications equipment and networks in Turkey and in Saudi Arabia, and have provided airplanes and services in Nepal, Kenya, and Peru. The great chartered banks are in place in Sao Paulo, Singapore, and Cairo. More than $2 billion worth of food products and agricultural commodities from Canada's farms and fisheries are exported to developing countries each year. The developing countries, for most of the decade of the eighties, purchased more manufactured goods from Canada than did either Japan or all the members of the European Economic Community combined.

Canada opened its first government office in a developing country in 1892 (a trade office, in the West Indies). Today, Canadian diplomatic, trade, and consular representatives are resident in developing countries in every region of the world. Ottawa is host to one of the world's largest resident foreign diplomatic corps: 105 embassies and high commissions, of which 73 are from developing countries. Canada's political independence and territorial integrity depend heavily upon the juridical recognition that these countries extend to it, as well as their adherence to the United Nations Charter.

Yet in a world dominated by the images of the industrialized countries, Canada and Canadians think all too fleetingly, and often in an unfocused fashion, of their vulnerability to the developing countries. Most Canadians would be flabbergasted even by the suggestion that they are other than peripherally affected by what happens in those countries. Vulnerable and dependent, however, we are, and increasingly so.

We are dependent for a wholesome global environment on the abilities of the four billion persons living in those countries to sustain themselves without destroying forests and rangelands, without fouling oceans and atmosphere, without changing the habitats of disease vectors and forcing their migration North.

We are dependent for international peace and stability on the ability of governments – often in newly independent countries – to deliver basic social services, to guarantee some minimum standard of living, to offer a credible alternative to the devotees of gangsterism and terrorism and the advocates of military interventions.

We are dependent for a buoyant world trading system on the economies of dozens of countries that are incapable of participating fully because of constraints, at least partially beyond their control, often instituted by the North in a mistaken endeavour to protect its privileges.

And we are dependent for a life of spiritual meaning and cultural values on a world that consciously chooses not to eliminate the needless deaths each day of thirty-eight thousand children under the age of five from malnutrition and preventable disease, preferring instead to spend the necessary funds on, among other things, weapons.

The economic downturn in the countries of the South during the 1980s led to the loss of 180,000 Canadian jobs. Should economic circumstances in the South not improve during the 1990s, there will be an estimated loss of 139,000 more jobs.

Since 1981, some 160,000 persons from developing countries have claimed refugee status in Canada for either political, economic, or environmental reasons. Those flows will undoubtedly increase unless conditions in the South become less punitive.

In the period 1945–89, 127 wars were fought. All but two of them have been in or between developing countries. Virtually every one of them has had the potential of escalating into a much broader conflict. Developing countries are importing weaponry (most often from enthusiastic exporters in the North) worth U.S. $39 billions per year. At least five of those importing countries have either attained or are close to attaining nuclear explosive capability. Several possess chemical weapons, and at least one is suspected of developing biological weapons. The consequences of that pattern took an ugly but predictable turn in the Persian Gulf in the summer of 1990.

Cocaine, marijuana, and heroin trafficking and possession have become major concerns for Canadian communities and their police forces. Injured by the depressed prices of most legal tropical agricultural commodities, but stimulated by the lucrative rewards for cultivating narcotics crops, farmers in country after country in the South have responded to the clear market signals generated in the North. We pay more for marijuana than peanuts, more for cocaine than coffee.

Far and away the most heinous crime ever committed in Canadian history was the destruction of Air India Flight 182, en route from Toronto to London on 23 June 1985. Two hundred and eighty Canadian citizens and forty-nine other persons died in that tragedy, the product of political turbulence in a developing country. At the time of the Iraqi invasion of Kuwait, there were more than seven hundred Canadians in Kuwait whose exits were blocked.

Inexorably, Canada's present and future is being shaped and influenced by events in the developing countries of the South. These influences are not incidental and they are not spasmodic; they are major and they are persistent. Nevertheless, Canada as a nation has acknowledged adequately neither the importance of the relationships nor the vulnerability of this country to events in the South. We seem unable to recognize that we cannot will ourselves immune to the unavoidable pressures of natural and physical laws, of economic certainties, and of political volatility – much of which now originates in the South. Inevitably, South–North relations will come to occupy a major segment of Canada's conscious attention, of its economic and scientific activity, of its foreign policy. As they will come to dominate the policies and activities of all the industrialized nations.

The only question is whether this recognition and this realignment of priorities will be in time to avoid the environmental catastrophes, the economic turbulence, and the political upheavals now gaining momentum. Our hesitancy to recognize what is real, our conviction that the palliative of foreign aid is an adequate response, our assumption that we in the North can somehow be shielded from events in the South – these are in large part manifestations of arrogance: that we are more capable, more knowledgeable, more experienced; that the nations of the North are suitable role models for those in the South. This kind of arrogance assumes that in this single biosphere, in this planetary economy, in this age of satellite communications and intercontinental ballistic missiles, a drawbridge policy and a withdrawal attitude can be effective. To think in those terms is nonsensical.

Without our fully having realized it, the world has changed and with it the rules of survival. This change is not one of the marginal realignments of power that occur from time to time and to which we have learned to adjust. We are now in the early phase of one of the major shifts of human relations, of a kind that has visited only occasionally in all of recorded history. Combined with this hinge of change and contributing to it is a technological capacity that is eroding our environmental capital base. That same technological capacity coincidentally informs billions of people worldwide that their wretched impoverishment is becoming worse even as the consumption patterns of the wealthy, most of whom reside in the countries of the North, are becoming obscenely excessive. We are required, in short, to overcome the errors of much of our own history.

Perhaps I am too harsh when I attribute our unawareness to arrogance. The preoccupation of the 'West' with the menace of communism has for four decades shielded us from the realities of events not directly linked with East–West tensions, and has persuaded us that our efforts and our resources had to be dedicated overwhelmingly to the defence of the 'free world.' Thus much of our intellectual attention, our industrial production, and our public purse was directed to defence-related purposes. Other issues, no matter how important, were relegated to lower priorities.

When, in a matter of months in 1989, the façade of 'monolithic' communism melted away, there was revealed a landscape bearing little resemblance to what we had for so long believed. We found a Soviet economy so weak that it was incapable of sustaining a major conventional war in Europe; a Warsaw Pact alliance so brittle and unstable that manifestations of popular discontent toppled the political regime in every single Eastern European country in a space of twenty-eight weeks; a support system to revolutionary movements in other parts of the world so tenuous as to be absurd.

As the haze dissipated from forty years of smoke and mirrors and myriad local conflicts, other images came into focus. We saw a world population growing so rapidly that it was destroying the habitat on which it depended for survival; a distribution of wealth so skewed that those living in the most privileged countries enjoyed average standards of living fifty times higher than those in the poorest countries; a gaping maw of poverty that could be identified as the true source of unrest, the principal threat to the survival of humankind; concentrations of weapons and of power that encouraged or permitted ferocious outpourings of resentment in places as diverse as Iraq and Liberia, Sri Lanka and the Republic of South Africa.

Now, surely, we are able in clear conscience to dedicate ourselves fully to the resolution of these challenges. Our technological prowess, our humanitarian instincts, and our financial resources can all now be harnessed to face the global realities that impoverishment is visiting upon the entire human species, and that is made much the worse by inequities and injustices. These latter we have long been convinced were unfortunate necessities. We now realize them to be the determinants of our own future. In the diminishment of threats of nuclear war, in the presence of immense scientific knowledge, and with the identification of new priorities, we can surely begin the corrective measures required.

This volume contains no grand design for wondrous outcomes. Nor is it intended to be a prophet of doom. Its purpose is to lay before the reader the empirical results of sound research that illustrate the extent to which Canada and the countries of the North now are vulnerable to events in the South, the enormity of the disequilibria now influencing our own future, and the range of options open to us to ensure for ourselves and the billions of human beings who live in the South a future of hope.

That we must choose from those options, I have no doubt. That there is an opportunity for unprecedented benefit if we choose promptly and wisely, I am confident. That we shall act with decisiveness and timeliness is the immodest purpose of this book.

I

The Setting

The pageantry of human endeavour reveals little uniformity, and even less continuity. For want of adequate information and common value systems, the interpretations of triumph and despair, of accomplishment and failure, have been wholly disjunctive and culturally enclosed.

The human condition has been the cause and the product of intense local endeavour, of introspection, and of rationalization. Ethnocentricity and xenophobia have been common to the species since it first rose on its hind legs.

Never have these divisions been more evident than between those sectors of the world that we describe so easily, and so inaccurately, as North and South: those communities and nations distinguishable not so much by parallels of latitude on the Mercator Scale as by the standards of living of their populaces.

In recent centuries, circumstances have contributed to an immense disparity of benefit between these divided portions of humankind, and contributed overwhelmingly to a false sense of superiority and invulnerability on the part of those more well-to-do. It is a fundamentally flawed perception of reality. On the eve of the twenty-first century, the ultimate balance of disadvantage appears increasingly to be in the South where burgeoning populations and wretched standards of living are contributing to a series of disequilibria that threaten the well-being of both North and South alike.

◆

The North has discovered the South any number of times over the centuries. It has given it – or parts of it – a variety of names, sometimes in error. It has defined its own interests almost always from its own exclusive perspective, but generally voiced in universal terms. Curiosity, greed, fear, evangelic fervour, the zeal to civilize: the motivation for contact or disengagement has ranged from the loftiest to the most base. Northern observers have generally chosen the more generous interpretation; Southerners much less often shared the same point of view. And always, we in the North have equated 'progress' with our own historical experience, have assumed that 'modernization' is desirable, have interpreted our dominance as 'earned.'

Our records of the odysseys of discovery were written by or about the adventurers, not by those 'discovered.' These chronicles almost always emphasized the exploits of the travellers in preference to the wonders they observed. In the result, schoolchildren of the North have gained some acquaintance with these exploits through the names of the expedition leaders – Alexander, Drake, and Vasco da Gama, for example – but learn all too little of the character or quality of the societies visited. The fact that many of the building blocks of knowledge essential to the North's development came originally from the South is now only vaguely remembered. Accounts of banditry and pillage assumed the tenor of folk tales, lauding the courage or determination of the Europeans who slaughtered and destroyed all that resisted them. They were told in a pejorative vocabulary that affects our thought processes to this day; it is dominated by words such as 'native' or 'pagan' or 'heathen,' even when those described had achieved the brilliance and accomplishment of the heights of the Ming Dynasty, the Inca Empire, the Kingdom of Benin.

The very language of modern technology – mathematics – is a product of Southern genius. The decimal system originated in India. It was assimilated by Arab travellers during the first, golden century of Islam (630–730 AD, a period in Europe described as the Dark Ages) and carried to the Moorish territories in Spain about 750. The essential concept of zero was first derived in China. Without it, none of the great advances in theoretical mathematic and scientific reasoning would have been possible.

Even the most erudite of Northern beneficiaries tended not to acknowledge these sources of technological transfer. Francis Bacon correctly perceived the impact of three major inventions that would revolutionize world history – printing, gunpowder, the compass – but he failed to record that each of these came from the South. Said he, 'these three have changed the appearance and state of the whole world:

first in literature, then in warfare, and lastly in navigation; and innumerable changes have been thence derived, so that no empire, sect, or star, appears to have exercised a greater power and influence on human affairs than these mechanical discoveries.'[1]

Brilliantly employed by practically minded craftsmen in the North, these inventions laid the technological foundation of the Northern states, equipping them to embark on their great navigational and other exploits of discovery and domination. From the late fifteenth century onwards, there has been woven a complex tapestry of political, economic, and social fibres, firmly linking North with South.

Of those three, economic linkages have proved the most enduring, and have taken several forms. Trade has been foremost, generally consisting of commodities from the South (spices, fibres, precious metals and gems, beverages, slaves, sugar, tobacco) and manufactured goods from the North (trinkets, cloth, weaponry, implements, machinery). During the industrial revolution of the nineteenth century, global patterns of trade evolved that continued with little variation until the Russo-Japanese War in 1904–5. The pattern was clear: the seeking of commercial advantage, not vis-à-vis the Southern trading partner, since that was assumed, but rather over Northern competitors. The protection and securing of obtained interests followed: initially, against Northern rivals and adversaries, local ruling classes, and occasional brigands, and later, against religious sects and sometimes entire local populations. From time to time the North settled segments of its surplus population in the South: forcefully, as in America and Australia; with encouragement, as in Canada and parts of Africa; voluntarily, as in Latin America.

Always from North to South, information and methods were passed, principles of governance introduced, technologies transferred – and always with the assumption that the Northern techniques and technologies were superior, were relevant, were transferable, were sustainable. Much more frequently than admitted, these assumptions have proved false.

In North–South terms, the year 1945 was a turning point both in activities and in expectations. Throughout the South, long-festering independence movements burgeoned into prominence. In the North, a sterile bifurcation began to divide East and West. Interests were defined increasingly in terms of security and stability. Not surprisingly, the interpretation of security and the criteria for stability differed between

North and South. Of the human attributes, arrogance has not been absent in either hemisphere. Humility, however, has seldom been present in the North as it looks South. Its absence has weakened the North in image in the past and threatens to weaken it in substance in the future.

Where once the Northern powers established with confidence their outposts of empire and influence in Africa, Asia, Latin America, in islands everywhere; where once they dealt mercilessly with pirates and assertively with adversaries; by the 1960s they gave the impression of fearing the South as a source of commercial rivalry, of contraband narcotics, of illegal immigrants, of debilitating diseases. Again and again, governments of the North came to measure those of the South not on a friendship scale denominated in terms of human dignity and democratic values, but on a barren template of allied commitment and anticommunist rhetoric. In the result, there began a process of withdrawal – North from South, South from North – that such intemperate events as the United States military invasion of Panama only exacerbate. In the North, fortresses of protectionism entice – for example, the transparently ludicrous assumption that this planet can be divided and quarantined effectively against one or more of unwanted goods, diseases, peoples, currencies, or environmental degradation; and that if the quarantine should fail 'surgical strikes' of paratroops and battle tanks will somehow right the balance. In the South, there continue to be heard the strains of the siren song of disengagement, of debt renunciation, of nuclear aspirations, of insensitivity to human rights. Indifference begets reaction.

The circumstances that contribute to these attitudes flow from the fact that Northern governments and peoples, much more than those in the South, reject reality with the time spasms of television programming, all too often embracing the familiar simply because it is, and ignoring the novel no matter how ominous or attractive. The peoples of the North observe the rapid destruction of the world's rain forests, the advance of the deserts, and the explosion of populations either with indifference or with a smugness rooted in their false assumption that *they* act otherwise in *their* hemisphere. In our understandable concern over issues of debt, the penetration by the newly industrialized countries in East Asia of Northern markets, and the maintenance of defensive alliances no matter how outdated, we in the North seem to be unaware of the diminishment of effective government in country after country in the South, of the growing strength and attraction of tribalism, of factionalism, of withdrawal and xenophobia. We encourage military solutions to socio-economic problems and vigorously promote weapons sales and defence industries even as terrorism proliferates and savage practices escalate. We miniaturize and multiply our weapons of mass destruction on the naïve assumption that their possession can be monitored and controlled indefinitely.

We seem equally oblivious to the abject misery of hundreds of millions of fellow humans and to the human rights practices of many Southern governments (so long as they profess to be anti-communist), just as we are to the extraordinary range of Northern dependencies upon the South. During the past decade, in one of history's most striking ironies, social and economic indicators have fallen in real terms in many countries of the South, at the same time as Northern vulnerability to Southern issues has increased. It is rare that we regard the peoples of the developing countries as individuals, even rarer that we treasure their genius, their talent, their potential as contributors to our own richer lives.

North–South is a web that is diverse and confusing. To understand, to respond effectively, to ensure a constructive outcome, is as demanding a task as any that faces humankind. It is as well the most important, for it subsumes – or inevitably will subsume – all the others. It is a task that is demanding not only because of its substance, but because of attitudes well entrenched in both North and South. We in the North may be most in peril (as those in much of the South have long been) because the momentum of events impacting upon us is still beyond our current willingness to respond. The term 'North–South' is itself misleading for it lends weight to the impression that the South is the diminutive. 'South–North' may now be more accurate.

◆

The phrase 'North–South relations' is said to have been employed for the first time in the late 1950s by Sir Oliver Franks, then British ambassador to the United States. In the three decades since, the definition of the term has become as elastic as the relationship it describes has been turbulent. The reason, perhaps, is the multitude of variables the term encompasses: the release from colonial status of tens of millions of individuals and the formation of a hundred or so newly independent states; the professed desire on the part of governments rich and poor that broad disparities in wealth be reduced; the hard evidence in a variety of places that violence is all too often still regarded as an acceptable option; the stark reminders of the strengths of atavistic social groupings; the ubiquitous obstacles to change – lack of awareness, absence of preparedness, inadequacy of commitment, retention of privilege. The term 'North–South' is imprecise. Yet it is resonant of human expectations and richer by far in its range of connotations than its contemporary, 'East–West.'

Consistently present in those connotations has been development. The word itself is now permanently associated with the non-industrialized, often recently independent countries. The letter 'D,' for development, has attached itself increasingly to acronyms, initially as an add-on – Organization for Economic Cooperation and Development, Paris (OECD) – later as an integral – United Nations Conference on Trade and Development, Geneva (UNCTAD), United Nations Development Programme, New York (UNDP). Economists of considerable renown have dedicated their efforts to the study of development issues, Raul Prebisch, Sir Arthur Lewis, and Wassily Leontief among them. Gradually, the concepts of 'economic advancement and social security' included in the 1941 Atlantic Charter by Prime Minister Churchill and President Roosevelt, and reformulated in the United Nations Charter in 1945, have come to occupy a central position in international relations.

They occupy a central position, perhaps, but are not accorded a uniform interpretation. Popes, politicians, academics, and journalists have put forward definitions and proposals. The phrase 'foreign aid' projected an indelible image of charity; Marxist historians formulated a sense of imprecise guilt; unexpected events, such as oil embargoes, brought a mixture of outrage and fear. Increasingly, the terms 'North–South' and 'development' took on a statistical form. The underlying concern for human well-being gave way to numerical accounts of Gross National Product (GNP) per capita, and economic growth assumed an importance independent of resulting human benefits. The determination of the International Monetary Fund to introduce structural adjustment programs into developing countries, often at immense social cost, is perhaps the most vivid current example of this dedication to economic orthodoxy.

In hindsight, the earlier perspectives from North and South were so distinct that it should not be surprising that they have led to tensions.

Official Development Assistance (ODA) transfers tailored by the countries of the North to include the reduction of their own agricultural surpluses or to create employment in their own sluggish manufacturing sectors not surprisingly are regarded in the South with at least equal cynicism. Governments in the South seemingly more attentive to their privileged élites than to principles of equity and freedom generate antipathy in legislatures in the North. Lengthy negotiations, encompassing in a single package a complex bundle of disparate issues as in the once-proposed 'New International Economic Order,' led to ennui on the part of observers and frustration on the part of the participants.

Withal, seemingly unobtrusive to national negotiators in their cocooned conference halls, there has emerged in the past decade a world economy with its own rules and structures, one not yet fully understood and even less wholly acknowledged or accepted, but one increasingly independent of national sovereignties. It brings with it perils that are in some instances unprecedented and that often make themselves visible only over a long time. Likely perilous, and certainly sad, is the image of the South that the general public in the North has seized upon. Those at the more generous end of the scale see the South as a series of idyllic winter vacation destinations populated by friendly people who cannot overcome their own poverty and who are dependent upon foreign aid to survive. Those at the cynical end see corrupt military dictators with overflowing Swiss bank accounts. Seldom do those with either point of view have an opportunity to become acquainted with the rich range of frustrations and accomplishments in the countries of the South, or with the intricate and sometimes contradictory elements of this ill-understood process called 'development.'

◆

Policy makers in the immediate post–Second World War period grappled with development issues framed by the experience of the colonial era and the anxieties of an increasingly polarized world. Initial development efforts emphasized, on the one hand, flows to the South of technical assistance and improved access to markets in the North for primary commodities; on the other hand, the strengthening of friendly, strategically located countries against the perceived threat of communist aggression or subversion. In all too many instances they failed to respond effectively to the underlying social and economic problems facing the developing countries. In the absence at that time of accurate diagnosis, the tendentious policies of the industrialized countries should not now be surprising. In particular, the rapid and vigorous employment by Western European countries of generous United States assistance in the late 1940s led to assumptions that similar activities in developing regions would be equally successful. The Marshall Plan was not, however, replicable in societies ill-equipped by experience and education to absorb massive inflows of capital and technology.

Much the greater number of developing countries attained political independence only in the post–Second World War period. The balance, for the most part located in the Western Hemisphere, were in many instances long-time economic surrogates of United States interests. In all these countries, the complex, and necessarily lengthy, process of acquiring governance skills is often still in its infancy. The turmoil of governments in Western Europe as they grappled with governance issues in the seventeenth and eighteenth centuries appears placid compared with the plight of these new states. In the twentieth century, modern communications technologies have acquainted the residents of even the most remote communities with a knowledge of the much higher standards of living enjoyed elsewhere. Alternative social and economic images are projected and debated with at least the ferocity of the antagonists within Europe during the period of the Reformation, but are joined by a supply of weaponry and an intrusion of ideology that turn local dissidents into pawns on a global chessboard.

As they attained independence, developing countries found themselves wooed by East and West, not always in benign fashion. Desperately short of trained cadres of public servants, dependent upon a physical infrastructure and an economy formed as a segment of a colonial empire, facing the unreal expectations of a politically unsophisticated electorate, and nursing real or imagined wounds inflicted by generations of insensitive expatriates, many were alternately confused and exhilarated by the apparent choices open to them. To governments ill-equipped to shape their own societies, and impotent to respond to such indignities as the Hickenlooper Amendment, which required suspension of United States assistance to countries that nationalized United States property without speedy compensation, the planetary struggle for hearts and souls appeared in many instances as a bargaining card. The development debate quickly transformed itself from local social and economic imperatives into broad political divisions argued out in regional and interregional assemblies. Western politicians rapidly sensed that more was involved here than the provision of rural health clinics or the importation of unprocessed primary commodities. North–South was no longer an engagement of cooperative activity. It had become a battlefield in which human ideals, vested interests, and concepts of strategic security tussled and jousted.

Throughout the 1950s, the legal basis for United States development assistance was security: The Mutual Security Act. South Korea and Taiwan became major aid recipients. Western financing for the Aswan High Dam was withdrawn when Egypt announced its acceptance of Soviet military assistance. During the same period, Canadian assistance was prompted primarily by humanitarian considerations but quickly 'Canadian content' assumed major proportions, ensuring that the Canadian economy be a major beneficiary of aid projects. The projects were largely channelled, at least initially, through the Commonwealth's system, called the Colombo Plan, which came into being in 1951. Prime Minister Diefenbaker championed Canadian aid as a means of distributing Canadian agricultural produce, setting a precedent that is followed to this day.

Stimulated by an alarmed World Council of Churches, the United Nations General Assembly accepted a proposal of President Kennedy and declared the 1960s to be the 'U.N. Development Decade.' A year earlier, the United Nations had adopted a target for the amount of assistance to be transferred from the North to the South: 1 per cent of the combined national income of the industrialized countries. This later came to be accepted as 1 per cent of Gross National Product. It was anticipated that 0.7 per cent would flow from public sources, and the other 0.3 per cent would take the form of private sector transfers. The creation of the United Nations Conference on Trade and Development (UNCTAD) in 1964 was in response to the contention of the South that its plight was anchored in the international economic structure. 'Trade, not aid' became a rallying cry, one that led to the formation of the 'Group of 77' (the number then of developing countries in the United Nations) and a determination by the nations of the South that they would form and maintain a unified bargaining position. If the North controlled the economic agenda, the South moved to assert the political agenda. Throughout the seventies, with mixed results, that agenda remained. The General Agreement on Tariffs and Trade (GATT) added Part IV to accommodate the particular problems of developing countries, and UNCTAD produced an important resolution on a generalized system of preferences favouring developing countries, which was later adopted by OECD members. The strident call for a new international economic order issued from a non-aligned summit in Algiers in 1973 on the eve of the successful move by the Organization of Petroleum Exporting Countries (OPEC) to quadruple oil prices within a year. The intensity of the North–South debate escalated during the two Special Sessions of the General Assembly (April 1974 and September 1975) until efforts were undertaken to mute the language and restore some orderliness to the dialogue.

The World Bank and the International Monetary Fund introduced new facilities to meet the needs of those countries grievously wounded by the rise in oil prices. The European Economic Community at a conference in Lomé, Togo, introduced Stabex, a scheme to stabilize the export earnings of certain former colonies. A 'Common Fund,' designed to moderate the effects of fluctuating prices for a basket of commodities, emerged in mid-decade as the dominant demand of the South, but diminished in importance as its complexity proved to be unmanageable and as the attention of the world turned increasingly to the fate of the low-income oil-importing countries. The South, wearied by the reluctant responses of the North, turned to South–South cooperative initiatives, but found its unity shattered with the second oil shock. At the end of the 1970s, the Independent Commission on International Development Issues under the chairmanship of former West German Chancellor Willy Brandt signalled alarm that Northern interests were imperilled by the inability of the South better to meet its needs, but it was unable to attract the attention of the new United States administration. The 1980s responded by ushering in the great international debt crisis, drought and famine in much of Africa, and, coincidentally, unprecedented economic vitality and export performance in the 'newly industrialized countries' (the 'NICs') of Asia (Hong Kong, Singapore, South Korea, Taiwan). The World Commission on Environment and Development, chaired by

Norway's Prime Minister Gro Harlem Brundtland, warned that, if the planet did not practise sustainable development, it would lose its ability to support life. As the decade closed it was clear that the governments of the North had not yet been able to muster resolve and respond effectively to the bewildering circumstances facing them.

◆

The multiplicity of these issues and their resistance to solution have attracted legions of analysts and developmental experts. As in the arcane and isolated world inhabited by arms controllers, so in the supercharged atmosphere of development, sheer quantity of activity can leave the false impression of accomplishment. In a number of sectors, accomplishment has indeed resulted. In the twenty-five-year period 1960–84, the average annual per capita growth of Gross Domestic Product for all developing countries, excluding China and the oil-exporting countries, was 2.8 per cent. If those other countries are included, the average was 3.4 per cent. In that same period, remarkable positive gains were recorded in literacy, in infant mortality, and in life expectancy. Cereal grain production increased; smallpox was eradicated. Yet in most developing countries, individual standards of living have dropped, political instability has increased, and the likelihood of sustained economic growth has diminished. From the perspective of hundreds of millions of inhabitants of developing countries, life remains a wretched, uncertain prospect. The likelihood of a dignified, fulfilling livelihood is as distant as it was a generation earlier.

From the actions of the governments of the industrialized countries, North–South relations seem to have resumed their earlier diminutive role, debated not so much in the earlier atmosphere of short tempers and frequent accusations, as in a sea of Northern unawareness; even, in the era of relaxed East–West relations, of growing indifference. Little noticed is the extraordinary imbalance that has developed between North and South, the immensity of the resulting disequilibria, and the dangers they present. Disequilibria are destabilizing in any dynamic where a controlled outcome is desirable, for they make unsustainable the continuance of the status quo. They lead to inevitable, often unpredictable, sometimes uncontrollable change. In North–South relations, disequilibria are evident in several categories. All of them demand some balancing or compensating mechanism if the often savage and unforgiving natural, economic, or social forces seeking balance are not to emerge and dominate.

The most obvious of the disequilibria in the relationships between South and North concern population, economic wealth, scientific activity, and military power. The most obvious consequences of those disequilibria are environmental degradation, economic uncertainty, social unrest, and political instability. As in the interaction of all phenomena when left unattended, momentum may become irreversible. In the most tragic of scenarios, error may become irremedial. Because of the complex interaction of these phenomena and the speed with which they evolve, the force of their impact and the unpredictability of the consequences are compounded synergistically.

The processes resulting from these or other disequilibria are not always predictable, sometimes not even discernible during real-time human observation. The political unit by which time is measured in the industrialized democracies is four, at the most five, years. Events that mature on a longer cycle are seldom visible, and are certainly not influential, in the time frame that occupies decision makers. Absent the political equivalent of time-lapse photography, governments of the North are unlikely to commit resources now to influence or control events in the distant future. If development is investment, as we encourage the developing countries to believe, we in the North offer all-too-little evidence of our own commitment or even of our prudence. All the while, inexorably, the momentum of events continues apace, threatening in some instances to become irreversible.

1 / Rising populations in circumstances of absolute poverty degrade the environment in an incessant quest for food, firewood, and forage. Planetary forest cover is being destroyed at an alarming rate, down from 25 per cent of the earth's surface to 20 per cent in two decades according to the Brandt Commission.[2] The Brundtland Commission estimates that for every tree planted in the tropical regions, ten are destroyed.[3] In sub-Saharan Africa the ratio is one to twenty-nine. Yet even these estimates may err on the low side. The United Nations Food and Agriculture Organization in 1988 doubled its earlier estimates of annual closed tropical forest destruction. The current estimates of loss are in excess of sixteen million hectares a year.

2 / Economic uncertainty in the South has a direct impact upon the current accounts of all the industrialized countries. Developing country markets are now at risk. Desperately poor countries can no longer continue to buy goods from abroad and at the same time service their debts. Rising standards of living, by contrast, would permit debts to be serviced, goods to be imported, social services to be provided. They would also lower fertility rates and reduce the incidence of social unrest.

3 / The inability of developing countries to solve their own problems through modern local applications of science and technology increases the likelihood of political instability. Those who see no likelihood of advantageous change, who have little to risk or to lose, are susceptible to the appeals of populism, bigotry, and extremism.

4 / A world model that exalts the triumphs of excess consumerism, that rewards weapons makers, and that interprets so erratically the political foment in developing regions sends clear signals to political decision makers and economic planners in countries of the South. The policies these persons will implement are unlikely to be of the sort that, over time, will enhance and strengthen stable civilian regimes. The experience of Iraq is stunning evidence.

The South–North matrix is extensive and complex. It does not translate readily into simple, patriotic imagery. It does not respond to simplistic solutions any more than it can be defined in purely statistical terms. Measured against the relentless momentum of current phenomena, indifference is not benign. Humility is needed, as is sustained dedication, if there is to be any reduction in magnitude of the disequilibria now evident. The crafting of a mutually beneficial dynamic relationship cannot wait for the emergence of a brilliant universal accord; it must emerge from a series of 'creative patchworks.'[4] In their absence, the present and growing imbalances threaten an uncontrollable Newtonian reaction of the kind prophesied by François Mitterand a decade ago. 'I am convinced,' he said then, 'that the balance between the two parts of the world, the industrialized nations and the others, will be one of the causes of the most serious tragedies at the end of the century, to be explicit, of world war.'[5]

II

The Roots

The human quest for survival and well-being has long been witness to two streams of activity that are at times inconsistent, at others synergistic. Coincident with activities to enhance production and commerce have been those that are designed to protect interests but that have often contributed to destruction and carnage. This civil-military linkage has roots in prehistory.

Roots of another sort reach deeply into those regions of the world now categorized as the 'South.' Through these root canals to the 'North' flowed much of the earlier applications of science and technology upon which industrialized societies still depend. Through them flowed as well a rich philosophical and cultural stream, of immense influence and of even larger potential.

The mutuality of benefit from these South–North transfers, evident for many centuries, largely waned in the infancy of the colonial era. That era has now concluded, and in its place is a new age of interdependence, one demanding the moderation of the great inequities that have arisen. What has become a mutuality of vulnerability must be transformed into a mutually sustainable life support system for all, whether they live in the North or in the South.

◆

The human species is a much more complex bundle of needs and desires, of aspirations and motivations, than is any other member of the animal kingdom. Humans are able to record their own present and past. In the result, they alone anticipate their own distant future, including post-mortality. The human quest for acceptable forms of social order thus incorporates elements much more sophisticated, and certainly more complicated, than are found (or yet understood) in any other living species. The quest may have roots in the territorial imperative, as Robert Ardrey[1] has argued so persuasively, originating in, or mimicking, 'lower' orders of primates but differing from them. It is likely coloured by aggressive instincts as described by Konrad Lorenz.[2] Two elemental distinctions which were long ago described by Aristotle ('Man is by nature a political animal') and Descartes ('I think, therefore I am') set the human species apart.[3] Still another distinction, one which in the twentieth century is ever more obvious, is the human skill as a toolmaker. Unlike the passive adaptation to their environment of all other living species, humans are active manipulators.

Yet in one basic sense, humans are not distinct. They share with every other living species the elemental need to provide for their physical requirements. The most basic of basic needs is food, quickly followed by some form of shelter (which, in the case of humans, means clothing as well as habitation) and the means to provide for the survival and nurturing of offspring. The discovery millennia ago of the benefits of sedentary agriculture and animal husbandry was the anthropological turning point and the first discernible step in the continuing ascent of man. The apple and the serpent have exerted an immense influence on human spiritual development but are relatively insignificant in the formulation of the species when compared to the overwhelming organizational consequences of a tilled field or a fenced pasture. With these humans sought self-sufficiency in ever-widening fashion, initially including forms of aggressive raiding and of barter. The alternative of 'guns or butter' has roots deep in prehistory as the dual pursuits of warfare and trade became universally commonplace. In the quest for physical survival and well-being, each activity became increasingly intertwined with the other. Today, on the eve of the twenty-first century AD, the model of the mighty United States military-industrial complex illustrates the extent to which the two forms of activity have become essentially one.

The earliest economies tolerated military expenditures to be protected from enemies; the modern economy depends for its vitality on its defence-related industries. Once fearful of enemies, many states now thrive on them. The advertising campaigns of military contractors actively promote xenophobia. United States Senator Moynihan has stated: 'The Cold War changed us. We used to be pretty much what we started out to be: a republic which expected normally to be at peace. With the Cold War, all this changed. We became a national security state, geared for War at all times.'[4] The celebrated Chinese military strategist Sun Tzu understood well this phenomenon. In his classic treatise *The Art of War*, written in the fourth century BC, he wrote: 'War is like unto fire; those who will not put aside weapons are themselves consumed by them.'

Somewhere along this twenty-five-hundred-year route other elements interceded, generally always to explain or support one form or another of social organization, but always including economic elements because of the centrality of the survival instinct. Thus did the creation myth become a powerful instrument for the justification (or the denunciation) of this or that human activity. It was in response to the survival instinct, however, not myth, that humans commenced their first organized activities – those that came to be described by a word with Greek roots, 'economics,' meaning in its origins 'the management of the household.'

From the depths of prehistory to the present, 'household management' has represented both the finest and the most bestial of human behaviour. The exquisite artistry of Benvenuto Cellini's salt-cellar, the utility of the telephone, the rapture associated with fastidious adornment, the excessive consumption of material goods, the enslavement of servants – these are all forms of household management. All are examples of the quest for creature comforts as represented by material gain. It is that acquisitive force in the nature of men and women that has been both a most powerful stimulus in the history of humankind and the source of many of the inequities that trouble us today. One of the earliest examples of technology – the plough – emerged from the desire to cultivate food crops more effectively. Another, even older – the club – was used first in hunting, then in warfare. So began the lengthy and influential contribution, first of technology and then of science, to human accomplishment and to human savagery.

Throughout history, no chapter has been more colourful, more influential, or more continuous than that written by the traders. Risk takers, merchants, adventurers, navigators, bullies – those engaged in commercial transactions capture to this day the imagination of those who in one way or another rely upon them. No other single element of society has been more influential in the shaping of political frontiers or the dissemination of religious influence. It was the economic treasure that lay in wait that prompted so many early expeditions of discovery and conquest; it was the richness of material acquisition that lay perceptibly below the surface of the great religious pilgrimages. The planet and its geographic mysteries came to be exposed one after the other as various communities sought in turn to extend their commercial activities and advantages.

This apparently innate instinct to extend political or religious influence for economic benefit was not limited to any single race or society. Historians have traced examples wherever the species has inhabited. The earliest instances of organized human behaviour – the societies along the Nile River, through the odysseys of the Greeks, the navigational feats of the Arabs from the Persian Gulf and those of the Pacific Island ancestors who voyaged from the South American continent, the far-ranging Malays, and the seemingly incredible treks of the Inuit – these are the exploits of humans who have sought to improve their livelihood in far-away places. Empires rose and fell in the course of these quests. Wars have been fought, legal regimes designed, societies have prospered and disappeared. The pennant of trade with its search for goods and for markets has in some instances fluttered at the masthead of armadas and has in others been resisted vigorously on the ramparts of foreign cultures. Withal, however, the history of human endeavour has been in the first instance the history of activity undertaken in pursuit of economic advantage. The gaining of such advantage has not always been at the expense of others, however alien such a concept might appear to many today, so common is short-term greed in markets of all kinds. In its earliest forms the sharing and exchange of knowledge and goods was most often undertaken with an evenness of intent and thus a mutuality of benefit.

So well entrenched has become the concept of competition in the countries of the North, however, that 'advantage' is now seen as a one-way phenomenon; winners create losers. A game theory has evolved in which a 'zero-sum' concept is central. (In zero-sum games, what one player wins, the others lose. The concept assumes conflict; in contrast is 'non zero-sum' in which players can gain – or lose – simultaneously, a circumstance which encourages cooperation.)

In the long saga of human development, the lengthy prehistoric period can be categorized in the absence of a zero-sum formula. Not for millennia did there arise evidence of marked disparities of accomplishment between regions or societies of the kind so clear at present. The several stone (or 'lithic') periods were virtually universal in their speed of advancement. Simple tools, pottery and weaving techniques, agricultural and animal husbandry practices, all reveal a marked similarity from continent to continent. In contrast to the North–South schism that much later was to evolve, the lithic period was 'one world' in which there occurred a continuing evolution, exchange, and assimilation of technologies, societal structures, and even religious concepts. In this early time, as modern archaeological discoveries have revealed, many of the basic elements of social organization, economic activity, and cultural expression evolved seemingly simultaneously in many parts of the globe. Evident as well in each of these societies was some sense of the human species' interdependent relationship with other species and with the natural environment. Animism was a common practice, even as aggressive conflict was present.

During the fourth and third millennia BC in Egypt and other countries in that region, and during the third and second millennia BC in China and India, various forms of settlement began to penetrate the great river valleys, and this in turn led to the use of water for irrigation and other purposes. Water-management techniques were the foundation for large hydraulic societies, in which sophisticated networks of canals and aqueducts permitted cultivation and settlement to take place a considerable distance from the river itself. Now began a new form of societal organization, no longer earth-oriented in view but sky-dominant (theocratic) in its interpretation of reality. Not now the norm of egalitarian social structures; instead, one that was hierarchical and most often patrilineal. In the period of what is now referred to as the 'archaic civilizations' (extending from the third millennium BC to Christian times), major technological advances took place, largely because communities could better control their environments. One immediate result was a burgeoning of larger and more complex economies, with greater concentrations of population. Metals were worked and combined (copper and bronze), techniques for spatial measurement (maps) and time reckoning (calendars) introduced, writing instruments invented, and advances made in mathematics and astronomy. Belief in celestial deities influenced architectural design, and expression assumed monumental size, often in the shape of pyramids or ziggurats.

These archaic civilizations were the progenitors of a number of the societies now defined as 'the South.' The oldest, continuous – and hence most populous – of these are known to the world today as China and India.

The roots of contemporary Northern societies tap the Greek and Roman experience. The benefits conferred by the Greeks upon later civilizations took several forms but perhaps the most influential was the development of rational thought processes to extend conceptual reasoning. Without the employment of this ability, the human species had remained – as much of it would for centuries still to come – in a visual and temporal cage, confined by the extent of sight-lines and the immediacy of events. The emergence of the rational mind from the flat plain of sensory perceptions changed humankind's attitudes indelibly. The process has been described as requiring several stages, moving from the 'heroic' (sensory) through the 'visionary' and the 'theoretical' to the 'rational.' John Finley[5] associates these stages with well-known Greek intellectuals. He relates Thucydides to the theoretical stage and Plato and Aristotle to the rational stage. Of the latter stage, he wrote: 'The consequences of this view are virtually limitless. It enthrones order at the centre of things and makes the mind's task one of discerning it by dialectic, with entire confidence that what the mind perceives will not contradict but further clarify the regnant scheme ... In sum, it gives assurance ... that the seemingly infinite variety of the world is not in fact wild and ungoverned but open to understanding and hence to control' (p. 93).

The rational employment of thought permitted the Greeks to articulate their view of the world in a fashion essential to this day in all scholarly endeavour: 'logos,' which perceives reason as the guiding principle to account for the cosmos and for humankind. 'It lies at the heart of philosophy, science, religion. Everything in the world has a "logos"; it says something, means something ... If we listen carefully we can understand.'[6] Another Greek term, 'metron,' meaning measure, is the fork in the road between North and South. To the Greeks, and later to the Romans, 'metron' was the application of measurement to the phenomenal world. Combined with 'logos,' this concept permitted the application of reason to a universe that was measurable. It was an essential element in Northern scientific thought, most notably in the works of Sir Isaac Newton, until early in the present century. Only then was it found wanting in certain respects by the quantum theorist Max Planck.

The Greek word 'metron' comes from the same Indo-European linguistic root as the Sanskrit word 'maya,' yet has a connotation far different. To the Indian mind, 'maya' meant more than the measurement of discernible, discrete phenomena; it reflected as well human inability to measure the ingredients of being, of pure continuity, and the consequent need to approach that task by other means.[7] Thus began one of the North–South schisms, the emphasis of the North upon quantification, logic, and scientific method to construct both epistemologies and technologies, and the increasing concern in the great region of the South influenced by Indian thought to understand better the supraphenomenal – the non-measurable.

The spread of Greek influence was accomplished primarily by the use of sailing vessels, with all the limitations that weather and distance intended. The Romans concentrated on overland communications as more reliable. Their highways were extended again and again over the centuries until, at the peak of empire, their length was equivalent to a distance ten times the earth's circumference at the equator. Along these roads passed troops and merchants alike. Cities were linked, and grew in the process. To facilitate that growth, a range of engineering marvels, many of them visible to this day, were constructed: aqueducts of immense capacity and reliability, terracing of agricultural lands, amphitheatres for entertainment and political education.

Still another intellectual phenomenon marks the progression of the human species from the earliest civilizations through the advances of the Greeks and the Romans in the Mediterranean region and the great societies of India and China: the sense of human worth, and thus the development of a body of values. Here emerged still another fork in the road, this time within the communities of the North, this time dividing scientists and philosophers. Virtue, human value, equitable treatment, and social recognition, while all estimable and worthy concepts, were difficult to measure, as they are to this day. Rather than endeavour to overcome this challenge, or even to include concepts of human worth within the construct of scientific research, scientists of the North departed from the holistic concept of the Greeks and began, from the time of Galileo onward, to espouse what has come to be called 'value-free' science. The separation of human activities into separate, seemingly impermeable boxes, each with its own set of 'absolutes,' had begun. Rational thought prevailed within the boxes; rationalization and sophistries among and between them. The endeavour of the Catholic church to influence the connections is perhaps most vividly revealed in the trial of Galileo. As described by Bronowski, 'Galileo was not tortured. He was only threatened with torture, twice. His imagination could do the rest. That was the object of the trial, to show men of imagination that they were not immune from the process of primitive, animal fear that was irreversible ... The result was silence among Catholic scientists everywhere from then on. Galileo's greatest contemporary, René Descartes, stopped publishing in France and finally went to Sweden.'[8]

◆

The North–South dynamic traces its recorded beginnings to the exploits of Alexander the Great in the fourth century BC. Evidence of his penetration is visible to this day. At Taxila, Pakistan, in the lower Indus Gorge, where to the east the expanse of the Gangetic plain extends for two thousand kilometres without physical barriers, Greek coins occasionally come to the surface of ploughed fields, and now and then a blue-eyed child is a reminder to observers that the Macedonians of Alexander's period were fair-haired. Three centuries after Alexander, the Roman emperor Augustus established direct commercial transactions by sea with ports on the Indian Ocean, using the then recently understood monsoon winds blowing across the Arabian Sea. An overland route came to link China and the Mediterranean using the Silk Road of central Asia. In the first century BC, silk began arriving in the West and soon thereafter the insatiable Roman appetite for luxury goods stimulated immense growth in trade.

The balance of trade was uneven, however, because Roman exports of wool, glass, linen, and metalwares were of much less value than the items imported from Asia: silk, perfumes, spices, gems. In the result, Rome was required to offset its adverse balance of trade with regular shipments of gold and silver. Pliny estimated that annual flows to China, India, and Arabia amounted to 100 million sesterces and declared: 'That is the sum which our luxuries and our women cost us.'[9] Later discoveries of large hoards of Roman coins in India support Pliny's estimate. This drain of economic wealth, from North to South, was a significant factor in the economic decline of the Roman Empire in the third century AD.

In subsequent centuries any number of innovations and technologies vital to an advancing society passed from Asia to Europe. In some instances, centuries were required for the transfer. During Marco Polo's thirteenth-century travels, he could have found printed books circulating in China on a range of subjects: warfare, religion, agriculture, philosophy, painting, economics. Yet on his return to Venice, his narrative accounts were handwritten on manuscript, and so copied a hundred times. Many of the technologies he described formed the building blocks for the later major accomplishments of European science and commerce. Yet few Europeans were even aware of the source of the inventions upon which they relied.

This flow from South to North ebbed and surged. The links were seriously and lengthily interrupted when in the third century AD there occurred simultaneously the fall of the Han Dynasty in China, turmoil in India, and the decline of the Roman Empire. Almost a thousand years were to pass before these contacts (which historians and Rudyard Kipling[10] were to label East–West, but which would today be called North–South) were renewed on the same scale. During that period of the Dark Ages in Europe, much of the knowledge of the outside world gained from Ptolemy and others had been lost. At the time of the crusades, myth likely exceeded fact about lands and climes beyond the immediate Mediterranean Basin. Medieval geographers usually placed Jerusalem in the centre of their maps and enlarged the area of Palestine disproportionately in order to accommodate all the biblical place-names.

This situation altered radically in the thirteenth century when the nomadic Mongol tribes of central Asia struck out in all directions. Like whirlwinds they spread, looting and conquering, and creating an empire more vast than any that the world had yet seen, one that extended from the China Sea to Eastern Europe. The significance of the Mongol empire lay not so much in its direct political effects, for these were fairly short-lived. Rather, its importance lay in the sudden efflorescence of contacts among the regions of Eurasia. Increased trade and travel, with the concomitant spread of technology and ideas, were opening new horizons. Throughout the lands of the Mongols and beyond, the late Middle Ages saw an increased tempo of cultural diffusion.

At the height of its power the Mongol empire stretched from the Danube to the Pacific. For the first time on record, Europeans crossed Eurasia to the Pacific. Travellers' accounts revealed that the Far East not only equalled but exceeded Europe in population and wealth. These accounts were not believed fully for several centuries, however, so confined and local were European attitudes. For example, Marco Polo's accounts of his travels and of the wonders he viewed were dismissed as fiction on his return by his Venetian contemporaries.

The Mongol era saw an increase in communication between scientists of different countries. The Yuan court of China favoured Arab mathematicians for the improvement of its calendar. Arab encyclopaedists recited accounts of Chinese science, particularly medicine. After his conquest of Persia, Hulagu Khan had an astronomical observatory built at Maraghah, south of Tabriz, where astronomers from China met with persons from as far away as Spain. As might be expected of such an era, exploration flourished; Kublai Khan even sent expeditions to determine the true source of the Yellow River.

But it was not improved knowledge in fields like geography and astronomy that was of major significance for the future. Rather, it was the diffusion of applied science and the mechanical arts. The spread of technology, like that of science, was not wholly in one direction. For example, during their conquest of south China, the Mongols imported from Mesopotamia Arab specialists in the use of siege-machines, which hurled huge blocks of stone or incendiary matter into fortified enemy towns. But a much more massive transfer of technology moved westward during the Middle Ages, reflecting the fact that until modern times Asia, particularly China, was considerably more advanced in this area. We may, as examples, single out three such technologies for which the modern North is indebted to the South.

Printing and Paper. Printing began in China some two thousand years ago, at first with carved seals of stone, then with page-sized blocks of wood and eventually of baked clay. The potential of printing took off only after Gutenburg invented cast movable metal type in Europe, about 1450, yet it was in China – long before – that movable type originated. Pi Sheng is credited with the design of movable earthenware type in the eleventh century. In the Mongol period, wooden type was used in China and central Asia. But it was in Korea, where bronze was employed, that printing with movable type flourished. In 1392, the government established a department with responsibility for casting type and printing books, and from 1403 onward there was a government foundry in existence, casting type from moulds. During the fifteenth century, the country was ruled by a strong dynasty that sought through printing to further education, the books published being devoted to history, morals, and classical literature.

The manufacture of paper from hemp, tree bark, and rags is said to have been announced officially to the emperor of China in the year 105, though recent evidence indicates the use of paper in China even before this. In Europe paper was not manufactured until a thousand years later. As with many other inventions, it was the Arabs who acted as intermediaries. In 751, Arab and Chinese armies clashed in what is today Soviet Turkestan, and among the captives carried away to Samarkand by the victorious Arabs were a number of Chinese papermakers. 'Paper of Samarkand' soon became well known in the Asian lands of the Abbasid caliphate, and at the end of the eighth century, Chinese workers were brought to start a paper factory in Baghdad. When manufacture began in Damascus, that city became the centre for the export of paper to Europe. In 1294, at Tabriz, the Mongol capital of Persia, there appeared an issue of paper money with text in Chinese and Arabic; this was an example of the needs of traders from differing cultures and regions and an early endeavour to meet the problems created by foreign exchange of currencies. Seven centuries later, the international community introduced the 'Special Drawing Right' (SDR) and the 'European Currency Unit' (ECU) as more modern solutions.

The secret of the actual manufacture of paper entered Europe from Muslim Spain, having reached there via Egypt and Morocco. The first known paper-mill in Christian Europe was established in 1157 in southern France. Nonetheless, paper only gradually replaced parchment as a writing material in Europe. Only after the coming of printing – first from blocks and then from type – did the use of paper became general for both writing and printing.

The Stirrup and Gunpowder. These two most important medieval innovations in warfare both came from Asia. The stirrup appeared in primitive form in India in the second century BC, and was perfected in China by the fifth century AD. The idea spread westward and by the eighth century arrived in the Frankish kingdom, where it was employed to advantage by Charles Martel in his organization of cavalry forces. The stirrup welded horse and rider into an effective fighting unit. It permitted more effective use of the sword and bow, and direct assault with a lance against an enemy without the danger of the rider falling off. The creation of a new class of mounted warriors became a central feature of European feudalism. The Mongols conquered vast territories on horseback, partly thanks to the use of the stirrup.

Gunpowder, which was to have such an impact on the world, arose from the investigations of Taoist alchemists in China. A military handbook of 1044 describes explosive grenades. About the early eleventh century the rocket appeared: an arrow to which was attached a bamboo tube filled with low-nitrate composition. With the Mongol conquests, the Arabs became acquainted with saltpetre (potassium nitrate), which they called 'Chinese snow,' and the rocket, which they called the 'Chinese arrow.' Very quickly the use of gunpowder became known in Europe, where it was mentioned in the writings of Bacon. The first European references to gunpowder composition date from about 1300.

In Europe it was the wealthy republics, or kings backed by merchants, that could command the resources and technical skill required for this new military technology. Gunpowder and cannon battered down the castles of the feudal nobility and speeded the triumph of the nation-state. Naval warfare, too, was revolutionized by gunpowder. But its effect was not limited to exploding the material bases of feudalism. It was written that 'Niter has made as much noise in philosophy as it has in war.' The European mind was confronted with something radically new under the sun, something the ancient Greeks had not imagined, and the practical problems in chemistry and ballistics that now arose were powerful stimuli to scientific thought.

The Compass and Maritime Technology. Knowledge of the magnetic compass arrived in Europe from China about 1200, probably through contacts made with Arab traders. Yet in Chinese literature there are references to south-pointing spoons carved from lodestone from the first century AD onwards. From the eleventh century on, there are descriptions of a fish-shaped piece of iron that floated on water, and that had been magnetized by being heated red-hot while held in a North–South position.

Another important Chinese contribution to sea voyaging was the stern-post rudder, which in Europe now replaced a steering oar fixed to the starboard side of the ship. Use of this type of rudder meant that from the thirteenth century onward the deep-keeled European vessels could hold a course with their sails set close to the wind, and voyages could be made in rougher weather. With the help of the compass, roundabout coastal travel could now be replaced by direct routes across the seas. The stage was now set for the fifteenth-century voyages of discovery. And here, too, the problems that open-sea navigation raised for astronomers and instrument makers became an important spur to the future development of science.

The list of technologies transferred from China to Europe is lengthy, as was the lead time in their development. Without this massive influx of applied knowledge, the mould of feudalism would not have been broken in the way that it was. Nor would there have been planted many of the seeds of entrepreneurial activity, the forebears of capitalistic endeavours. This latter has been a powerful force in the evolution of systems of social relations and material production. These, in turn, exercised an immense stimulus to the European scientific revolution of the sixteenth and seventeenth centuries. In the North, in the twentieth century, we tend to forget the extent of our technological indebtedness to the South, and this ignorance is a factor that colours our attitudes and our relations.

◆

For many centuries commerce was conducted by trade because coinage currencies were either non-existent or non-negotiable. Barter transactions demanded skill and experience. Central to them, however, as to any commercial transaction, is the concept of mutuality of advantage. In most instances, each contracting partner should assume benefits of roughly equal value. To achieve that end, much depends on accuracy of information and on the good faith and honesty of the other party. The elasticity of the definition of good faith in these circumstances is legion. Unlike social undertakings, which are considered to be an indicator of honour, economic transactions favour the most intrepid. The accomplishments of certain groups are legendary, as is the quid pro quo in certain instances now infamous. Manhattan Island was obtained by the Dutch in 1626 from the Indian occupants for sixty guilders, then worth about one and one-half pounds of silver. In 1670, the Hudson's Bay Company ('The Governor and Company of Adventurers of England Trading into Hudsons Bay') gained exclusive rights of a wide-ranging nature throughout a vast expanse of what is now Canada on payment to the Crown of a fee consisting of two elks and two black beavers 'Whensoever and as often as wee our heires and successors shall happen to enter into the said Countryes Territoryes and Regions hereby granted.'[11]

Over the years, the examples notwithstanding, there is ample evidence to indicate that in day-to-day transactions benefits could be calculated and exchanged on a basis of mutual satisfaction, thus laying the groundwork for sustained and profitable commercial relationships. Some of the great trading partnerships flourished for centuries: Phoenicia with Iberia, Jutland with Italy, Rome with China. On several continents, well-travelled trade routes became highways of commerce, often with camel caravans linking far distant communities as in the Sahelian region of Africa between Northern Senegal and the Sudan, or along the Silk Road of central Asia. The sea route from the Persian Gulf down the east coast of Africa to Zanzibar carried the dhows of traders back and forth for a thousand years.

Undoubtedly, instances of opportunism and deceit occurred, but these in the main were either self-correcting or so inconsequential as not to be meaningful. Benefits were balanced; advantage was not at the expense of the other participant. This traditional practice, accepted for centuries, was not to persist beyond the age of discovery, however. With the sudden entry into world markets of the great European maritime powers, there disappeared any concept of mutuality of benefit. Now began the capricious era of mercantilism and the entry of savage practices to gain and maintain commercial advantage. The colonial period got under way, the wholesale commerce in human slaves reached its peak, the famous real estate transactions between the 'wily' Europeans and the 'innocent' indigenous natives took place, the Spanish and Portuguese looted the civilizations of the Western Hemisphere, the gunboats of Europe and America forced their way into Asian harbours, the English became the world's first international narcotics traffickers as they created the opium trade between India and China. Fuelled by superior armament and buoyed by the arrogance of their religion, these European 'merchants' displayed none of the characteristics of their earlier counterparts; guile, force, and greed became the common attributes of the day. No atrocities were too heinous, no conduct too scandalous for the stomachs of these 'business representatives.' Daniel J. Boorstin describes the 1502 activities of Vasco da Gama off the coast of India:

> Arriving off the Malabar coast, when he sighted a large dhow, the *Meri,* carrying Muslim pilgrims home from Mecca, he demanded all the treasure on board. When the owners were slow to deliver, the result was recorded by one of his crew. 'We took a Mecca ship on board of which were 380 men and many women and children, and we took from it fully 12,000 ducats, and goods worth at least another 10,000. And we burned the ship and all the people on board with gunpowder, on the first day of October.' On October 30, Gama, now off Calicut, ordered the Samuri to surrender, and demanded the expulsion of every Muslim from the city. When the Samuri temporized and sent envoys to negotiate peace, Gama replied without ambiguity. He seized a number of traders and fishermen whom he picked up casually in the harbor. He hanged them at once, then cut up their bodies, and tossed hands, feet, and heads into a boat, which he sent ashore with a message in Arabic suggesting that the Samuri use these pieces of his people to make himself a curry. When Gama departed for Lisbon with his cargo of treasure, he left behind in Indian waters five ships commanded by his mother's brother, the first permanent naval force stationed by Europeans in Asiatic waters.[12]

Sir Francis Drake's famous sixteenth-century voyage in the *Golden Hind,* for example, was precedent setting in a business sense, as well as a navigational one. The voyage was financed through the world's first joint-stock enterprise, the forerunner of all English – and later Canadian and American – corporate activity. Writing of the expedition in 1930, John Maynard Keynes said that

> the booty brought back by Drake in the *Golden Hind* may fairly be considered the fountain and origin of British Foreign Investment. Elizabeth

paid off out of the proceeds the whole of her foreign debt, and invested a part of the balance (about £42,000) in the Levant Company. Largely out of the profits of the Levant Company, there was formed the East India Company, the profits of which, during the seventeenth and eighteenth centuries, were the main foundation of England's foreign connections ... the £42,000 invested by Elizabeth out of Drake's booty in 1580 would have accumulated by 1930 to approximately the actual aggregate of our present foreign investments, namely £4,200,000,000, − or say 100,000 times greater than the original investment.[13]

So much for the deeply held belief that the roots of British wealth are found in prudent, fiscally conservative landholders and factory owners. Piracy and imperialism are more accurate, with a dash of compound interest.

The age of the European empires, complete with scattered colonies on all continents, communities of expatriate governors and officials, and tightly controlled trading and investment regimes, continued for four centuries. Massive transfers of wealth took place, initially by plunder as was the Spanish practice in the New World, later by contrived market and pricing systems that concentrated value-added activities and profit margins in the hands of the colonial power and its business community. The quite improbable map of Africa has nothing to do with demography and African cultures, and little enough with natural geographic features, but everything to do with competing European colonial claims. The present hodgepodge of national boundaries was produced not by the Africans or their representatives but by European diplomats during the protracted Berlin Conference of 1884–5.

Some empires were more accomplished than others both in the value obtained by the colonial power − which was geopolitical as well as commercial − and in the advantages gained by the populations of the colonies in education, health, governance, technology, and infrastructure. Over the years, an increasingly aware population in Europe began to demand more humane practices on the part of their own governments. Wilberforce's successful crusade against slavery is one example; the cocoa procurement practices of the Cadbury enterprises, which were revised in an endeavour to force more socially acceptable labour policies in Angola, is another.[14] The grip of some imperial centres was shaken off relatively early. In South America, neither Spain nor Portugal had the stomach for an extended political presence and so withdrew as Simon Bolivar and his contemporaries sought independence and self-government. The globe-girdling British Empire on which the sun never set dissolved almost completely in less than a century, commencing with Canada's initial, and partial, steps toward independence in 1867 and concluding with the flood of newly independent states in the decades following the Second World War. In the 1990s, only the odd remnant remains. Hong Kong (to be absorbed by China in 1997) and Bermuda are the most prominent, but British islands are still able to provoke international incidents such as The Falklands/Malvinas in the South Atlantic and Diego Garcia in the Indian Ocean. Of the colonial powers, those most reluctant to withdraw from active governance of their overseas possessions bequeathed continuing turmoil and an inadequate preparedness for independence, with dreadful consequences and civil strife: France from its Indo-China colonies of Vietnam, Laos, and Cambodia, Belgium from the Congo, Portugal from Angola and Mozambique, and the Republic of South Africa from Namibia.

Not all the colonial powers were European. The United States of America, describing its occupation of subservient territories at the turn of the century, chose self-indulgent terminology. Its acts, however, sprang from the same motivation that European nations had evidenced for centuries. Puerto Rico, Guam, Cuba, and the Philippines were all obtained as a result of the Spanish-American War of 1895–8. A half-century earlier, war reduced by some 40 per cent Mexico's land claims in North America. Much of what are now New Mexico, Arizona, Nevada, and California passed from Mexican to United States sovereignty. In the period 1898–1989, United States military forces physically invaded and occupied for varying lengths of time six sovereign states in the Western Hemisphere: Cuba, 1898–9; Nicaragua, 1912–13; Haiti, 1915; Dominican Republic, 1965–6; Grenada, 1983; Panama, 1989. Well into the twentieth century, exaggerated exclamations of 'manifest destiny' were heard from the American side of the Canada–U.S. border, conveying the impression that the entire continent was fair game for U.S. conquest.

The end of the colonial period was signalled in 1941 by Prime Minister Winston Churchill and President Franklin Roosevelt in the historic Atlantic Charter drawn up aboard HMS *Prince of Wales* steaming off the coast of Newfoundland. There, during the darkest days of the Second World War, these two statesmen envisaged a postwar world with qualities far different from those that had held sway previously:

> ... they respect the right of all peoples to choose the form of government under which they will live; and they wish to see sovereign rights and self-government restored to those who have been forcibly deprived of them.
>
> ... they will endeavour, with due respect for their existing obligations, to further the enjoyment by all States, great or small, victor or vanquished, of access, on equal terms, to the trade and to the raw materials of the world which are needed for their economic prosperity.
>
> ... they desire to bring about the fullest collaboration between all nations in the economic field, with the object of securing for all improved labour standards, economic advancement, and social security.[15]

These aims and undertakings formed the basis for the later Declaration dated 2 January 1942[16] which employed for the first time in its modern context Byron's phrase from *Childe Harold's Pilgrimage* – 'United Nations.'[17] Still later, at San Francisco, on 26 June 1945, the United Nations Charter was signed, and came into force following ratification on 24 October 1945.

III

The Economics

The steady evolution of self-sufficiency anticipated by the United Nations Charter has not materialized. During the 1980s, the economies of most of the countries of the South stopped growing, and many of them declined. Yet during this period none of the populations declined; all grew, some of them more than doubling since 1960. This combination has profound implications for the countries of the North. Massive disequilibria have developed: unprecedented imbalances of capital flows, of merchandise, of people. All of these impact now upon the interests of the North, and will do so increasingly in the future unless the underlying causes of the imbalances are identified and rectified. The abilities of the developing countries to invest in their own futures, to pursue simultaneously the desired goals of economic and political liberalization, are sharply constrained by the international barriers that face them and by their preoccupation with the servicing of past debt.

The global economy is now a reality. Its complexity arises out of commercial linkages subject to severance or upset as unpredictable events occur anywhere in the world. The pursuit of narrow, national policies in these circumstances not only frustrates harmonization but inevitably jeopardizes national interests. A universal economic and social value system must be derived to overcome the systemic malfunctions still evident in current practices.

◆

The lofty precepts of the United Nations Charter and the generous idealism of the Churchill-Roosevelt vision led to major changes in the international community following the Second World War. The four and a half decades since have been witness to an unprecedented effort on the part of the industrialized countries to assist the newly independent states – and their older, but economically frail, associates – through major programs of economic support. Historians, without question, will acknowledge these efforts to be among the most laudatory of any in this or previous centuries. The rationale has not always been universal or consistent, the assistance not always practical or without fetters, but the instinct was uncommonly decent. Raising the standard of living of the developing countries was seen as a contribution to human dignity, a contributor to economic buoyancy, a counter to social turbulence and political instability. All this was consistent with the preambular language of the United Nations Charter, which contained the determination to 'promote social progress and better standards of life in larger freedom.' The obvious fact that those goals seem now in many instances to be even more distant than they were forty-five years ago prompts, however, and properly, many questions and much criticism.

Starting at modest levels, the annual volume of Official Development Assistance (ODA) rose from U.S. $4.6 billion in 1960 to U.S. $49.7 billion in 1988,[1] an immense increase but ever so much less than what was needed, and what had been promised. The United Nations Economic and Social Council and the General Assembly had both addressed the issue of quantum of assistance and adopted in 1960, as mentioned in chapter I, a target of 1 per cent of the combined national income of the industrialized countries, to take the form of capital transfers. At the United Nations Conference on Trade and Development in 1964, the types of flows to be considered as eligible were enumerated and 1 per cent of Gross National Product (GNP) was made applicable to each of the industrialized countries individually. The resolution to this effect was approved by 107 of the countries in attendance. Twenty-five years later, the World Bank revealed that only one industrialized country met that goal in 1989 (Norway at 1.02 per cent) although one other (Netherlands) has in the past surpassed it and was still close at 0.93 per cent. Even closer in 1989 was Sweden at 0.98 per cent. The world's largest ODA contributor on a basis of percentage of GNP is Saudi Arabia, which has ranged as high as 5.95 per cent in 1976 and was, in 1988, at 2.70 per cent. In 1987 Kuwait was also well over the U.N. target, at 1.23 per cent, but dropped to 0.41 per cent the following year.

'ODA' may have a clear meaning but it has a bureaucratic ring to it. The press quickly gave it a catchier name: 'Foreign Aid.' This may be better street language, but it generates all kinds of images, many of them inaccurate; it also invites governments to use developmental assistance funds for what are really non-development purposes. 'Foreign aid' smacks of charity and so is subject to the not unreasonable adage that charity should begin at home. 'Foreign aid' also projects a false sense of philanthropic generosity to governments endeavouring to find a noble description for such activities as the overseas disposal of surplus agricultural products. Indeed, 'foreign aid' is such an all-embracing term that it can contain without apparent embarrassment military weapons, massive public works projects, humanitarian relief, and university scholarships. Not all of them, obviously, are developmental.

'Development,' in essence, is a single concept: investment. Development decisions are – or should be – investment decisions. They are decisions of today intended to create benefits tomorrow. If this future element is not present, any assistance offered is not developmental, no matter what other purposes it might serve. There may, of course, be specific goals attached to any development decision but 'investment' must be understood. The International Development Research Centre (IDRC) has long used a clear definition: 'a process for the benefit of people ... consistent with human dignity ... best fostered in conditions of adequate nutrition, sound health, independence of spirit, pride in indigenous culture and respect for human rights.'

ODA transfers are clearly important to the developing countries in terms of both quantity and quality. The contribution they can make to the abilities of those countries is generally undeniable. If the contribution is basically military, however, or if the cost-effectiveness of some of the assistance invites deserved criticism, then the whole concept of aid comes under attack. It is important to understand as well that ODA transfers do not by any means reveal the full range of financial flows between the countries of the North and those of the South. To capture that larger picture, one must look as well at trade and investment statistics. From these, it becomes quickly evident, as the developing countries have long argued, that they are not net beneficiaries. The most dramatic circumstances are revealed in terms of debt. Of the 119 indebted countries in the South, the net flow in their external borrowing accounts decreased from a positive, or inward, flow of U.S. $423 billion in 1981 to a negative, or outward, flow of U.S. $58 billion in 1989. This net flow from South to North has been described by the New York Council for Foreign Relations as 'a massive, perverse redistribution of income.' The turnaround was the result of a significant drop-off in new borrowings and a major increase in interest payments. In the result, the outward financial flow of these countries exceeded by some 17 per cent (U.S. $8 billion) the total ODA flows to all developing countries. This means exactly what it says: the poor countries are paying considerably more money to the rich countries than they are receiving in the form of ODA.

For the small, low-income countries, these circumstances are especially desolate. From 1981 to 1989, ODA incoming flows increased by U.S. $3.1 billion while outgoing interest payments increased by only a slightly smaller figure, to U.S. $2.7 billion. But that is not the whole picture. In the same period, borrowings by developing countries from private banks decreased by U.S. $2.5 billion and International Monetary Fund (IMF) transfers dropped by U.S. $1.5 billion. A modest increase in long-term official borrowing of U.S. $1.1 billion did not begin to make up the drop-off in funds available for development purposes. The net result for those countries was less money, a whole lot less – U.S. $2.5 billion less.

Trade statistics are equally bleak. In 1986, the last year for which final World Bank figures are available, the net terms of trade (that is, the relationship between the prices of exports and the prices of imports) for the developing countries revealed a year-over-year percentage *drop* for almost every country grouping (only South Asia showed an improvement) while the OECD countries recorded an *increase* of 12.4 per cent. Comparable IMF data show that between 1982 and 1989, the terms of trade of the developing countries as a whole fell by 20 per cent. During the same period, the terms of trade of the industrialized countries improved by 16 per cent.[2] Imbalances of this kind are destabilizing, and so preliminary figures for 1989 trace the beginning of a balancing trend, but the balance remains heavily to the advantage of the North.

Since 1955, worldwide, there has been an immense increase both in trade volumes and in financial flows. Global scale economies have increased considerably, but the growth has not been distributed evenly between countries in the North and the South and this, too, leads to instability. While worldwide trade increased in real terms by some 600 per cent in that period, the trade of the countries of the South increased by only 12 per cent. (In comparative terms, the developing countries' share of world trade dropped from about one-third of the total to one-quarter of the total.) Not surprisingly in these circumstances Canadian exports to, and imports from, the developing countries reflected a substantial drop. Canada's favourable balance of trade with the developing countries, which is substantial in volume and value and on which the Canadian economy's health relies to an important degree, is decreasing. Not at all well known to Canadians generally is the fact, mentioned earlier, that, for much of the 1980s, Canada's exports of manufactured goods to developing countries exceeded in value our exports to either Japan or all the members of the European Community combined. This market in the South is massive and is significant. Should it continue to diminish, there would be major deleterious consequences for Canadians. It is one of many illustrations of the North's dependence on the South.

Export earnings are dependent on two factors: volume and price. This means that they cannot ever be entirely within the control of an exporting country, no matter how efficient or productive it might be. Especially subject to price fluctuation are commodities, as Canadian exporters of unprocessed minerals and agricultural produce well know. This fact explains the extreme vulnerability of the economies of so many developing countries that depend in many cases almost entirely on the export of this kind of primary good. To illustrate the volatility in this sector, the world index of these items, minerals and agricultural crops in most instances, registered a year-over-year drop of 17.3 per cent in 1989.[3] In a single, dramatic instance in that period, Colombia's coffee exports earned U.S. $192 million *less* than in the previous year despite a 14 per cent *increase* in volume.[4]

Price fluctuations reflect in the first instance basic supply and demand, but these are all too often only one element of pricing mechanisms that include as well industrial countries' insistence on protecting either their own consumers or their own producers through special interventionist measures. And so the developing countries face two powerful circumstances that work against their interests. The first is their understandable inclination to overproduce, which drives down commodity prices and which acts as a disincentive to efficient producers. The second is the protectionism of the North, which attracts the support of powerful domestic interest groups even when these function at the expense of Northern consumers.

The enormity of the impact on a developing country economy of plummeting commodity prices is beyond any possible comparison with events in the industrialized countries. In Canada and the other countries of the North, there are without question occasional factory closures or industry shut-downs that have widespread, tragic consequences. The closing of a mine, for example, can turn a thitherto thriving community into a ghost town as happened for a period at Faro in the Yukon, or, still, at Sept-Isles in Quebec. A downturn in a major industry such as the Atlantic fishery can have major repercussions through a broad geographic region; so can widespread crop failures in the Prairie Provinces. These are calamities with deep implications for the well-being of thousands of people. Yet the social and economic effects are limited and softened by the buoyancy of the Canadian economy in other sectors and regions. Governments at various levels, the private sector, and voluntary organizations are all able to offer assistance. This combination extends and anchors the mutual safety net so as to break the fall of those in jeopardy. As a result, not in the past half-century has there been an enduring, national-scale economic depression in any industrialized country.

In the countries of the South, by contrast, there is in all-too-many instances an overwhelming dependence on a single economic activity. Simply stated, most economic eggs are in one basket. And to make the dependence even more keen, more often than not those eggs assume the form of a single agricultural commodity – coffee, cocoa, sugar, sisal, ground-nuts, etc. – or a single mineral – tin, copper, gold, as examples.

Should world prices collapse in one of these commodities, or should access to a major market be blocked, the results can be catastrophic. If the bulk of foreign exchange earnings is derived from that product, government income falls, social programs suffer, all related economic activity (transportation, processing, etc.) stagnates, and the country finds itself in desperate circumstances. This is the reality of an undiversified economy. This is the disadvantage of a seller in a buyer's market.

In circumstances of this kind, the efforts of the developing country itself, no matter how stalwart, can be woefully ineffective. Take the case of Ghana. Encouraged by external advisers, assisted by technical experts from the World Bank and other organizations, Ghana directed itself in the period 1983–9 to the doubling of its production of cocoa. Acreage dedicated to cocoa was extended, new cultivating techniques were introduced, scales of economy were increased. The goal was achieved. But to what end? World cocoa prices plummeted (partly as a result of oversupply) and in the result, Ghana's cocoa earnings were less than at the outset. All that effort, all the disruption to subsistence farmers as they were displaced to make room for cocoa production, all the forest destroyed by those small farmers as they sought to clear land elsewhere for the seeding of food crops, all the financial investments made – all these paid off in the negative for Ghana: environmentally negative, economically negative, socially negative.

The great agricultural industries of Europe and North America pride themselves on their efficiency and their productivity. Yet virtually none of their crop sectors are willing to engage in free market practices. Most depend on heavy state subsidies. Again and again some of these crop sectors are responsible for blocking entry within their national borders of competitive products produced more efficiently elsewhere. In the result, an uncompetitive, high-price sugar-beet industry in North America is instrumental in maintaining a highly discriminatory quota system that restricts entry of cane sugar from developing countries and is able, because of the government subsidies it receives, to depress artificially world sugar prices. The effects on developing countries are devastating. At the request of high-price domestic rice producers, the United States effectively bars entry of Asian rice, in some instances from countries that have increased the efficiency of their agricultural sector following the advice of U.S. experts. The much-heralded Caribbean Basin Initiative launched by President Reagan in 1983, which was designed to stimulate the economies of selected countries by offering improved access to United States markets, concluded its first six years with a negative contribution (–4.0 per cent for the period 1983–9). The welcome rise in export earnings in a number of non-traditional industries, including light manufacturing, was more than offset by lower world sugar prices, itself a manifestation of United States interest groups, and lower United States petroleum imports.

More is on display here than the obvious contradictions in policies of the industrialized countries, and the resulting costs to consumers and to taxpayers in those same Northern countries. Terms of trade function in these circumstances to the distinct disadvantage of most of the developing countries. If world prices for agricultural produce are determined by the strength of demand (however manipulated by the imposition of subsidies and trade barriers), by contrast the world price for manufactured goods is generally a compound of cost of production plus profit margin because oversupply is seldom encountered and is quickly corrected. In the result, manufactured goods tend to become more expensive each year, even as agricultural prices tend to be stagnant or to decline. The most eloquent of those who revealed the results was President Nyerere of Tanzania. Again and again in international forums, but perhaps most forcefully in the biennial gatherings of Commonwealth heads of government, he would relate the continuing – and increasing – spread in prices between Tanzania's exported crops and its imported requirements. How could societies such as his ever improve the welfare of their people in the face of such widening imbalances, he would ask; how, when it would take more than twice as many tons of sisal to pay for an imported farm tractor in 1975 as in 1965, and four times as much by 1985. Contributing to Tanzania's sisal marketing problems, of course, was the increasing use throughout the world of synthetics such as nylon. Contributing to the marketing problems of many developing countries is another factor, one that has much less to do with synthetic substitutes than with protectionism. It is the quota system imposed by the industrialized countries, designed to limit the penetration of Northern markets by Southern textiles and natural fibres, which took form in the Multi-Fibre Arrangement.[5] The disappointing economic performances of developing countries have been extensively examined by any number of analysts. The fact is that in developing countries there is present a multiplicity and an intermingling of external and internal factors. Not all are within the control of the developing countries.

The most influential of all those persons in the South seeking some solution to this (agriculture commodity) export versus (manufactured goods) import paradox was the brilliant Argentine economist Raul Prebisch. He observed that world demand for commodity exports was limited and very price sensitive ('elastic' in the terminology of economists) while developing country demand for manufactured goods was seemingly unlimited and quite independent of price ('inelastic'). To overcome the disadvantage that these realities presented to developing countries, he recommended to the governments of Latin America, in his capacity as the first director general of UNCTAD, that they embark on an import substitution policy: that they use their power in the form of government subsidies, tax holidays, and protectionist tariff mechanisms to favour local manufacturing sectors. In this way, Prebisch postulated, the imbalances could be contained within a national economic framework for the benefit of each country.

So attractive was this proposal, and so highly regarded was its proponent, that the Prebisch Doctrine was enthusiastically embraced by country after country in Latin America. Manufacturing flourished, but of a derivative kind. Based on imported technologies and machine tools, in many instances reflections of industrial activity elsewhere, the goods-producing sector quickly revealed all the manifestations of a 'branch-plant' economy. With the major exception of Brazil, manufacturing took the form of automobile assembly factories, soft-drink bottling plants, and small-scale machine shops. In the absence of competition and markets of adequate size, costs rose, efficiency and productivity stagnated, creativity failed to appear. With the arrival of the debt crisis in the early eighties, the need for foreign exchange earnings forced these governments to turn to export-oriented industrial policies. It was a necessary, but wrenching experience, catastrophic for hothouse enterprises and their investors. The export economies of the successful Southeast Asian nations became the new model, first in Chile, then elsewhere in Latin America. The Prebisch Doctrine had proved to be an expensive error.

These contrasts illustrate the dilemma of the South. In the sixteenth century North–South trade was composed of agricultural and other commodities paid for with primitive forms of manufactures or in currencies. This practice shifted almost entirely in the late eighteenth century to reflect the marvels of the Industrial Revolution. And so shifted as well North–South terms of trade. Thus began to build up the immense disparities in wealth between the industrialized societies and the others. This is well illustrated by estimates of GNP per capita in countries North and South before the Industrial Revolution (measured in terms of 1960 U.S. dollars): England (1700), 150–190; American colonies (1710), 250–290; France (1790), 170–200; Japan (1750), 160; India (1800), 160–210; China (1800), 228.

It can be said that Europe, before the Industrial Revolution, was less wealthy than the territories it had colonized and was exploiting. Perhaps more important, the range of disparity was limited. It was a circumstance that came firmly to an end with the Industrial Revolution. The North–South wealth imbalance shifted absolutely in the late nineteenth century as shown by total GNP calculated in billions of 1960 U.S. dollars:

	1750	*1860*	*1880*	*1900*	*1976*
North	35	115	176	299	3,000
South	120	165	169	188	1,000

Fernand Braudel, who compiled these figures, writes that the European Industrial Revolution 'was not merely an instrument of development in itself. It was a weapon of domination and destruction of foreign competition. By mechanizing, European industry became capable of out-competing the traditional industry of other nations. The gap which then opened up could only grow wider as time went on.'[6] When population disparities are added in (in 1750 the population of the world was roughly in balance between North and South; in 1976 it was 75 per cent in the South, 25 per cent in the North) the per capita contrasts become considerably greater. The reorientation of the economies of the South to reflect these realities is now under way. Immense self-discipline is evident in the more successful countries as in East Asia. Elsewhere, social suffering is widespread. Everywhere, however, economic success is dependent on external factors as well as sound domestic policies. The most important of these, of course, is continued access to the markets of the North. That access is often stoutly resisted because it can lead to disruptions and relocations in the North. What must not be lost from sight, however, is the fact that in the long run those disruptions in the North will become much more severe if the economic paralysis of the South leads to social turbulence and political instability. That is the result of interdependence. That is what is meant by mutuality of vulnerability.

The frustration of the South in the face of Northern protectionism was forcefully vented by President Sarney of Brazil to a small group of visitors who called on him in Brasilia in 1987.

You demand that we pay our debt, and do so in your currencies. To earn the foreign exchange necessary, we must sell our products to you. You won't buy them unless they are competitive. Because we don't possess novel technologies or processes, our only competitive advantage is our lower cost of labour. Since 1982, we have kept wages down even as worldwide inflation continues. For five years, in order to service our debts to your banks, Brazilians have endured a steadily decreasing standard of living. And social services have deteriorated as well because my government is told by the IMF to reduce spending on health and education. We are impoverishing ourselves in order to benefit your banks. Yet what are you now telling us? That our lower wages are unfair to *your* workers; you are now resisting entry of our goods. What do you expect us to do? How are we to pay you? You offer no advice, only criticism.[7]

Where lies the balance in this struggle? What is the extent of the penetration of the markets of the North by manufactured goods from the lower-wage countries of the South? What volume of developing country manufactures are in fact entering the industrialized countries? Not very much in the aggregate: only 2.36 per cent of all manufactures consumed in the North in 1982-3 was imported from the South, and most of that was represented by clothing. Four years later, the figure had risen slightly, but still only to 3.5 per cent.

How far do we fall short of our capacity to enrich human life worldwide when we are willing to contribute to child mortality in the South because of our fear of imported shirts. How much do we injure the future prospects of our own children by these short-sighted policies. How greatly do we damage our development assistance programs and reduce their effectiveness by our inconsistencies. How hypocritical do we appear to the nations of the South as we offer them a hand while standing on their bootstraps.

◆

Necessary as is a dynamic manufacturing sector, agriculture has, nevertheless, retained its importance in the economies of all the industrialized countries, even though it is less dominant than it once was. The recent struggles within the Uruguay Round of the GATT and the negotiations among members of the Western Economic Summit both reflect the political sensitivity as well as the economic importance of the food production and food processing industries. In the North, as these industries have become more efficient, the anomalous situation has arisen that they have become increasingly subsidized. The intention of the subsidies in large measure is to maintain the structure of the 'family farm' at a time when efficiencies of scale make these operations increasingly less viable. The subsidies have two results offshore. The first is to permit Northern agricultural produce to enter the world's markets at much less than the cost of production, which penalizes all exporters but particularly the more efficient. The second result is that a large quantity of this often-surplus produce finds its way into the food-aid programs offered by the North to the South. Unless carefully designed and soundly administered, food aid can have a depressing effect on agriculture in developing countries; an artificially low pricing structure takes hold, which is a disincentive to local farmers.

Farming in the countries of the South is of two broadly different kinds. One embraces the production of food for local consumption (which is often described as 'subsistence' agriculture) and consists of food products that are consumed by the farmer and his family, with any excess entering the local market. The products vary from place to place but generally belong to one or other of the families of roots, tubers, pulses, and fruits. The second type of farming is large-scale plantation cropping, much more akin to the big operations in the Prairie Provinces of Canada. The produce from these plantations is destined for the export market and consists of items familiar the world over – sugar, bananas, tea, cocoa, rubber, cotton. There are, of course, crossovers. For example, several crops grown by smallholders in some countries enter into international commerce – ground-nuts (peanuts), coffee, cocoa, and rice are among them – while some of the produce of larger-scale operations is locally consumed.

Because of the dependence of the countries of the North upon agricultural produce that can be grown only in tropical climates, it is in the interest of Northern consumers that the agricultural-export sector of the South be supported and bolstered. This means that there be respected there the same economic principles critical to farmers in the North and that can be summed up as 'reasonable return on investment.' The same principle applies, although in somewhat different form, to the small farmer upon whose output the burgeoning populations of the South increasingly depend for their food. There is a popular saying heard everywhere in developing countries, and which could have had its origins in the Canadian prairies a century ago, that well describes the situation:

'There are millions of farmers in the world who may not be able to read, but there are none who do not know how to count.' In most developing countries there is no form of crop insurance, no dependable credit facilities for small farmers, no welfare provisions. Life is precarious for that small farmer and he or she (in Africa, women are often the farmers) must know how to count, and count accurately. Small farmers in developing countries are historically most averse to undertaking any kind of discretionary risk; this is understandable because a successful crop year is necessary for survival. As a result, this large segment of the food production system is resistant to any innovation, no matter how promising, unless it is accompanied by some form of safety net, which developing countries are seldom able to offer. This is a major challenge to agricultural policy makers in developing countries. The enemies of increased production are by no means confined to pests, drought, poor seeds, and inappropriate cultivation practices. Deep-seated and entirely defensible social and economic stigmas must also be overcome. The entire complex of pricing structures and marketing mechanisms, so familiar to countries in the North, must be designed, introduced, and maintained.

As the appetites of Northern populations for tropical produce extend and increase, the mutual advantage of sustainable agriculture – sustainable both economically and environmentally – is self-evident. But theory and practice are far distant one from the other. The agricultural sector worldwide has historically been subject to wild price fluctuations as weather conditions intervene in the market mechanisms of supply and demand. In the countries of the North, governments and populations have long accepted the desirability of some form of mechanism to moderate these fluctuations and, in so doing, protect the income of the producer and the supply of produce to the consumer. The challenge in doing so is to avoid the introduction of subsidy practices. Marketing boards of one form or another are familiar and functional, and can be subsidy-free. In the countries of the South, there is little evidence of this kind of activity and, as among producer countries, few with a successful history. Not unexpectedly, with all emphasis given to production, a massive oversupply (as in the case of Ghanaian cocoa) depresses prices catastrophically. Equally, freak weather conditions can diminish output and cause prices to soar (as happened when frost decimated the Brazilian coffee crop in 1975–6 and world prices consequently increased almost tenfold).

The case clearly exists for modulating mechanisms. The initial international endeavours of the developing countries in this direction were quite unsuccessful, however, and there has been little evidence of South–South cooperation since. Those earlier attempts took the form of proposals for a mammoth 'common fund' to permit the creation of buffer stocks for eighteen different commodities. Coming as these proposals did hard on the heels of the successes of the OPEC cartel, which both reduced production and increased prices, there was widespread resistance in the North. The political aversion to cartels, when combined with the extraordinary technical problems associated with the regulation of such a comprehensive basket of individual commodities, rang the death-knell of this scheme. First introduced by the South during a Special Session of the United Nations General Assembly in April 1974, later discussed at the fourth UNCTAD Conference in Nairobi in May 1976, the common fund proposal finally gained international acceptance in principle through a resolution of the General Assembly in 1989. By then, however, there was virtually no chance that it could be successfully implemented.

Yet the need remains for a common understanding of the benefits to be gained both North and South from a healthy, reasonably predictable agricultural sector in the South. The benefits are not just environmental or economic: two major consequences, both discussed later, are social tranquillity and political stability. The tropical regions as well have a considerable comparative advantage in the production of a range of sometimes exotic plant varieties. Especially as Northern demand increases for tropical fruits and vegetables, nuts, and cut flowers, and as the new discipline of biotechnology advances, there is a promising future with a number of attractive applications, including the medicinal. These opportunities must not be pursued to the detriment of subsistence agriculture, however. Wise and innovative management practices and reforms are demanded. These will be difficult to design and administer as our experience has proved. One major barrier is the still all-too-common assumption that Northern agricultural practices are, or should be, transferable to the South.

A common hazard in tropical climates is the negative impact of intensive agriculture on soil quality and terrain. The destructive environmental effect of crops varies and is not confined to those cultivated for export, although the long-term negative results of monocropping (as distinct from traditional mixed cropping) are well known. Soil erosion and exhaustion can result from inappropriate small-farm practices such as intensive tillage, just as forest clearing, pesticide residues, fertilizer applications, and curing or drying techniques associated with such plantation crops as cotton and tobacco can be devastating for long-term environmental health. Only geographically broad, regional policies will be adequate, not the immediate pressures of this or that market.

Broad-scale balancing of the dedication of crop lands to export crops and consumption crops becomes, therefore, a necessary starting point. The advantages to be gained include a better equilibrium between food crops (often inadequate to meet local needs) and export crops (all too often in excess supply) as well as soil protection. In this kind of complicated and long-term exercise, the developing countries will have to cooperate among themselves (including traditional competitors in the various crop sectors) as well as with the industrialized countries. And as necessary as anything else will be the choice of the most appropriate forum within which the research and discussions can take place. A territorial feud involving a number of specialized U.N. agencies would send sorry signals to publics long sceptical of the effectiveness and speed of response of multilateral institutions. There is good reason to be impatient, for becoming increasingly clear year by year is the debilitating effect of non-cooperation. The population increases in the countries of the South are placing severe strains on the carrying capacity of the natural habitat. Much of the destruction of the natural forests is by destitute families moving further and further afield, clearing land as they go in a desperate and futile attempt to grow food for their own survival. As one example of many, worldwide, the last major segment of tropical rain forest in Mexico is now under such sustained pressure that it will disappear by the turn of the century in the absence of effective remedial measures. At the present time, none are in sight.

An essential element in determining the most efficient as well as the most effective of mixes is research. A multiplicity of disciplines must work together to compose a better body of knowledge of all the key ingredients – biological, economic, and social. The contribution of a broad range of scientists and technologists is required, all working within well-understood policy guidelines. The old Northern arrogance of technological fixes, determined independently from the peculiar social and cultural environments of the developing countries, must be avoided. The extensive knowledge gained through the network of international agricultural research centres, both those within and those without the Consultative Group on International Agricultural Research, as well as the rich experience of IDRC, provides a sound basis for further work. For twenty years IDRC has assisted the developing countries in imaginative ways to enhance their own scientific competence and thus solve their own problems in a wide spectrum of disciplines. The groundwork is now firmly, and often adequately, in place in many developing countries to permit a series of integrated interdisciplinary studies aimed at providing policy makers with the information and options necessary to take wise decisions. The role of the North increasingly must take the form of sympathetic support, not intrusive technical involvement. Obvious as this fact is, it is not favoured by the Northern aid community. In sub-Saharan Africa at the present time, notwithstanding the presence there of a vigorous, large, and well-trained number of African agricultural and some other scientists, fully two-thirds of all aid from the North (U.S. $400 million of the U.S. $600 million currently dedicated to research) takes the form of salaries paid to expatriate experts. How unwilling is the North to relinquish its self-imposed parental relationship.

◆

Of the many elements that bind the countries of the world together, it is the economic that has made itself most evident. In a remarkably short period of time, the realization has grown that no nation, no matter how large or how powerful, is able to manage its economy without major reference to events elsewhere. The case was stated cogently by Peter Drucker in 1986: 'From now on any country – but also any business, especially a large one – that wants to prosper will have to accept that it is the world economy that leads and that domestic economic policies will succeed only if they strengthen, or at least do not impair, the country's international competitive position.'[8] Not surprisingly, national political leaders are reluctant to embrace such a statement. Notwithstanding that the respected and experienced U.S. investment banker Robert Hormats had stated, 'More than at any time in this century, U.S. economic well-being depends on conditions abroad,'[9] UNCTAD found that: 'In the 1980s, countries' policies, on the whole, have been framed without regard to their international consequences.'[10]

One of the challenges faced by governments as they design policies is the increasingly difficult task of obtaining and analysing relevant information. This is so not because of an inadequacy of data, but because of its overwhelming volume and because of the difficulty of managing the key ingredients. An example is found in the area of capital flows. Critical to the performance of any economy is the availability of capital. Capital flows involved in investment, as in the repayment of debt, are the lifeblood of economic activity. Not long ago, capital flows were not only measurable, they were subject to governmental management. Now, increasingly, they are neither. One reason is that they now include a disproportionately large speculative element. Another reason is that the recent introduction of marvellous new technologies that permit high-speed transfers of information and data, computer to computer via satellite, continent to continent, has led to massive financial flows and virtually instantaneous, non-stop stock-market activity. 'Goods' of all sorts, their producers in the form of shares of enterprises, and their countries of origin in the form of national currencies, are now subject to speculative trading around the world and around the clock.

As recently as thirty years ago, 90 per cent of foreign exchange transactions funded trade in a direct sense. That is no longer the case. Of the total volume of flows in the principal world capital markets today – estimated to be in excess of u.s. $430 billion in each twenty-four-hour period – less than 10 per cent can be characterized as trade financing or as investment. The rest is trading in currencies, a form of futuristic speculation. It is largely uncontrolled because so many national jurisdictions are involved, and because few governments are as yet willing to surrender to an international regulatory body what they believe to be their sovereignty, ineffective though they are in exercising it. These transactions make little distinction between unprocessed primary commodities, frozen orange juice concentrates, or national currencies. In this kind of environment, human benefit, whether in North or in South, is simply not a factor. The world's economy has assumed the form of a mammoth electronic dice game in which meteorological conditions are a much more important factor than is human wisdom. Technology in the form of telephones, computers, and earth-orbiting satellites is a driving force; governments are scrambling to understand the impact and are far from able effectively to monitor or regulate these flows, let alone to make full use of the information available as they construct their national policy frameworks. In the result, orderliness and preferred outcomes are quite uncertain.

If the desired outcomes of a global economic system are to include such positive factors as stability, predictability, and sustainability, there is little evidence that present practices are contributing to those ends. Indeed, much conventional doctrine – continued economic growth on present terms, for one – provides guarantees that those desired qualities, sustainability in particular, will not be attainable. Perhaps more so than at any previous point in history, it is clear that economic activity is taking on a form and thrust of its own, indifferent to the efforts of elected governments to influence it, bearing little relation to its origins as 'household management.' The effect of this evolution is clearly evident in the broad disparities of living standards among different populations and communities. A tragic irony is found in the fact that in this recent era of global access to information, the use made of that information, and the acquisitive ethic that drives its transmission, appear blind to the changes – not all positive – that these economic activities are creating.

To understand the momentum of these processes, it is necessary to reflect in some detail on the immense expansion of international trade, investment, and bank lending that has taken place in the past half-century, and on the unevenness of that expansion. As mentioned earlier, world trade has expanded in unprecedented proportions: sixfold if measured in real terms, thirtyfold if measured in current dollars.[11] Comparable data for international investment and credit flows are not available, but some sense can be gained from a look at the United States experience. Between 1970 and 1986 alone, U.S.-owned overseas assets of all types rose 6.5 times to U.S. $1.07 trillion, while foreign-owned assets in the United States rose 12.5 times to U.S. $1.3 trillion.[12] Stocks of foreign direct investment in the world as a whole appear to have risen from U.S. $68 billion in 1960 to U.S. $714 billion in 1985.[13]

This huge increase in the volume of international transactions is a daunting challenge for all economic managers. The volume of financial flows in particular is a major problem. Of the U.S. $430 billion figure of daily capital flow mentioned above, the turnover in the Eurodollar market alone each working day in 1986 was estimated to be U.S. $300 billion. (Annualized, that converts to U.S. $75 trillion, a sum twenty-five times the value of world trade.)[14] Not surprisingly, volumes of this magnitude have not gone unnoticed. The search for some means to coordinate policies to reduce disequilibria is perhaps most concentrated in the mechanisms of the annual Western Economic Summits. To be overcome are those difficulties that find expression in national rivalries and competition and are evident in the huge trade and payments imbalances between the principal industrial countries of the North. It was this situation that prompted Paul Volcker, near the conclusion of his term as chairman of the U.S. Federal Reserve Board, to portray the world economy as suffering from a 'massive international disequilibrium.'

Whatever solutions are chosen to deal with these imbalances, they will be of intense interest to the countries of the South, countries that are not always present at the table. For them, the immense expansion of international trade and financial flows has not led to an even distribution of benefits. With the exception of the period 1966–75, the growth of the value of the external trade of the industrialized capitalist nations has consistently exceeded that of the developing countries. The South's share of world trade fell from about 36 per cent in 1955 to about 25 per cent in 1987. Three-quarters of the investment activities of multinational corporations are in the North;[15] transnational banks have lent 75 per cent of their stock of loans in the North.

A partial disaggregation of overall global financial flows reveals that, as a group, the developing countries have fared much less well than the industrialized countries in the thirty-five years or so since many of them attained independence. Disaggregating further, one finds that the small number of newly industrialized countries (NICs) has succeeded much better than most. All countries, North and South, have been influenced during this period by the decision of the major industrialized countries early in the seventies to commit themselves (more or less) to floating exchange rates and then, a decade later, to adopt policies of monetarism. The immediate result of the latter was a depression of demand in those countries that was exacerbated as interest rates rose to record levels. These rates inflated beyond recognition the debt problems faced by many countries in the South.

The new monetarist policies had the effect of ending one well-known social system and beginning another, one that was the product more of improvisation than of thoughtful design. Governments consciously chose to venture into uncharted territory in an endeavour to overcome the economic crisis in which many of the countries of the North found themselves. In the process, Keynesian employment policies were abandoned, credit was tightened, social spending cut back, organized labour attacked, and income redistributed in a new and often inequitable manner. All this was done in an effort to assist Northern recovery in the rates of profit, and to lay the foundation for a period of sustained economic growth. The objectives were to shake out uncompetitive companies, to reduce the cost of labour, and to create a new climate for growth and acquisitiveness. The effects on most developing countries have been catastrophic and long lasting. From 1981 to 1988 real per capita incomes of Southern countries fell by 18 per cent as exports declined, debt servicing costs rose dramatically, and real flows of official assistance fell. Only the countries of Asia escaped relatively unscathed because of their larger domestic economies, their lower external debt burdens, and their proximity (in some cases) to Japan. A major, initial impact on the South of all these factors has taken the form of huge balance-of-payments deficits. These are the result of a rapid increase in the service charges of their foreign debt and a fall-off in their export earnings as demand for their products has fallen. This combination of factors precipitated the debt crisis of the eighties. The current account deficit of the fifteen most heavily indebted countries rose to U.S. $50 billion in 1981; by 1989 the accumulated debt of all developing countries had reached U.S. $1.3 trillion. With the exception of the oil exporters, who were to enjoy large surpluses until prices dropped, and the NICs of East Asia, who came to be called the 'Four Tigers' (Hong Kong, Singapore, South Korea, and Taiwan), a period of considerable economic difficulty settled over the developing world. For all countries, the major challenge became one of managing money flows.

For the oil exporters, the collapse of oil prices led to a deterioration of their current account balances of some U.S. $64 billion between 1981 and 1986. The drama of this turnaround placed in shadow the circumstances of other countries. Although the industrialized countries were able to halve their deficits during this period, the developing countries, over all, stayed about the same. Individual performances varied considerably, however. It was the extraordinarily dynamic performance of the 'Tigers' that balanced much of the deficit of the others.

Not surprisingly, the means by which the developing countries sought to control their balance-of-payments problems was quite asymmetric. The successful performance of the Tigers was almost entirely the result of expanding exports; the large debtors, in contrast, chose to reduce their imports. Overall, import compression became the single most important policy characteristic as the debtor countries sought to adjust to the circumstances facing them in the period 1981–6. Real imports fell by an astonishing 35 per cent as domestic demand was dampened through policies of austerity.[16]

This overall reduction of economic performance by the countries of the South affected the North very much. Markets in the South for exports from the North contracted sharply. For Canada, 12 per cent of total exports in 1980 were to the South. By 1987, the figure dropped to 7.6 per cent, with a huge number of jobs lost as a result. Fully one-half of all United States sales to Latin America disappeared. The South's intake of world exports declined from 33.4 per cent in 1980 to 24.8 per cent in 1987. Apart from their trade with the NICs, the countries of the North looked to one another increasingly as markets, not always successfully and certainly not without major sectoral disruptions.

A major contributing factor to the lower value of trade was the drop in oil prices, but prices for commodities other than fuel fell as well, by 25 per cent between 1981 and 1986. Terms of trade for developing countries deteriorated significantly throughout much of the eighties. The aggregate drop was shared between oil exporters (42.2 per cent) and non–oil exporters (7.4 per cent).[17] In the last three years of the decade there was some modest recovery (1.7 per cent) in terms of trade for non–oil exporters. On the whole, however, the decade recorded relative price changes very much to the detriment of the South. In two major regions of the world, Latin America and sub-Saharan Africa, the 1980s have been dubbed the 'lost decade': ten years of shattered hopes, increasing despondency and frustration, and seeds of bitterness among millions of youngsters, many of them well educated, who remain unemployed and without hope. They represent a brooding, ever-growing challenge to the future stability of the entire world.

If not necessarily the dominant element in the desperate economic plight of so many developing countries, the debt issue is perhaps the most visible and the most explosive in terms of generating passion on both sides of the 'debt-divide.'

◆

No single North–South issue has likely attracted so much sustained public
attention as has the 'debt crisis.' The sheer size of the debt itself – now
approaching U.S. $1.3 trillion – is as baffling to the layman as it is enti-
cing. Seldom, however, does any detailed discussion of the issue appear
other than in the financial pages of newspapers. There, assuredly, there
is no translation into human terms of the effect of huge interest payments
on daily life in the debtor countries, no indication of the hopelessness that
descends on a society whose resources increasingly are channelled into
debt servicing for the benefit of foreign creditors, yet seem to accomplish
nothing in debt reduction. Canadian parliamentarians prefaced a 1990
special report on debt with the statement: 'Most developing country
debtors were undertaking painful economic "adjustments", often at the
expense of the already poor and vulnerable members of their societies,
but with little evidence of sustained recovery being achieved.'[8] In the
absence of major turnarounds, the future prospects for major regions of
the world are dismal, to the benefit of no one. Two comments by experienced observers are telling. Speaking of Latin America, Pedro Pablo
Kuczynski, a former minister of energy and mines of Peru, now chairman of the large New York financial house First Boston International,
told an international conference in Japan in October 1989: 'The problem is not just the obvious fact that we are dropping behind, far behind,
but also that the time lost – in terms of living standards, modernization
and social welfare – for the generation that has entered the labour market
in this decade is lost forever.' Adebayo Adedeji, executive secretary of the
United Nations Economic Commission for Africa, told a press conference in London, England, in July 1989: 'Africa must take charge of its
own future. If we do not set our own house in order, if the economic
deterioration continues, Africa could be completely marginalized in
international relations, of interest only to welfare agencies.' In terms
uncharacteristically foreboding for politicians, the Canadian Standing
Committee warned that 'the unfinished business of Third World debt
pose[s] a grave threat to our common future on the planet.'[19]

More, of course, than debt lies behind the current, floundering
economies of so many developing countries. Current circumstances are
not, as sometimes simplistically depicted, the results of either Draconian

measures taken by hard-hearted banks on the one hand, endeavouring to reverse their earlier lending errors, or ill-conceived and partly corrupt development projects on the part of the borrowing countries on the other. Other factors there certainly are, numerous, complex, and interlinked, yet debt must be recognized as a major determinant of poor economic health in many developing countries. Just how central this issue is to modern economic planners is the fact that the IMF–World Bank Joint Library acquired 435 books and 2,940 articles and working papers under the catalogue heading 'external debt' in the eight-year period 1982–90.[20]

In retrospect, it is quite clear that the extraordinary changes in the global economy that came to pass in the early eighties could not have been anticipated by either lenders or borrowers when the great percentage of the present stock of loans was negotiated. At a time of great fluidity resulting from high oil prices, and a desire on the part of the oil-exporting countries to put to work their ballooning incomes, immense pressure grew within the world's financial system to recycle the funds. The IMF took several steps to alleviate these pressures, two of them in the form of temporary oil facilities to assist governments as they struggled with a balancing act of unprecedented dimensions. Both the government-funded international financial institutions (IFIs – the World Bank and the several regional Development Banks) and the private banks turned to the developing countries as potential borrowers of sufficient magnitude to absorb the immense sums suddenly flowing into the banks. Over a short period of time, one of the world's largest-ever exercises of redistribution of wealth took place.

The loan contracts were negotiated without duress and without any special conditions. The IFIs and the private banks all lent money at prevailing interest rates with the normal provision that service charges be calculated over the term of the loans on the basis of actual, as distinct from fixed, rates. Should rates change, then the borrowers' obligations would vary correspondingly. In the period 1975–8, yearly averages for three-month loans at the London Inter-Bank Offered Rate (LIBOR), on which all lending rates are based, varied from a low of 5.55 per cent to a high of 8.85 per cent. During this period, outstanding debt increased by U.S. $146 billion, made up of loans to the developing countries by private sources ($95 billion), governments ($33 billion), and the IFIs ($18 billion). The intended purposes of the loans were the financing of a broad range of projects, primarily in the form of infrastructure in the case of the sovereign loans. In the private sector, the money was to be used most often for the normal range of industrial, resource extraction, and commercial types of activity.

The conventional wisdom in financial markets during this period assumed that interest rates would remain stable and low as a result of the anticipated massive flows into the market of petrodollars. Low interest rates are generally of advantage to both institutional lender and borrower. It is the depositor, not the bank, that profits most from high rates.

In 1981–2 the unpredicted happened. Interest rates began moving sharply upward, peaking at a LIBOR of 16.78 per cent in 1981 before sliding downward somewhat, and in August 1982, Mexico announced that it could no longer service its debt. The debt crisis had arrived.

In 1980 the global stock of Third World loans totalled approximately U.S. $731.5 billion. Each rise of 1 per cent in the interest rate represented therefore an additional annual interest charge of U.S. $7.31 billion. By 1981–2 the annual service charges on foreign debt for which the developing countries were responsible had risen to U.S. $124.1 billion. In country after country, the percentage of export earnings dedicated to the servicing of the foreign debt rose alarmingly. In some instances it represented one-half or more of all foreign exchange earnings. For example, Mexico employed 55 per cent of its foreign earnings to service its debt, Equador 66 per cent, and Argentina 72 per cent. The poorest of African countries were affected even more seriously. The ratios for Somalia and Mozambique were 167 per cent and 205 per cent respectively.

As discussed earlier, most governments chose to sacrifice imports to service their debts. Again and again, national strategies took the form of reduction of imports, with far-reaching impact on those economies in the North that had exported goods (often manufactured goods of a high value-added nature) into those markets. In the United States alone, in the period 1980–5 it has been estimated that reduced U.S. exports to developing countries were responsible for the loss of 1.7 million jobs.[21] In Canada, the losses were of the same magnitude. From 1981 to 1989, according to the North South Institute in Ottawa, Canada lost Can. $40.5 billion, equivalent to 180,000 Canadian jobs, in exports to the seventeen most highly indebted countries alone. Those private banks in the North with considerable Southern exposure found themselves holding a large stock of sometimes overdue and sometimes non-performing loans. In due course a painful series of exercises commenced that involved, within individual banks, the establishment of reserves and, internationally, endeavours to negotiate broad, all-party accords on a country-by-country basis.

As with disruptions and variations in merchandise and investment flows, so did (and does) the Third World debt crisis affect different countries in different ways. For purposes of analysis, it is convenient to divide the developing countries into four distinct groups: (1) the four NICs, (2) the oil exporters, (3) the fifteen largest debtors, and (4) the poorest countries. At the beginning of the eighties the first two categories, overall, had relatively low debt burdens measured against either Gross Domestic Product (GDP) or exports, and very low annual debt service burdens. Even here, however, there were exceptions. Mexico and Venezuela were problem debtors, and South Korea was close to becoming one. The debt crisis was felt most acutely by the second two categories. In some instances, debt approached or exceeded 40 per cent of GDP and 200 per cent of annual exports. A major difference between these two groups was apparent, however. Because some three-quarters of the debt of the poorest countries was to official agencies (both multilateral and bilateral), and much of this on concessional terms, the debt service burden for this group was only one-half that of the largest debtors.

In the course of the decade, developing country debt in its entirety grew by 63 per cent as a result of missed payments, rescheduling, and the relentless effect of compound interest. Fresh inflows from the North were so insignificant that transfers as a whole assumed a perverse and entirely unintended net flow from the poor of the South to the rich of the North. Of the four groups, only the NICs have been able, since 1986, to reduce somewhat their indebtedness. For the group of largest debtors, debt burdens at the end of the decade were no lower than at the beginning in terms of GDP, and had risen considerably measured as a percentage of export earnings. This was the position notwithstanding ten years of massive and painful service payments. Servicing for this group has now stabilized at about 40 per cent of exports. The debt burden of the oil exporters has increased significantly over the decade, to the point that several members of this group must now be regarded as problem debtors. The debt service burden of this group has more than doubled since 1981, and is now at about the same level as that of the poorest countries. Those latter, once relatively better off because of the concessional nature of their debts, are now in the worst position of all as defaults and compounding have combined inexorably.

As the nineties commenced, interest payments (not charges, which are much larger, but actual payments) on foreign debt amounted to U.S. $100 billion a year. Over the nine-year period 1981–9, interest payments totalled U.S. $773 billion, a sum larger than the total Third World debt outstanding at the beginning of the decade. The figures for individual countries reveal the dilemma. Brazil, for example, paid interest on its foreign debt in the amount of U.S. $176 billion between 1972 and 1988. Nevertheless, in 1990, the debt stood at U.S. $113 billion. Interest payments are now twice as large as the balance-of-trade account for the South as a whole and almost seven times the size of trade balances for the net debtor countries.

Perhaps no other issue has revealed in such startling and immediate fashion the interpenetration of the economies of countries North and South, and the vulnerability of the North towards the South. Environmental, social, and security questions are either so diffuse or so distant in their impact as to appear fuzzy to the public eye. The debt crisis, by comparison, is here and now. The money is owed to the governments and the banks of the North; defaults have an immediate impact upon bank earnings, upon dividends to shareholders, and upon the confidence levels of depositors. The inability of countries in the South coincidentally to buy Northern goods and to pay interest to Northern banks means the loss of Northern jobs.

Quite remarkably, most debtor nations have continued their payments, often at immense cost in social terms and individual standards of living. In the absence of adequate foreign funds to service foreign debt, governments incur debt domestically in their attempt to provide necessary services. The scant domestic savings pool is monopolized and overrun, creating immense inflationary pressures. In sub-Saharan Africa and Latin America, incomes and living conditions deteriorated over the decade. Perhaps most telling of all, and most distressing, is the daily deaths of tens of thousands of children from preventable or treatable diseases.

Nevertheless, repudiations or unilateral alterations of loan conditions have been rare. Perhaps the most widely publicized reaction was that of

Peru where the government of President Alain Garcia declared Peru's unwillingness to pay service charges in excess of 10 per cent of export earnings. In Zambia, President Kenneth Kaunda introduced a similar policy. Nevertheless, the 1985 siren song of Fidel Castro imploring the debtor nations of the South to renounce their debt obligations as part of a common stand-off negotiation seemingly fell for the most part on deaf ears.

During this period, some of the public pronouncements in the North, and the general political indecisiveness, betrayed a disturbing absence of leadership. Some of the biggest creditor banks threatened withdrawal from any Southern countries that might dishonour or repudiate debt agreements. Some lending institutions expressed indignation when they belatedly discovered that loan proceeds had been diverted to inappropriate uses. Less was said of the active involvement of branches of these same banks in some of the practices now criticized: the unauthorized transfer of funds to overseas accounts in Miami or Zurich, the investment of funds in illegal pursuits and the subsequent laundering of profits, the use of funds for politically inspired and wholly inefficient enterprises. Several Canadian banks expressed their intention to introduce sanctions in the event of non-performance. 'I'm suggesting that we don't just walk away and smile ...' said the chairman of the Canadian Imperial Bank of Commerce.[22] (Similar reactions by the Canadian chartered banks toward the debt-strapped Prairie Provinces during the depression of the 1930s created an attitude of hostility towards 'Eastern' banks that plagues to this day political attitudes in Canada.) On the whole, however, the banks regarded their management of the debt crisis as a success. Success it was in terms of avoiding a major crisis in the international financial system, but credit for this should surely go to the impoverished developing countries who manfully continued their interest payments. By contrast, the banks themselves more often than not did little more than take advantage of attractive tax laws to create reserves.

As disturbing as any of the debt-related pronouncements, however, were those of American politicians who maintained that Congress was not about to 'bail-out' the banks. No reflection was shown here of the encouragement given to the banks by all Northern governments in the early eighties to participate in recycling. No reflection was given, either, of the social circumstances of the developing countries, of the deterioration in political stability, and of the increase in security-related turbulence. Probably not surprisingly, no mention was made either of the immense coincidental bail-out of domestic U.S. savings and loan institutions, which, during the laissez-faire Reagan administration, had acted so imprudently as to make publicly funded assistance necessary, now frequently estimated in the hundreds of billions of dollars, before all accounts are settled sometime in the future.

Discreetly, bank representatives in the United States, Canada, and other Northern countries seldom mentioned the fact that public funds, indirectly in the form of legal deductions from the banks' taxable income, were, in effect, 'bailing out' the banks. Canadian tax law, for example, permits banks to deduct provisions against loan losses up to 45 per cent of the total exposure. It is not that these laws or these uses of public funds are inappropriate in these circumstances – indeed the case can be made that other, additional, mechanisms be made available – it is the process that must be criticized. This kind of unexplained, almost invisible activity leaves members of the public uninformed and uninvolved, which in democratic societies is both wrong and unforgivable. It permitted public servants in testimony to legislators to argue that these issues were for the private sector to address. And it allowed the private bankers to argue that the blame for this difficult situation lay upon the developing countries. Seldom was there any admission that the loans were freely negotiated in open circumstances ten years earlier, presumably with the involvement of informed and adult bank officials. Infrequently in Canada were there balanced observations by senior bankers that recognized the shared responsibility and the plight of actors both North and South as a result of the economic circumstances in which they found themselves.

The position of the banks certainly has improved, and their exposure been reduced, owing to a multitude of individual actions. Reserves have been increased; the weakest of the debts have been discounted and sold in secondary markets, allowing the initial lender to recover some of its money; some loans have been 'swapped' (traded) for equity positions in national enterprises in the developing countries. But in none of these circumstances have the developing countries gained any net advantage. The face value of the paper representing the loan remains the same. Canadian banks have not written off or written down the debts, as the popular press in error so often reports; they have set aside reserves, compensated by income tax benefits.

These loan-loss reserves are not insignificant in size. During the fourth quarter of 1989 alone, reserves were built up by Can. $4.1 billion. Canadian chartered banks in the period 1986–9 reduced their total exposure to developing country debt by Can. $9.4 billion, or 37 per cent, and improved their reserve coverage from 12 per cent to 67 per cent. Their net exposure on their developing country loans fell from 5.4 per cent of total assets in 1986 to 1.1 per cent in 1989. Without question, this is a noteworthy achievement, but none of it has been done without the co-operation of developing countries at great cost to their own populations, and none of it is worthy of the pious self-congratulations of some bank executives.

The 'socialization' of bank debts has taken an additional form in each of the (abortive) Baker Plan of 1985 and Brady Plan of 1989. The first sought to increase much-needed credit flows to the developing countries on the part of the World Bank, the IMF, and the private banks. The latter institutions refused, in effect, to act. The Baker proposal was important, however, for it was the first acknowledgment by the Reagan administration that developing country debt was a problem. The Brady Plan went one step further: it proposed converting loans to grants. The Canadian government agreed to these conversions in 1987, and then later extended them to a number of debt-distressed countries on condition that these would undergo IMF supervised structural adjustment programs.[23] The 1988 Western Economic Summit in Toronto supported a menu of debt relief options that included grace periods, interest rate reductions, rescheduling, and actual debt reductions in a variety of combinations. All this was welcome but is subject to IMF agreements, country by country. As a result, national economic policies are conditional on IMF approval virtually annually with all of the uncertainty and continuing inconvenience that this entails for creditors.[24]

It must be stressed that the provisions apply only to bilateral public debt, not to private bank debt, or to multilateral debt. The World Bank and the IMF are not constitutionally capable of either rescheduling or writing down their loans. Their role is therefore restricted to the establishment of new facilities for the refinancing of debts.

Of as much concern to the debtor nations as debt relief is their need for fresh financial flows. During the eighties, net flows diminished dramatically, down from U.S. $43 billion in 1981 to U.S. $7.3 billion in 1989.

Annual flows of official loans are now back up to about the same level as they were in 1981. The most dramatic changes, however, are in the form of private transactions. Foreign direct investments (net) are down U.S. $4.5 billion per year relative to 1981; borrowings from private banks have fallen by U.S. $94 billion in the same period.[25]

Net flows of IMF credits have never been a significant source of finance for developing countries. Their importance is found in their trigger effect, releasing funds from other sources once IMF loan conditions are met. Nevertheless, during the years 1986–8, IMF flows turned negative (–U.S. $5.9 billion in 1987). IMF approvals also trigger reschedulings. These latter, in the period 1981–9, totalled U.S. $276 billion, evidence of the extraordinary weakness of so many developing country economies and the unpleasant fact that many countries, quite incapable of ever retiring their debts, face a seemingly never-ending future of interest payments.

This modern form of South to North tribute shapes and limits the economic and political freedom of developing countries. Coincidentally it shapes the image in the South of the North. As social and economic conditions deteriorate, as they do in so many countries, and political stability and security become less certain, so too does this tribute payment limit the policy options of the countries of the North.

If the nations of the South are to be able to lift themselves by their own bootstraps, more is required than simply their own efforts. The economies of the North must be sufficiently vigorous, and open, to absorb increasing volumes of developing country exports. There is no guarantee (some would say that under present policy circumstances no likelihood) of this happening. The immense United States balance-of-payments deficit (U.S. $152 billion in 1989) discourages any likelihood of an early turnaround. In the meantime, a myopia continues that is wrongly accusatory of the developing countries, blaming manufacturers in the South rather than U.S. military spending for the U.S. deficits. Harris has stated: 'it suited everybody to blame the foreigners and their wretched manufacturers for the difficulties rather than presidential war mongering ... Without foreigners it would have been necessary to invent them.'[26]

A successful passage into the twenty-first century for both North and South surely depends on more enlightened – and more accurate – analyses. Equally important, it demands a reduction in finger pointing and an increase in cooperative policy making. In the words of the House of Commons Standing Committee: 'dealing with the unfinished business of international debt is a political responsibility shared by the developed and the developing world. It is, moreover, a matter of enlightened mutual interest and public justice not charity, which calls for actions that are democratic, human-centred, and in harmony with the environment.'[7]

◆

The terms 'North' and 'South' are a convenient form of shorthand to group large numbers of countries that share in broad fashion certain characteristics, some of them of an economic nature. There is a danger, however, that this classification may be interpreted in ways that mask major dissimilarities among countries in either grouping or within individual countries. Canada and the United States, for example, are clearly countries of the North: politically independent, industrialized, active participants in world capital markets. Yet in each country there can be found geographic pockets of poverty where there is little evidence of vibrant economic activity, where incomes are determined by the vagaries of natural resource exploitation (often controlled by 'outside' owners), and where the range of economic and social indicators reveals a marked disparity from the national averages. These are 'developing' regions within 'developed' countries. So, too, in certain countries of the South, there are vibrant economic regions that set the region and the country apart from others. In these circumstances, the diversity of social group interests – as among gender, class, or race – tends to become hidden in aggregated statistical data. This clouds the true picture, and complicates the task of policy makers. Critics in countries of the North, for example, who quite understandably become enraged at the breadth of wealth disparities in the South, often tend to overlook the presence of the same phenomenon in the North.

At the onset of the 1990s, an immense heterogeneity in economic performance is evident among the countries of the South. It is important to distinguish among the different groups in order to understand better the reasons for the varying patterns of growth and disequilibria, for the implications of various types of international policies, and for the assessment of development prospects. Statistics reveal, for example, that the four NICs and the eighteen oil exporters together account for over 75 per cent of investment in the South by multinational corporations,[28] and for over 80 per cent of foreign lending to developing countries by transnational banks and by other private sector lenders.[29] Partly as a result, the trade performance of the NICs has been extraordinary. They increased their share of world exports from 7.2 per cent in 1970 to 12.5 per cent in 1987. Their trade in real terms was an astonishing 9.3 times as high in 1987 as in 1955, more than 50 per cent higher than the growth in world trade as a whole.

By sharp contrast, the share of world export trade for forty-five small, low-income countries (most of which are in sub-Saharan Africa) has fallen steadily from 3.2 per cent in 1955 to 0.6 per cent in 1987. Although the global increase in world trade was 600 per cent in real dollar terms in that same period, these countries increased their exports by only 12.7 per cent. They account for less than 6 per cent of the stock of direct foreign investment in developing countries and for only 2.8 per cent of foreign private loans there. These countries are highly dependent on flows of official development assistance. Their plight is an agonizing one: increasing poverty, declining literacy, worsening health.

Such contrasts as these make clear how inappropriate it is to extend general theories to all developing countries. The success of the NICs and the evidence in some other instances of increased manufacturing capability, as in Thailand, have led to observations that there is a growing 'new international division of labour.' This trend is marked by a shift of capital from North to South to take advantage of new forms of work organization that use the pools of comparatively cheap labour found there as well as innovations in transportation technology that lessen the importance of industrial locations. A closer examination reveals that these tendencies are found in only a few countries, however, and are limited to certain individual industries, of which electronic components are the best example. More important, it can be shown that this form of manufacturing with its high import content, its low local-value added, and its high rates of profit remittance often simply re-creates underdevelopment in a new, industrialized form.[30] Dependency remains, as does the inability of these countries to generate production or decisions which reflect in the first instance local interests.

The assumption that the Northern industrial model is a desirable one for replication in the South is now widespread and forms the foundation for planning policies in most developing countries. It is an assumption that must be challenged, however, just as the Northern model itself must undergo significant alteration. Not to challenge it is to overlook the massive environmental damage now accumulating from energy-intensive, consumer-driven societies, and to minimize the destructive social repercussions from such phenomena as underemployment, substance abuse, and the decay of many large cities. The all-too-common tendency within industrialized societies to accept as normal gross inequalities in income and wealth, pollution and waste, the alienation of differing classes, and the relegation of moral values to the pursuit of private gain is simply not a pattern that should be transferred into a South where 4 billion now live and where population levels will reach as high as 6.3–6.8 billion in the next twenty-five years. Neither political stability nor natural ecosystems can absorb those numbers if the production and consumption patterns of the North continue and are imitated elsewhere.

In its arrogance, the North has not thought through these contradictions, has not recognized its own responsibility and its own need to change, has not well examined the alarming circumstances and trends now evident in the South, and has not understood the implications of the economic heterogeneity now present in all regions of the world. If there is such a phenomenon as a 'global manufacturing system,' for example, as the popular financial press seems to suggest, it certainly excludes the poorest countries. At most, some developing countries have been able to reduce their import dependence upon the North by creating a degree of manufacturing competence to meet domestic demand. Trade statistics do not yet reveal, however, a major shift from North to South of industrialization. In 1984, the share of global industrial production of the developing countries was 13.9 per cent, slightly below where it was in 1948! The changes that have occurred in this period, and they have been dramatic, have not been from North to South, but have been within the two groups of countries. In the South, the NICs have benefited at the expense of South American countries; in the North, a significant shift of global industrial production has taken place towards Japan and the centrally planned economies.[31] This is further borne out by the fact, as earlier stated, that the penetration of developing country manufactures in the total consumption of manufactured goods in industrialized capitalist economies (including Japan) was only 3.5 per cent in 1987,[32] and at that was significant only for clothing. Perhaps the most striking evidence of all to illustrate the extraordinary North–South imbalance in industrial capacity is found in the fact that in the period 1970–85 the increase in value of real manufacturing GDP in the United States alone greatly exceeded that of the whole of the South.

Nevertheless, in selective fashion, structural changes are occurring in the world economy. There is a trend towards concentrating capital, skill, and research-intensive industries in the North or 'core,' and shifting labour-intensive and standardized technology-intensive activities to the periphery, sometimes in the South, sometimes to economically depressed parts of the North.[34] The lesson to be derived from the pattern of these shifts seems to be that the relatively few countries in the South benefiting are those that have been the major recipients of capital and credits in the 1970s. They now dominate the growth in export earnings of the South. By comparison, the foreign exchange shortages facing so many developing countries have actually dampened those countries' manufacturing activities because of their dependence upon imported components and machine tools. Between 1980 and 1985, eighteen of the fifty-seven low- and middle-income countries for which data are available experienced absolute declines in their manufacturing sectors, while several others had growth rates of less than 1 per cent per annum.[35]

The global economy is now much more complex than it was even twenty-five years ago, with widespread repercussions flowing from events and activities in one region or another. The pursuit of narrow, national interests now not only frustrates broad attempts to harmonize, but guarantees as well the failure of these national policies. Unfortunately, the immediate victims of policy fragmentation in the North are the weaker economies of the countries of the South. In such powerful forums as the Western Economic Summit, decisions are taken without any consultation with the South and with precious little awareness of the ramifications of those decisions on either a North–South, or a South–North, axis. One result has been that for the majority of the developing countries patterns of production are reverting to earlier configurations. The countries themselves are becoming increasingly dependent on flows Northward of primary products. As has been seen, single-commodity economic systems are vulnerable to cyclical world prices, which themselves are often the result of the supply responses of the developing countries.

Should the Northern development model remain unchanged and continue its dominance, reflecting as it does a Northern, rather than a universal, value system, there is every reason to be deeply worried about the future of all humankind. The continuance and acceleration of environmental degradation, the infectious nature of social and political instability, the tragic implications of populations so large that basic human dignity is jeopardized, the epidemic nature of mysterious diseases, and the threatening growth of criminal activities – these are all non-economic manifestations of the current malfunctioning world economy. The ill effects of these and other phenomena can now be seen within Northern societies. The more thoughtful of Northern political leaders, bankers, and industrialists recognize these linkages and that Northern economic policy management cannot be successfully pursued without full awareness, involvement, and attention to the needs of the developing countries of the South. Those persons remain, however – and tragically – in the minority.

The Environment

Since prehistory, a dominant characteristic of much of the human species has been its ability to 'improve' the natural habitat for the benefit of humans. The erection of dwellings and monuments, the harnessing of technology and natural resources, the subjugation of resistant aboriginal tribes: these are all fibres in the fabric of human 'accomplishment.' If there is a single, conformist element common to dominant populations everywhere, it is the sense of triumph associated with the transformation and utilization of the Earth's resources.

The vast size of the planet, the harshness of climatic circumstance, and the vulnerability of humans to disease combined for millennia to curb the zeal of these assaults on nature. Until relatively recently it mattered not that the great civilizations often tailored their moral philosophies to support these materialistic quests. In the past century, however, the balance has shifted. The Industrial Revolution has been followed by extraordinary achievements in science and technology; in unexpected fashion these have contributed to an immense surge in the world's population. What was once a noble venture to humanize the natural habitat has become a destructive onslaught: the Earth's surface is being transformed and the atmosphere poisoned. The initial endeavour to contribute to the human condition has become a guarantor of its diminution and possible extinction.

◆

The degradation of the environment is a human practice with ancient origins. Of the present generation, few persons, anywhere, are unacquainted with unsightly assaults on either rural beauty or urban

orderliness, most often as a result of dumping of waste products. All too
many contend as well with the down-wind effects of industrial smokestacks or the discharge into lakes and streams of effluents and sewage. But
until relatively recently, these practices have been regarded as nuisances,
not hazards. This, not because of the absence over the years of toxins or
pathogens in the discharges (or of the means to detect them), and certainly not because of society's lack of interest in orderliness or natural
beauty, but because it was assumed that these pollutants were local, were
containable, and so were finite in their impact.

As well, there has always been something triumphant about these
kinds of activities, an interpretation of them as proof of humankind's
ability to survive and prosper in a hostile setting. And so, in an ironic
sense still evident in many communities, massive junk-yards, chimneys
belching obnoxious gases, and poisoned rivers are all regarded as evidence of human accomplishment: the quid pro quo necessary to generate
employment and other material benefits. So, too, have been accepted
such other examples of organized human toil as open-pit mines and
clear-cut forest tracts. These have been seen as reflections of the ability of
humans to wrestle from nature the hidden resources that have lain there
for millennia awaiting the ingenuity and daring needed to turn them to
useful ends. Some of these exploits have been nothing short of marvels,
among them some major Canadian initiatives in frontier regions.

The interpretation of waste and despoliation as proud testimony of
human accomplishment enjoys a secure philosophic foundation. John
Locke, the brilliant eighteenth-century intellectual who contributed so
much to the emergence of democratic theory and practice, and whose
seminal works are still quoted with praise and approval, looked upon
natural resources as a challenge, and upon the failure to use them as a
negative. 'The negation of nature is the way toward happiness,' wrote
Locke; humanity must be 'effectively emancipated from the bonds of
nature.' 'Land that is left wholly to nature ... is called, as indeed it is,
waste,' he wrote.[1]

Locke was on solid theological ground in his reasoning. The Book of
Genesis (1:29) makes that clear: 'God said to them, "Be fruitful and
multiply, and fill the earth and subdue it; and have dominion over the
fish of the sea and over the birds of the air and over every living thing
that moves upon the earth."'

This is a potent combination: the relentless demand for economic

activity as a survival tool, and the biblical assurance that God intended
man to exercise dominion. In the period before the Christian era, and for
much of the two thousand years since, man's environment, in theory as
well as in practice, was his to exploit with few questions asked. These
practices were acceptable in large measure because of the limited number
of human beings and the dispersed nature of their communities on a
planet of gigantic proportions. Even following the age of discovery and
the beginnings of a global awareness, the vastness of the globe and the
seeming inexhaustible nature of its resource base encouraged more, not
less, exploitation.

One of the earliest scholars to address issues of a global dimension was
the Dutchman Hugo Grotius, who lived from 1583 to 1645, and who is
generally regarded as the 'father' of international law. In his treatise *Mare
Liberum*, published in 1609, Grotius argued that the open sea could not be
the property of any state for it was in the interest of all states to enjoy
freedom of navigation. He then extended his argument to fisheries on the
simple premise of sufficiency: that because there were enough fish for all
– the stocks being able to regenerate themselves indefinitely – there was
no reason why any state should endeavour to claim jurisdiction or to
exercise control. This conviction of sufficiency continued over the centuries even in the face of growing incontrovertible evidence to the
contrary. Whether driven by arrogance, optimism, or by a sense of
religious destiny, humankind has imposed relentlessly a servitude on the
environment and its resources even while exhibiting a naïvely innocent
sense of wonder at the richness of each succeeding frontier. The early
explorers of the Great Plains areas of North America marvelled at the
proliferation of bison (as they did of the passenger pigeon) and observed
that the wasteful practices introduced by the early white hunters were of
little moment because the supply was so much in excess of the demand.

There were, of course, some early expressions of alarm and caution-
ary admonitions, but in the cut and thrust of the immediacy of survival
and, later, in the creation of vast fortunes, these critical voices gained few
followers. In one of those peculiar alliances that is known to this day, the
interests of the wealthiest of industrialists and of the least skilled of
workers combine to insist upon the continuance of even the most environmentally detrimental of manufacturing or resource exploitation
practices. Labour unions have been historically cautious about deman-

ding the abandonment of commercial activities except where they represented a hazard to the health of the workers. And so, today, in all regions of the world, those most engaged in – and therefore most dependent upon – the wise stewardship of natural resources are among the most vociferous in their opposition to the introduction of any production constraints or conservation practices. Among miners, loggers, and fishermen, environmental safeguards are seen more often than not as inimical to their own interests.

Measured against the information now available about the state of the planet's ecological health, the warnings of the earliest environmentalists take on fresh meaning and display a remarkable insight. The nineteenth-century English social theorist John Ruskin employed language that has not been improved in the 150 years since. He wrote: 'God has lent us the earth for our life; it is a great entail. It belongs as much to those who are to come after us, and whose names are already written in the book of creation, as to us; and we have no right, by anything that we do or neglect, to involve them in unnecessary penalties, or deprive them of benefits which it is in our power to bequeath.'[2] Ruskin's North American contemporary Henry David Thoreau is now regarded as his country's pioneer environmentalist. He emphasized the essential quality of nature with his simple statement: 'In wildness is the preservation of the world.'[3]

Not in Thoreau does one find expressions of confidence that the planet is so large, its resiliency so great, its inherent wholesomeness so strong that human activities can never do more than scar the surface here and there. Thoreau worshipped pristine nature with a passion that has stimulated and inflamed generations of environmentalists since and, in the process, pitted many of them in irresolvable conflict with persons not so committed to their cause. There are few disputes today so bitter or so heroic as those that pitch environmental activists dedicated to their lofty cause against desperate loggers dependent for their livelihood on the felling of giant trees. These conflicts are today a matter of daily record in Canadian and American newspapers, as are opinion polls that reveal that 'the environment' is an issue of greater concern to the publics of Canada and Western Europe than any other. In a dramatic vault over such perennial fears as war, unemployment, or crime in the streets, environmental issues are now the pre-eminent worry of millions of residents of the industrialized world.

There was no single event or moment that precipitated this concern and it is that fact that has probably contributed a good deal to the widespread and profound sense of unease that the opinion polls have recorded. The very word 'pollution' has itself been transformed from a descriptor of intensely personal activity to one of broad public implications. The origin of the word and its employment until relatively recently related primarily to uncleanliness of a moral (usually sexual) kind, and most often to individual acts of corruption or defilement. The images thrown up by that concept are a far cry from current reports of hundreds of square kilometres of spilled crude oil floating toward rich oyster beds or scenic beaches, or descriptions of thousands of biologically dead lakes in the Canadian wilderness. It is these more recent images that have so weakened the earlier precepts both of local impact and of biblical authority. The rapid transmission of photographs and descriptions of events of widespread environmental degradation have contributed much to the current awareness. One of the most vivid of such photographs was that taken by the crew of the Apollo 11 lunar mission in 1969. Viewed from the surface of the moon, the impression of the planet Earth as an integral whole was persuasive and memorable. Distributed worldwide three years before the pioneer United Nations Conference on the Human Environment in Stockholm in 1972, the photograph contributed to a global mind-set open to warnings of environmental hazards. Remembered, too, and quickly introduced into everyday usage, was the wonderfully descriptive word 'biosphere,' first coined by the Austrian Eduard Suess in 1875 in a short book on the genesis of the Alps,[4] and later used by the Soviet scientist Vladimir Vernadsky whose lectures were published in French in 1929 under the title *La Biosphère*. The integrity of the planet, the singleness of its atmospheric canopy, and the systemic nature of all biological life forms had at last penetrated the consciousness of the general public.

And so environment as a concept has taken on a multiplicity of dimensions. One concern is for endangered species of wildlife, ranging from giant elephants and whales to microscopic and numerous plant forms. Another form of concern arises out of the challenge of waste disposal, whether this be management of litter and household garbage or the safe disposition of toxic chemical and nuclear by-products from giant industrial plants. Still another worry arises from forecasts of the exhaustion of non-renewable resources (and the wanton destruction of irreplaceable renewable resources). These elements of concern combine to challenge the future quality of human life. When added to the solemn pronouncements of respected scientists about such atmospheric phenomena as global warming and ozone depletion, these impressions present to a worried public a sense that the wholesomeness of their environment cannot be taken for granted.

There is something quite different in all this from the earlier worries, at the height of the Cold War, of atmospheric fall-out from nuclear weapons tests. In contrast to that pervasively militaristic period, there is no longer any persuasive reason why human beings should be exposed to such risks. There is less confidence, too, by publics in the explanations of governments, and their soothing assurances that all is under control. Recent revelations of the cavalier attitude of successive United States administrations toward safety measures in atomic weapons plants have contributed to both alarm and cynicism. Finally, as important as anything else, there is visible evidence of what has been happening. The public today has in its possession much more demonstrable evidence of toxic poisoning from a number of sources than had those who worried about strontium-90 in their children's milk in the mid-1950s.

Perhaps the tide of public opinion began to turn with the widespread introduction of detergents and the beginning of the era of plastics. Gradually did the term 'non-biodegradable' enter into vocabularies, as omnipresent evidence of these miracle products crept into the consciousness. Increasingly rare were streams or rivers not revealing the scummy froth of detergent bubbles; even rarer were ocean coastlines not marked by an unbroken border of plastic containers, styrofoam cups, nylon rope fragments, or fishermen's gear – a far cry from the often romantic and infrequent nautical flotsam and jetsam of bygone years.

The popular awareness strengthened with the incidence of massive tanker breakups. Oil spills and the irresponsible dumping of tanker bilge slops had been known for decades, but it was not until such infamous incidents as *The Torrey Canyon* off the Scilly Isles (1967) and *The Arrow* in Chedabucto Bay (1970) that those shiny black lumps of tar so common on so many beaches began to be associated with oil tankers. As the size of these vessels increased monstrously, from the 80,000-ton range in the 1950s to the 500,000-ton range two decades later, public consternation increased proportionately – and appropriately. By January 1975, the Ocean Affairs Board of the United States National Academy of Sciences estimated the volume of petroleum products entering the world's oceans to be 6.1 million metric tons each year, the largest single portion coming from tanker operations.[5] A decade later, a review study estimated the total ocean input of petroleum from all sources to be within an annual range between 1.7 and 8.8 million metric tons.[6]

A final element in this accumulative phase of public perception was the remarkable news that a New Zealand scientific team had detected 2,4-D residues in the fat of Antarctic penguins. The nearest point where this chemical compound had been employed was in New Zealand, some 2,500 kilometres distant. Now could be understood the infectious and spreading incidence of environmental neglect: of toxins and pathogens, oil spills and garbage dumps, forest destruction and spreading deserts. As is often the case, public perceptions and public concerns were far ahead of the willingness of governments to act.

Perhaps not surprisingly, the attention paid by governments to the 1972 Stockholm Environment Conference was uneven. The Soviet-bloc countries (with the exception of Romania) refused to participate as a signal of their impatience over the non-recognition of East Germany. Brazil and some other developing countries expressed opposition to the conference because of their contention that it was a conspiracy by the economically advanced countries to deny to others the opportunity of industrializing. Yet, irrepressibly, public awareness spread, and with it concern, as the evidence mounted.

And evidence there was: of acts of negligence, some of it criminal in nature, as toxic wastes were clandestinely introduced into heavily populated areas with no regard for the hazardous conditions so created; of acts of conspiracy, as information pertinent to the health of communities was purposely held back by governments; of acts of greed and acts of desperation as well. All, however, were seemingly unconnected and apparently isolated. Few seemed to note the alarming statistics that had been gathered by the Brandt Commission in 1979 that 'the combined demand for firewood, farm land, and increased exports of forest products to industrial countries is causing a deforestation of 11 million hectares each year in the Third World. That is half the area of the United Kingdom.'[7] The speed with which these events were taking place nevertheless struck responsive government chords only here and there. Brandt pointed out that forest cover had decreased from 25 per cent to

20 per cent of the earth's surface in a twenty-year period. Individual examples were staggering: Thailand lost one-fourth of its forest cover in a ten-year period; Costa Rica lost one-third in ten years; Ivory Coast lost one-third in eight years.

A decade was to pass, tragically, before the deeply felt worries of the 1970s increased to the level of alarm, when forest and other conservation movements gained strength, when environmental hazards increasingly began to be seen as threats to the health and safety of the species. Lulled by reassurance from many sources that technological destruction could be reversed by technological accomplishment, most governments and many publics had responded only slowly to the warning signals. Then in short order came the calamitous 1984 explosion of a chemical plant in Bhopal, India, killing 3,663 and injuring 170,000, and the emission of radioactive fumes in 1986 from a nuclear reactor at Chernobyl in the Soviet Union with incalculable long-term effects. Now publics and governments alike were ready to listen, even if not always to respond, to the evidence of worldwide environmental degradation, much of it arising from the desperate attempts of developing countries to enhance their economic performance. No longer were these of local impact. Combined, they were of a magnitude to affect all parts of the globe. Yet it was not until the 1987 report of the Brundtland Commission that the world took notice. Brundtland stated the case starkly: 'environmental trends ... threaten to radically alter the planet, ... threaten[ing] the lives of many species upon it, including the human species.'[8] The 1988 Toronto Conference on the Changing Atmosphere, sponsored jointly by the Government of Canada, the United Nations Environmental Programme, and the World Meteorological Organization, was equally blunt. In its concluding statement, it said: 'Humanity is conducting an unintended, uncontrolled, globally pervasive experiment whose ultimate consequences may be second only to a global nuclear war.'[9]

Now was the message clear. Now, too, was South–North vulnerability made manifest.

◆

The human environment on planet Earth is subject to continuing natural change from a range of geologic and biospheric phenomena including variations in the sun's intensity and in the earth's orbital path. Mighty natural forces imperil human settlements and devastate landscapes with regularity, as they have for millennia. Volcanic eruptions, earthquakes, hurricanes, tidal waves, and lightning strikes are manifestations of the stupendous power of natural events. Their consequences illustrate the widespread havoc associated with natural disasters. Some, like earthquakes, strike suddenly and virtually without warning. Others, such as drought, are gradual and persistent, extending in some instances over several years. The impact of these events is enormous; the destruction and change associated with them is immense. Yet the forces of nature are relatively impotent compared to the forces unleashed by human activity. It is humankind, not nature, that threatens to make this planet uninhabitable.

The key is human behaviour: our instinctive need to reproduce and our acquired desire to enrich our diet and enhance our creature comforts. Ours is not the first species to increase rapidly its numbers to the point that its habitat is overburdened. Any number of examples can be cited: lemmings, migratory locusts, the Japanese beetle, and the Gypsy moth are all familiar. In each such case, profound biological repercussions resulted as imbalances were overcome, sometimes with effects limited to the species itself, sometimes not. Ours is, however, the only species that alters its habitat in permanent, or near-permanent fashion. One of the means it uses is the harnessing of energy, generated for the most part by the burning of wood and fossil fuels. The combination of increased numbers of humans – 220,000 net each twenty-four hours (in the approximate three minutes and forty-five seconds required to read this page of print, the world's population increases by some six hundred persons) – and the release into the atmosphere of the fumes produced by the burning process imperils our future. The peril is the consequence of gaseous imbalance – the greenhouse effect – with likely adverse effects upon biological systems worldwide. In the absence of any known, or likely, means of neutralizing those imbalances, some form of self-denial is necessary.

The challenge is awesome. The biblical admonition to 'Be fruitful, and multiply' (Genesis 1:28) is still rigidly interpreted by major elements of the Christian faith. The anthropological reality of high rates of infant mortality combines with economic reality to encourage couples in many parts of the world to raise large families as insurance against old age and as a means to increase income through available labour. The standard of living of the 5.3 billion persons on the planet is starkly divided – roughly along South–North lines between the industrialized and the developing countries of the world. Gross National Product per capita (far from a perfect illustration but a reliable economic indicator nevertheless) varies from upwards of u.s. $17,500 in Canada and the United States to less than u.s. $200 in a number of countries in sub-Saharan Africa. Governments on both sides of this poverty divide are endeavouring to overcome the worst aspects of this contrast through economic development policies and programs. One of the anticipated results, indeed one of the sought-after goals, of these policies is an increase in energy consumption in the developing countries. Unless wisely carried out, even though apparently successful in statistical terms, the results could be horrific. An undue concentration on economic development may well produce negative social results and disastrous environmental consequences.

At present, per capita energy consumption in Canada per year is the equivalent of 9,155 kilograms of oil. In the United States it is 7,265.3 kilograms, and in the People's Republic of China 570.4 kilograms. To generate the desired volumes of energy for a population that now exceeds one billion, and that continues to grow despite strict policies to control fertility, the government of China proposes the construction of several megascale power projects. One is a huge hydroelectric facility in the gorges of the Yangtze River, which would flood a vast upstream area to create the necessary head of water above the turbines. Several other projects will take the form of coal-fired generating facilities, designed to burn indigenous coal. China is already the world's largest coal burner. To fuel the new plants, coal production will increase from the 1980 level of 450 million metric tons to 1.2 billion metric tons in 2000, with a corresponding increase in fumes released on burning. It is not possible even to estimate what that volume will be except to say that it will be greatly in excess of the current total release of fumes from all Canadian smokestacks (those used to generate electricity, those employed for industrial purposes, and those required for residential and institutional heating): estimated to be 120 million metric tons annually. Should these Chinese facilities begin to operate, they will not by themselves close the South–North energy consumption gap, or come close to it. They will, however, create a major worldwide environmental hazard.

Populous as China is, it represents only a quarter of the population of the developing countries. A neighbouring country, India, is every bit as energy hungry and equally engaged in preparations to meet the demand. By the end of the current decade, the population of India will pass the one billion mark. Like China, its most readily available fuel is soft coal.

Carbon monoxide fumes from motor vehicles have been reduced gradually during the past two decades, evidence that progress is possible, but are still at dangerous levels. In 1988, in the United States alone, highway vehicle emissions were 34.1 million metric tons annually. (The total emission for all forms of transportation in the United States that year was 41.2 million metric tons.) It is not anticipated that the people of China or India, or the two billion persons living in the other developing countries, will all operate motor vehicles or will consume electricity at the same rate as those in the industrialized countries. Nevertheless, assumptions that Northern lifestyles should be regarded as normative and that technological 'fixes' are workable are a combination that guarantees disappointment and futility even were populations not increasing. Given the present rates of population growth in the South and the present bent to consumerism in the North, fundamental reappraisals of values and attitudes will be necessary if disaster is to be averted.

Burning takes place frequently in developing countries for purposes other than energy production. One of the most widespread agricultural techniques is the 'slash and burn' cycle practised by those engaged in shifting agriculture. The clearing of forest cover makes land available for sedentary cultivation; the burning of the felled trees contributes certain nutrients to a generally deficient soil mass, permitting two or three years of production before yields drop to the point where it is necessary once more to move on and repeat the cycle. Practised on a limited scale and in widely dispersed circumstances, this activity is not particularly harmful: the burned-over areas will in time regenerate their forest canopy and the soils will recover to at least the preburn level; the smoke emissions, while bothersome, are of a magnitude of the (now often outlawed) neighbourhood burning of fallen leaves in a Canadian city or the destruction of agricultural waste and trash on a small farm. Burning on a massive scale, by comparison, as is now under way in the Amazonian rain forests of Brazil, produces an impact far different. In that region, in a desperate attempt to form land tracts for either cropping or pastoral purposes, vast fires are now burning which coincidentally destroy the habitat for indigenous peoples and countless biological species, and pour into the atmosphere massive quantities of smoke and particulants.

The numbers are so large as to border on the incredible. Seventeen million hectares of forest cover were destroyed in the ten-year period from 1978 to 1988.[10] The worst year, 1987, saw a total of 240,000 fires, more than 8,000 burning each day of the burn season. In total that year, more than 10 million metric tons of particulants were released into the atmosphere in the form of smoke.[11] Happily, in the years subsequent to 1987, burning has been reduced considerably through a combination of Brazilian government interventions and wetter weather. There may be as well a spreading awareness that this activity is in pursuit of a futile cause. Had the largely uninformed and unskilled waves of Brazilian immigrants paused to question the much wiser indigenous tribes they have killed or driven out, they would have learned that the jungle soils are not capable of sustaining food crops without huge and costly recurring applications of fertilizer. Neither farming nor ranching in this region is either economically or environmentally sustainable.

Burning of this kind and on this scale has a second effect, one as dangerous to the health of the biosphere as the deposit into the atmosphere of poisonous waste products. This other effect is irony writ large. The trees that are destroyed are habitat to a biological resource of immense potential and value. Its destruction, even marginally, reduces markedly the future source of many benefits to humankind. Because the forests that are destroyed are old growth, it is biologically impossible to restore them in less than several centuries. Their burning destroys with the trees innumerable species of insect, plant, and animal life with their incalculable potential contribution to pharmaceutical and other scientific endeavours. This diminution of biological diversity may well be the most harmful result of the Amazonian deforestation. By its very nature, however, the extent and value of the loss can never accurately be determined.

Distant as are Canadians and the residents of other industrialized countries from these events, they are inescapably affected by them. The burning of rain forests is but one item in a long list of activities taking place in the countries of the South that affect the quality of life worldwide, even if indirectly. What must be understood is that the range of endeavours by 4 billion people to sustain themselves and to enhance their standard of living is extensive and often environmentally degrading, even as are the activities of the billion residents in the North.

These activities, and the issues they raise, are not of a kind that will simply disappear with benign governmental neglect. Nor are they susceptible to either simplistic or permanent solutions. We are now engaged with fundamental problems that will affect, sooner or later, in one way or another, the life of every human being on this planet. Involved here are not just basic issues of equity, of the disproportionate exploitation of resources, and the despoiling of the biosphere. We are face to face with circumstances that will diminish human life everywhere unless the human species, for the first time ever, recognizes that all members are interdependent and that cooperation is the only mechanism that will permit solutions. Greed must be understood to be, as the great religions have always taught, self-destructive. The human race is on the eve of a period exactly opposite to that of Ulysses and his companions who lived in a world 'whose margin fades forever and forever when they move.'[12] In today's world, the margins are closing in upon us with discernible speed. On reflection, we should not be surprised that this is so, or astonished to learn that major adjustments are now necessary. After all, no generation in history – before our own in the industrialized countries – has ever dared to think that standards of living could rise ceaselessly.

◆

It is not likely that any society anywhere is more sensitive to its physical environment than the Inuit of northern Canada. Atmospheric changes affect not simply their way of life, they affect their very lives. An Inuit chant repeats the words 'I keep walking along, looking for the other side of the weather.'

Science is now able to reveal to us that the 'other side of the weather' may be quite different from what we have always believed. No longer can humans disclaim any responsibility, or settle back into the idyllic mood of James Whitcomb Riley who could write a century ago, 'When God sorts out the weather ...'[13] We now know that the content and the dynamics of the giant atmospheric envelope surrounding the Earth are very much affected and provoked by human activity. We know that the atmosphere functions as a giant mixer, blending together on a planetary scale all the gaseous effluents and suspended matter that we in our industrious fashion send skyward. Those smoky events that could once be dismissed as of momentary impact, or avoided as of a purely local circumstance, we now know to be lasting and widespread. On the 'other side of the weather' is not God, but humans. Yet in this vast, cumulative exercise in which humankind is unconsciously engaged, we display little original wisdom, and virtually no sensitivity to the extensive and enduring impact of our activities. We seem to assume that the atmosphere is of such immense size, and of such a resilient nature, that it will be able to recover from our indifference and our malfeasance. We are wrong. And in our wrongness we have put ourselves and future generations in peril. Neither the inherent wholesomeness nor the apparent stability of the earth's atmosphere is able indefinitely to absorb in benign fashion the ever-growing assault that the human species has launched on this precious resource. It is folly to assume that the atmosphere is beyond our ability to alter. In altering it, we endanger ourselves.

The false impression of atmospheric durability stems in part from the fact that the average temperature of the atmosphere on the earth's surface has remained remarkably constant, hovering near 15°C for many thousands of years. The same constancy has been evident in the chemical composition of the atmosphere. This stability is partly a reflection of the inherent self-sustaining rhythms of biological systems as they utilize solar energy and photosynthesis for self-maintenance. So powerful and so extensive are those systems that the results of human activity have been of only marginal significance – until recently. Beginning with the Industrial Revolution, and increasingly since, we now realize, human-driven economic systems have become so environmentally intrusive that they now draw down the environmental capital by exhausting or destroying natural resources more rapidly than they can be replaced. Because of the diffuse nature of these activities, and the scientific difficulty of measuring change on a global scale, inadequate attention has been paid to this imbalance until relatively recently. There is no question, however, that it has atmospheric consequences.

It was for these reasons that the 1988 Toronto Conference on the Changing Atmosphere chose to describe humankind's onslaught on the environment as an 'unintended, uncontrolled, globally pervasive experiment.'[14] That experiment is the more dangerous because of the narrow range of earth temperatures living species can tolerate. Our margins of error are not flexible, nor are they wide. This is well illustrated by comparing the planet's climate today with that of the worst ice age of the past one hundred thousand years. The temperature difference is only some 5–8 degrees Celsius. A drop in temperature of that magnitude would lead to devastating changes in agricultural production, as the theorists of 'nuclear winter' have postulated. A rise in global temperatures of the same amount would lead to equally disastrous results, but of a different kind.

Climate change is, by its nature, an issue of global concern. It is, as well, a stunning example of the interconnections of all societies, wherever located on this planet. An exchange of nuclear weapons between the two superpowers, using only a tiny fraction of the nearly sixty thousand warheads that they possess between them, would lead to catastrophic consequences worldwide, not simply in the target areas. This would be because of the cooling that would follow from thermonuclear ground bursts and the dense clouds of smoke and dust that they would throw up, casting the earth's surface into deep shadow. Although the earliest estimates of these effects have been refined and reduced, a recent study by the International Council of Scientific Unions nevertheless reveals the still likely magnitude of effect. It estimated that several billion people might starve to death from the climatic consequences of nuclear war.[15] Those deaths would extend well into the Southern Hemisphere, even if no nuclear weapons were exploded there.

Although not so instantaneous, and therefore not so dramatic in the description, *rising* temperatures could lead to equally destructive, though different, consequences, again on a global scale. The warning signals are already in place: rising atmospheric carbon dioxide levels and as yet not fully understood regional weather anomalies. Our inability so far to measure accurately and interpret wisely these signals should no more be accepted as a reason for doing nothing than should our doubts about the full impact of a 'nuclear winter' encourage us to test the results of an actual nuclear exchange. Global temperature changes take place over a long period of time. Though no one can be certain of their extent, the potential impact is of such magnitude that prudence dictates we be cautious.

It is unlikely that any other single environmental issue contains a potential hazard to human well-being as great as climate change. No other circumstance could affect so profoundly the economic base of nations on all continents. This, increasingly, is understood by political leaders. With accelerating frequency, communiqués are released, protestations uttered, and conferences held. Again and again there are admissions of the need for international cooperation, of the damage that can be done by national or individual actors who are irresponsible, of the limits of freedom of landowners. In disrepute now is the old common law doctrine of 'ad coelum et ad inferos,' which attached to the surface owner unhindered rights of occupancy and enjoyment extending to the heavens above and to the centre of the earth below. Beginning with the findings of the Canada–United States International Joint Commission in 1931, and repeated by various judicial and arbitral tribunals since, legal liability extends now in certain instances to those who allow the escape from their territory of environmentally damaging substances of a number of kinds and forms. The age-old practices of discharging wastes into flowing streams, and fumes into the atmosphere to be blown away by prevailing winds, are now subject not just to criticism but, increasingly, to censure and judicial constraint. There are, of course, expense factors: to stop discharging, to overcome the damage done by past discharges. Estimates of the cost of remedial steps worldwide to overcome the effects of pollution range as high as U.S. $300 billion annually. If the costs of prevention and clean-up are high, however, so are the stakes. Chemical, nuclear, and biological wastes create major health hazards. Global warming of even a few degrees would threaten the entire socio-economic fabric worldwide.

Indisputable evidence of what is happening to the temperature of the atmosphere is made difficult because climatic changes that result from human activity are superimposed upon natural cycles of change. The human-induced atmospheric adjustments are masked by the 'background static' of local and short-term climate variations. Science does not yet possess the means accurately to distinguish the two, or to forecast with precision the results of changing compositions of atmospheric gases. The immensity and the complexity of the atmosphere make this impossible. Nevertheless, ample evidence exists revealing at least two hazards demanding immediate attention. The first is the phenomenon known as atmospheric warming. The second is the depletion of the ozone layer.

The atmosphere consists of a mass of gases that surrounds the earth and is bound to it by the force of gravity. The composition of the atmosphere consists overwhelmingly of nitrogen (about 78 per cent) and oxygen (about 21 per cent) that coexist in a constant, fixed proportion. The balance of 1 per cent or so is a mixture of several gases – carbon dioxide (CO_2), water vapour, argon, neon, helium, and methane (CH_4) among them. The atmosphere serves several functions essential to the maintenance of organic matter. The two major gases are primary contributors to plant and animal life: nitrogen passes from the air into the soil where bacteria transform it into nitrates to be taken up as nourishment by plants; oxygen is our primary source of energy, responsible for the respiration of living organisms and the combustion of fuels. Other gases, referred to often for convenience as the 'greenhouse' gases, trap the reflected energy of the sun as it radiates outward from the earth's surface. The mix of these greenhouse gases at any given time determines what proportion of the radiation is contained and held close to the Earth. This in turn determines the temperature of the surface itself. Human activities in recent years have increased dramatically the concentration of the naturally occurring greenhouse gases and have added new, man-made chemical compounds such as chlorofluorocarbons (CFCs). Independently, but simultaneously, these gases are altering two of the atmosphere's primary functions: trapping the heat from the sun, and blocking some of the sun's harmful radiation.

Because of the mixing effect of the atmosphere, it is a matter of planetary indifference from which point on the earth's surface gaseous substances are released. Smoke from burning forests in the Amazon mixes eventually with fumes from factory chimneys in Poland; exhaust from vehicles in Tokyo mingles with emissions from chemical factories in the Great Lakes basin of North America. The atmosphere is simply incapable of distinguishing between the developing countries of the South and the industrialized countries of the North. In this gaseous global 'commons,' the innocent foolishness of some thus combines with the conscious greed of others to affect all living organisms – and in huge volumes. As populations increase, and economic activity burgeons, the assault on the atmosphere becomes ever-more massive and ever-more intrusive. According to the World Resources Institute, human activity in

1987 caused the release into the atmosphere of the equivalent of 14.6 billion metric tons of carbon – in the form of carbon dioxide or other heat-trapping 'greenhouse' gases. Because natural processes remove some of these substances from the atmosphere, the net residue added to the atmosphere in 1987 was the equivalent of 5.9 billion metric tons of carbon, representing well over one metric ton for every human being alive that year. This must be compared with the net figure for 1957, only thirty years earlier, of 2.2 billion metric tons.

Because the greenhouse gases are invisible, and in some instances inert, they tend to be unnoticed by publics generally, and so by politicians. Even the presence of visually evident, smelly, respiratory-irritating smog is easily disregarded. A more startling image is necessary. Were carbon releases transformed into a solid mass, they would appear as a huge block of intensely black matter. Canadians produce 4.3 metric tons of carbon dioxide per person annually. Were the lawn in front of Canada's Parliament Buildings to be chosen as an illustrative repository, the annual carbon equivalent for just those persons who are present on Parliament Hill each day, 295 elected members, some 100 senators, 3,450 officials and support staff, 50 or so journalists, and 1,000 visitors (the daily average) – about 4,900 in total – that black mass would occupy in solid form 8,415 cubic metres.[16] That is a mass equivalent to one-half of the Peace Tower! A startling, constant reminder of that kind might prompt governments to appreciate the magnitude of these issues and to act effectively, and in time, to contain them.

Atmospheric Warming. The human activities responsible in largest measure for the emission of greenhouse gases are (1) the burning of fossil fuels, and (2) agriculture (including deforestation and livestock production). Notwithstanding the extent of deforestation and biomass burning in the developing countries of the South, the industrialized countries of the North remain far and away the major sources of atmospheric pollution. If these emissions could be measured on a historic, cumulative basis, the North's share would be proportionately even greater. At present, the United States, with 17.6 per cent of the total, is the world's largest single source of greenhouse gases, followed by the member states of the European Community, which are together responsible for 12.8 per cent, and the Soviet Union at 12.0 per cent. Brazil comes fourth and at 10.5 per cent is the South's largest source. Thereafter, on this black list, come China, India, Japan, Indonesia, Canada (2 per cent), and Mexico. But Canadians can take little comfort in the relatively low position. The rankings are for *total* emissions. On a per capita basis Canada in 1987 was the largest net contributor of greenhouse gases and the fourth largest emitter of carbon dioxide from fossil fuels of all the industrialized countries (after Luxembourg, East Germany, and the United States). Canada is regarded as an inefficient user of fossil fuels.

In terms of greenhouse gas *net* emissions, the countries of the South are already major sources, and have the potential to be even larger contributors unless present use patterns and technologies are radically changed. In 1987, according to the World Resources Institute, Brazil was the world's largest single producer of carbon dioxide emissions, owing primarily to the burning of the Amazon rain forest. That burning has since declined. Deforestation in the tiny country of Laos made it the largest per capita source of emissions (10 metric tons) while fossil fuel use and gas flaring in Qatar (8.8 metric tons) and the United Arab Emirates (5.8 metric tons) made them second and third respectively. Bahrain at 4.9 metric tons per capita was fourth. Worldwide, Canada ranked fifth at 4.5 metric tons per person.

Carbon dioxide emissions are derived, in the North, primarily from the combustion of fossil fuels, while in the South, still, from the burning of biomass (including animal dung). Coal and synthetic fuels derived from coal are far and away the greatest polluters. For the same amount of usable energy, coal emits 72–95 per cent more CO_2 than does natural gas; oil, 38–43 per cent more. Emissions from synthetic fuels are 200–300 per cent those of natural gas. All told, the burning of fossil fuels is estimated to put some 5 billion tons of carbon into the atmosphere each year, some of which, as stated, disappears naturally. Estimates of burning deforestation emissions – from biomass, wood, other vegetation, dung – vary considerably, from 1 to 4 billion tons annually.[7]

We must now anticipate the possibility that the developing South will overtake the industrialized North in total emissions sometime during the twenty-first century unless there are introduced major reversals of present practices. This is clear from the list, already cited, of the world's ten largest climate polluters in terms of net emissions of greenhouse gases. Already five out of ten are nations of the South, even though the per capita energy consumption of those countries is a fraction of that of the industrialized countries of the North.

The Ozone Layer. The thin ozone layer on the upper edge of the atmosphere is a shield that diminishes the harmful effects on living species of the sun's ultraviolet radiation. A decrease of only 1 per cent in ozone concentration can lead to an increase of approximately 2 per cent in the effective irradiance of ultraviolet B (UV-B) light at the earth's surface. (It is this portion of the sun's radiation that has far-ranging effects on biological tissue, damaging both protein and DNA.) For humans, such a change would mean an increased incidence of skin cancer. Those at greatest risk are persons with fair skins, the residents in largest proportion in the industrialized countries of the North.[18] The United States Academy of Sciences estimates that each 1 per cent reduction in the ozone layer would cause an increase of 2 per cent in skin cancer cases.[19] UV-B has also been implicated in suppression of the immune system,[20] which fights diseases in humans, and is known to induce cataracts in the eyes of humans and animals alike.[21]

Health hazards are not the only consequences of higher UV-B transmissions, however. Reduced crop and forest yields are likely; plankton and the larvae of some species of fish seem to be susceptible; many common synthetic materials such as plastics, paints, and window glazing tend to deteriorate.

These dangers prompted a gathering in Montreal in September 1987 of a number of countries to examine the possibility of common action to reduce the risk. The resulting 'Montreal Protocol on Substances That Deplete the Ozone Layer' is a valuable legal precedent. It was the first international agreement to limit 'well-established and profitable activities even before disastrous effects can be seen.'[22] The protocol aimed to halve consumption of five chlorofluorocarbons (CFCs) by 1998 and to freeze consumption of three different halons by 1992, yet gave a ten-year grace period to developing countries.[23] These substances are employed in the production of a number of commercially valuable products and tend to take a number of years to break down. Once dispersed into the atmosphere, as occurs when they are used as aerosol propellants, they remain active in their attack on the ozone layer for decades.

Even with the decade of grace, a number of developing countries rejected the Protocol as an interference with their own, often youthful and promising, plastics, refrigeration, and electronics industries. At the follow-on London Saving the Ozone Layer Conference in March 1989, twenty additional signatures were attached to the Montreal Protocol, a number of them of developing countries. China, however, supported by India, set out its terms for adherence: industrialized countries must themselves first make dramatic reductions; restraints on developing countries must be tailored to levels of economic development and to progress in finding CFC substitutes; an international fund must be established to finance research and to facilitate technology transfer from North to South. The adherence to the Protocol of these two heavily populated countries (which between the two of them account for nearly 40 per cent of the world's population) is critical, not the least because of the increasing and entirely justified demand in each of them for, among other things, more broadly accessible refrigerants and coolants. They are understandably not prepared to deprive their own people of the refrigerators enjoyed by people of the North.

It quickly became apparent that ozone depletion was considerably worse than scientists had feared, and that the Montreal Protocol needed strengthening. Even an immediate ban on the particular chemicals in issue would not stop damage to the ozone layer. In a remarkable demonstration of the speed with which governments are able to reach international agreement when once the need is demonstrated, and which augurs well for other environmental cooperation, a number of steps quickly followed the 1989 London ozone conference. Agreements were reached, the most important of them including the support of China and India, to accelerate rapidly the preventive steps needed. These agreements culminated with an accord in London in June 1990, to which India and China will accede in 1992, to phase out totally all CFCs and ozone-depleting chemicals by the turn of the century: 50 per cent by 1995, 85 per cent by 1997, and 100 per cent by 2000. India changed its position because agreement was reached for the North–South transfer of needed technologies, and for a fund to assist the developing countries to make the transition to a world without CFCs.

The ozone problem will not, however, immediately disappear. As with a number of activities now known to contribute to global climate change, the accumulated effects of past emissions will continue to increase and be felt for years to come. The British Antarctic Survey predicts that the ozone 'hole' will get bigger for some time, as chlorine levels rise. Not until the year 2030 will the chlorine level in the atmosphere be back to its 1984 level, the year that the hole in the ozone layer was first detected. Not until the end of the twenty-first century is it likely that world ozone levels will return to their earlier, precrisis state, and then only if strict timetables are adhered to.

Scenarios of Change. It is one thing to speak of a polluted atmosphere in planetary terms, but quite another to forecast the consequences of that pollution for any specific geographic location. Global warming of only a degree or two would undoubtedly affect snow and glacier depth in the Arctic and Antarctic regions, sea levels, precipitation patterns, and wind conditions. Each of these would combine to alter the physical circumstances on which biological life depends. Scenarios of change, not surprisingly, can be as numerous as the variables that scientists choose to include in the studies they undertake. There are still wide-ranging uncertainties about the complex interplay of natural systems: of the oceans' capacity to retain heat and to absorb CO_2; of the behaviour of water vapour, clouds, and ice; of the fertilization effects of CO_2 on plants; of the effects of the phenomenon known as 'albedo' (the reflectance from different surfaces). Of particular interest to Canadians is the possible disintegration of the great expanses of permafrost, with the resultant release into the atmosphere of massive quantities of CO_2 and methane, thus furthering the warming process. Each of these uncertainties leads to differences in predictions of winds, precipitation, soil moisture, and regional temperatures.

Perhaps the most important of all uncertainties is what scientists describe simply as 'surprise' – the modern discovery of unexpected or greater than expected phenomena. One such was the finding of holes in the ozone layer in 1984. Some respected scientists even conjecture that the twenty-first century could experience a modest, net, cooling, part of a natural two-hundred-year cycle, enough to offset the effects of the anticipated increases in CO_2 emissions.[24]

Clearly, the difficult determination of extent and effect depends on the mathematical models employed. In the past two decades, scientists have developed a hierarchy of models to measure atmospheric chemistry and climate processes. These range from simple, zero-dimensional models, useful in the study of chemical reactions, to extremely complex, three-dimensional models known as 'general circulation models' (GCMs) that are used to study climate changes.

Global warming would not evenly affect all regions. Generally, the effects would increase with distance north or south of the equator. South of the equator, the great ocean expanses will have a moderating effect. Studies commissioned by the Canadian Department of the Environment suggest that warming will be greater in the northern parts of Canada and greater in winter than in summer. Scientists used scenarios of climate change adopted from two United States 'General Circulation Models' to investigate the effects of these changes. In these scenarios, most of southern Canada might warm by about 4 degrees C, but the far north could experience winter temperature increases of as much as 10 degrees C.[25]

The Canadian economy seems most likely at risk in the forest sector, a matter of deep concern because 10 per cent of the Canadian labour force is dependent upon forest-related industries.

Because climate belts suitable for particular ecosystems will be displaced northward some 100 kilometres for each degree Celsius of warming, and this at rates of speed too rapid to permit tree species to adapt, the boreal forest will be particularly endangered. One study predicts that in the Prairie Provinces and the Northwest Territories the southern boundary of the boreal forest will retreat by 250–900 kilometres and be replaced by grassland in less than a century; meanwhile the northern boundary will advance only 80–700 kilometres. In these regions, the boreal forest could largely disappear.[26] This kind of prediction poses immensely important challenges to forest management that must be addressed immediately. Expensive silviculture decisions will have to be taken with incomplete information, simply because of the long time frames involved in the forest industry. What species should be planted today when we do not know what climatic conditions will prevail at the end of their life cycle?

The impact on agriculture will be mixed. There will certainly be benefits derived from a longer growing season, and perhaps from CO_2 fertilization effects in some plants. Crop substitutions and the introduction of innovative agricultural practices could permit corn to be seeded in Northern Ontario and horticulture and fruit growing to be extended through the south of the province.[27] In the prairies, winter wheat might replace spring varieties.[28] Yet with the possible exception of the valleys of the Peace and the Mackenzie rivers, areas in the northern prairies which would become warm enough for agriculture are possessed of soils unsuitable for the cultivation of anything but low-value forage crops, probably not worth producing.[29] Moisture stress could offset benefits in many parts of the country, moreover, while pests might flourish. One study of Ontario predicts reductions in crop production of Can. $100 million per year.[30] A study of Manitoba suggests that the increased frequency and severity of drought that could accompany global warming would be more damaging than would the warming itself.[31]

The net economic effects of such changes will depend as much on conditions elsewhere as on those in Canada. One study that considered only temperature rises showed that Canada could improve its comparative position in the world wheat trade.[32] Were drought to increase, however, the worldwide effect on cereal grain stocks could be very serious.

The impact of warming on Canada's water resources, both fresh and marine, would be considerable. Lower amounts of precipitation over southern Canada could reduce water levels in the Great Lakes by 30 centimetres to 2 metres[33] and could considerably reduce water stocks available for irrigation. In the St Lawrence River, outflow could be reduced by as much as 21 per cent. Overall, pollutants would be concentrated and water quality reduced. Competition for available water resources would increase. Warming would lengthen the ice-free shipping season on the St Lawrence and in the Great Lakes to eleven months, but the lower water levels would increase shipping costs for the four major cargoes because the allowable draft would be reduced, thus forcing more trips to transport the same tonnage as before.[34]

Ocean changes would be overwhelmingly negative and problematic. Were sea levels to rise, as is likely from the melting of arctic ice, low-lying parts of cities such as Charlottetown and Saint John would be flooded, with considerable damage resulting.[35] Water supplies would be harmed by salt-water intrusion into water tables and aquifers. Beaches would be eroded.

The effects on the fishery are much less certain. The tidal wetlands, a nursery for some of Canada's fisheries, would be inundated, but adjustment may be possible if the rise is slow and the land is flat. Aquaculture could benefit from a warming of the seas. One positive change would be a lowering of Atlantic coastal navigational costs where ice-breaking currently costs between Can. $15 and $20 million each winter.

In sum, Canadians would probably suffer economically as a result of climate change. GNP and disposable income could fall, living costs could rise, and regional differentials could increase because of damage to the resource base.[36]

In the tropical and subtropical regions of the world, in which the developing countries for the most part lie, temperature changes would be less than in Canada, but would undoubtedly cause much more human suffering. Much less research has as yet been dedicated to the effects on developing countries; what has been conducted has mostly focused on the impact of rises in sea levels and of the changing storm patterns on coastal communities. A number of states are vulnerable to catastrophic damage because their land is so low. Some small island states such as the Maldives might not be able to survive.[37] Other countries such as Egypt and Bangladesh would be very seriously affected because so many of their people live within a few metres' elevation of high-tide levels. Bangladesh is already beset with perennial flooding that will increase. One study estimates that up to 19 per cent of the habitable land of Egypt could be affected by 2050; by 2100 the figure could rise to 24–26 per cent, with concomitant effects upon the GDP.[38]

Worldwide, the tropical tourist industry, which is of such importance to so many developing countries, would suffer terribly as beaches erode. The destruction of mangroves and coral reefs would increase, exposing coastlines to storm surges and reducing the fisheries on which coastal populations survive. Many of the developing countries' most populous cities are located next to the sea. Pressures and tensions in these already overburdened places will only increase. Overall, the impact on human health, partly because of the spread of tropical disease vectors, will be considerable.

In agricultural terms, not enough is yet known of the exact effects of increased temperatures, ultraviolet light, and CO_2 levels, and of altered moisture regimes. Those persons most affected and least able to adjust to even marginal change will be those dependent on subsistence agriculture. In many instances, these persons now eke out their living on lands poorly suited for food production. Any negative change would force these people to migrate elsewhere, adding to the already large numbers of 'environmental refugees.' Their plight will be discussed in chapter v.

The difficulty of foreseeing the future, and of adjusting current behaviour in anticipation of distant need, is both a burden and a challenge to mature societies. It is not of recent origin, even if these environmental hazards are themselves novel. One of the modern testaments to the foresight and dedication of our forebears is the presence in many Canadian communities of large shade trees, planted carefully and with pride by pioneers who did so knowing that these slow-growing species would not reach maturity until long after the death of those who lovingly placed the seedlings in the earth. This gentle commitment to the environmental betterment of future generations is a precedent that must now be replicated by us, sometimes in novel fashion, as a mark of our confidence and our dedication.

◆

As with all elements of the world's ecosystem, the forested areas both contribute to environmental change and are affected by it. The presence or absence of trees anywhere is a major factor in the world's environmental health everywhere. The forests of the South are sometimes classified as either 'open' or 'closed.' The first are common in many parts of Africa; the second, generally, are tropical rain forests of the kind associated with the Amazon region in South America or with the countries of Southeast Asia. Each type can be found, or more properly once could be found, in each of the continents of Africa, Asia, and South America. Each, but especially the rain forest, is the habitat of an extraordinary number of diverse biological species, many of them still unknown. Open forest is more likely to attract the efforts of nearby dwellers seeking firewood. Closed forests attract the attention of governments seeking to create resettlement areas for surplus populations or to increase revenues from plantation agriculture or commercial forestry activities. Seldom are alternative arrangements made to ensure the continuing existence of diverse forms of animal, bird, insect, and plant life. Perhaps as much as 75 per cent of the world's flora and fauna concentrated in tropical forests is now at risk.

In all of these instances, and in all regions of the world, both North and South, trees are felled for one of two reasons: either they are of greater value down than growing, or the land they occupy is assumed to be of greater value cleared than forested. Tropical rain forests are under assault for both these reasons, and in many instances the incentive originates in the industrialized countries of the North. Markets in the North demand a wide range of tropical products, sometimes wood and wood derivatives, sometimes animal or plant products grown in the clearings. The hard currency earned by the export of these items is a powerful incentive to entrepreneurs and governments in the South alike. In the quest for immediate returns, sound environmental practices can easily be disregarded. The evidence is that this is often the case. The insatiable desire of consumers in the North for wood panelling, for hamburgers, and for cocaine is imperilling the future of forests in several tropical countries.

'Value-added' can be more apparent than real if all costs associated with tree felling are not honestly calculated, or if anticipated gains fail to be realized. There is much experience in many parts of the world in each respect. In the now industrialized countries, over the centuries, forests have been looked upon as an adversary, an obstacle to be removed, or a challenge to be met. In some instances they were logged for commercial purposes, including, on occasion, for firewood; in others they were removed to clear the land for farming or ranching. Seldom have replacement costs been calculated, almost never – until relatively recently – were royalties or fees of any kind charged to those destroying the forests. Concessions of one form or another tended to be negotiated, if at all, on a rough-and-ready basis that failed to reflect accurately either the risk to those seeking the concession or the opportunity cost to those granting it. In such circumstances, forestry management was an obscure concept. To gain access to quality trees, others of less value were laid waste. In North America, in the period 1860–1920, more than 400 million acres of trees were felled east of the Rockies.[39] Only recently has any effort been made to calculate with any degree of precision the full worth, including environmental worth, of forests. In light of such a record, there should be little surprise that developing countries are often reluctant to accept either criticism or advice from 'experts' in the North.

Sometimes mimicking and following Northern examples, sometimes stimulated and directed by Northern investors, countries of the South have engaged in the past quarter-century in an unprecedented assault on their forests. The reduction of timbered areas, touched on above, is of a magnitude difficult to comprehend. And the results, predictably, are unfortunate. Thailand has moved from being a net wood exporter to a net wood importer. Its rich stands of teak, logged for generations with the aid of domesticated elephants, have been ravaged in a single decade under the onslaught of mechanized equipment. There is no longer in Thailand any teak for commercial harvesting. Nor will there be for centuries to come, given the period required for these magnificent hardwood species to mature even under protected plantation conditions. Elsewhere in the tropics, the immediate impact of short-term policies is evident in various forms. At its most extreme, as in much of Haiti and parts of Madagascar, the careless destruction of forests has led to the loss of productive topsoil – so much so that agricultural uses of the formerly forested lands are severely constrained. In other countries, such as Malaysia, there are similarities to the Canadian experience where the most destructive of practices occur in the most remote of regions and affect initially the indigenous, less politically influential, elements of the population.

The experience of developing countries reveals the difficulties they face in designing and administering sound policies for forest use. Most begin with a reasonable intention: to make more wood available domestically while at the same time fostering an export industry to earn foreign exchange. Generally they progress from initial, limited-cutting regimes under local control, answerable to local interests, to a concession operated by alien parties regulated by the national government. Such concerns tend to be most profitable in the early stages, when a combination of factors encourages the destructive practice of 'high-grading' – the removal of only the most valuable species; this all too often takes place in the absence or non-enforcement of regulations to meet sustainable requirements. Often, too, in these early phases the export product takes the form of unfinished logs. This is much the preference, for example, of Japan and some members of the European Community, which endeavour to reserve to themselves both quality control in the manufacturing phase and the economic advantages of value-added activity. As a result, investment in local milling facilities is postponed and, with it, incentive for long-term reforestation practices. In these circumstances the economy of a complex tropical forest resource is arbitrarily and artificially limited to access roads and removal on the cost side, and to taxes and profit on the revenue side.

The apparently attractive alternative to these wasteful practices – the banning of the export of logs – is not always successful and in some instances contributes to even more destructive activities. Now a complex of interests and effects merge and conflict, tending to make difficult the attainment of both long-term profitability and sustainability. Among these are overcapitalization, corruption and greed, the inadequacies of controls in the international market-place, and the absence of hard competing data on ecological and social implications. The experience of Indonesia, which banned the export of logs in 1982, is illuminating in these respects. In the period 1982–7, Indonesia moved from the position of an insignificant plywood producer to the world's dominant tropical plywood supplier, capturing almost one-half of the total world trade in plywood. The capital investment required for this quantum leap was immense and so, necessarily, was the demand placed on the resource base. In the understandable desire to seize and hold the market, Indonesians have reduced prices much below where they should be, which forces additional productive exploitation on the one hand and encourages profligate consumption practices on the other. Japan is Indonesia's primary market for plywood, and imports have risen rapidly since the mid-1980s, accounting for 20 per cent of the country's total supply in 1988. Almost all of the rest of Japan's plywood requirements is met by tropical hardwood logs imported from Malaysia. Close to one-third of this inherently valuable product is used to fabricate concrete forms for the construction of building foundations. These panels, amounting to 135 million square metres in 1987 alone, are often discarded after being used just once.

Not surprisingly, in an economic activity of this value, the size and composition of the country's foreign debt becomes a consideration in any investment. In Indonesia, the linkage between foreign debt and forest depletion can be illustrated dramatically. The current Indonesian requirement for foreign exchange to service its debt to Japan is some U.S. $2 billion per year. The value of Indonesian forest product exports is approximately the same. On the premise that Indonesia's timber-cutting practices are not environmentally sustainable, a premise shared by the World Bank, it can be said that this rich resource is being exhausted to service debt. On the further premise that forest depletion to the extent now under way in Indonesia has a worldwide negative effect on the environment, the climate of societies in many regions is being sacrificed in the interests of the Japanese banking community.

Though located exactly on the opposite pole of the globe, the interests of Canada and Canadians are not unaffected by these Indonesian experiences, and in many more ways than the environmental impact. Although Canada imports very few unprocessed tropical logs, and is not by world standards a large purchaser of Indonesian plywood, its imports of these products have dramatically increased in recent years, from zero in 1980 to more than Can. $42 million worth in 1988. Of importance as well, Canada is a major exporter of wood products to the same destinations as Indonesia. If one views in holistic fashion the world trade in forest products, including pulp and paper, Canada is a principal player. From the perspective of Indonesia, economic likenesses abound even if species similarities are rare. Canada's exports of all forest products, for example, represent in value 14 per cent of all Canadian exports, are of an annual worth in excess of $22 billion, and represent almost 25 per cent of the world total.[40] Indonesia, for its part, commands fully 49 per cent of the world trade in plywood, a commodity in ever-increasing demand: world plywood exports have almost doubled in the past decade.

Canadian imports of tropical forest products, although not huge, are nevertheless not insignificant, a clear indication of Canada's reliance upon them, and of Canada's interest in their continued availability. The Canadian market thus transmits pressure to Indonesia and other tropical producers to maintain current competitive price levels whatever the environmental impact. Eleven per cent of Canada's imports of wood and wood products, of a 1988 value of $139.6 million, came from tropical and East Asian countries, as did 5 per cent of all paper and paperboard imports of a 1988 value of $86.8 million. Principal sources in the first category are, in order of importance, Indonesia, Taiwan, Brazil, Malaysia, and the Philippines; in the second category Japan (as intermediary), Brazil, Taiwan, and South Korea.[41]

Of much greater significance to deforestation in Canada's merchandise trade accounts are those tropical products grown in circumstances where, for the most part, the forests first have to be cleared. In 1988 the value of these products was: coffee, $432.2 million; citrus, $391.2 million; cocoa and products, $153.8 million; natural rubber, $134.2 million. Of these, only citrus comes in part from an industrialized country, the United States. For these commodities, plus others of lesser value such as palm oil, nuts, and spices, Canada is heavily dependent upon functioning tropical country ecosystems. Still another burden on tropical forests is the fast-food industry in North America which has created an immense market for lower-quality beef. A decade ago, this market stimulated cattle production in Central America, often on pastures cleared from the forests. The demand of Canadian teenagers for hamburgers and chocolate milk shakes thus reaches back to the tropical environment.

If one adds to this list of tropical products the street price of narcotics produced illegally in the developing countries and sold illegally in Canada, another category of commodity is added with a value greater than that of all forest-land imports. In the Andes, in the Caribbean, and in Southeast Asia, forests are cleared to permit the cultivation of coca, marijuana, and opium poppies for heroin. The Northern market demand has a devastating effect on the environments, the economies, and the political stability of many developing countries.

As a member of the immensely powerful industrialized country market system, Canada is at once dependent upon the developing countries as sources of goods and influences their national policies. Demand and price within Canada, as within the other major consuming nations, is reflected back to the tropical forests. Much more than is immediately apparent to even a discerning Canadian at breakfast – drinking orange juice and coffee, glancing at the morning paper, seated in a kitchen adorned with cabinets with tropical veneer panelling – the countries of the North are deeply engaged in the rain forests and highlands of the countries of the South. That interest must be pursued responsibly.

There is yet another linkage between the forests of the North and the South. In the Western Hemisphere, as in other longitudes, the annual migration of bird species serves an essential biological purpose. The forests of the United States and Canada depend to a considerable degree upon such birds to keep in balance insect populations that are often potentially destructive. Should the habitat of these birds disappear in the South, the forests of the North will suffer.

From Rachel Carson came an early, poignant appeal for the restoration of environmental balance. In 1962, her *Silent Spring* was one of the first popular observations of the loss of bird life in North America.[42] The more recent study by John Terborgh, *Where Have All the Birds Gone?* chronicles in some detail the diminution of these important members of the natural life chain in this hemisphere. Some 250 species of North American birds migrate regularly to the neotropics. The migrants constitute as much as 85 per cent of local populations. Once in their winter habitats, these birds become fully integrated members of the local communities, often altering both diet and behaviour to conform. Migration patterns are well mapped, and numbers and destinations reasonably accurately accounted for, but not yet to the point where meaningful long-term comparisons are possible. Canadian songbirds from the eastern part of the country fly deeply into the Caribbean and Central America. Birds from the west reach into Mexico and Guatemala. Deforestation in any of these southern destinations is of considerable significance. Sadly, those regions that most suit people (often the mountain slopes between 500 and 2,000 metres altitude), and are therefore under the most intense attack from human exploitation, are those most favoured by birds.

Any decrease in the numbers of songbirds visiting Canada has both ecological and economic implications. As migrant numbers decline for whatever reason, there does not appear to be a compensating increase in resident birds. Because most of the migrants feed on insects, their absence will mean less pressure on the insect species that make up their diets. The disappearance of predators signals an increase in insect pests and a corresponding destruction of valuable Canadian forest and agricultural growth. Thus does destruction of forests in the Caribbean and Central America – whether for cattle ranching, plantation crops, or smallholder agriculture – affect Canada and Canadians.

There is no accurate means of estimating the value to residents of the industrialized countries in the North of plentiful forests in the developing countries of the South. The contribution of trees and the many and diverse species of biological life dependent on them extends not only to a sustainable environment but as well to a treasure house of organisms of immense present and potential value to science, medicine, and industry. Our attitude towards forest resources in our own country reveals just how irrational and contradictory we are. In the Queen Charlotte Islands of British Columbia and in Oka, Quebec, the aboriginal peoples who have protected the natural forests for millennia recently have found themselves engaged in armed conflict with communities wishing to harvest trees for lumber or simply to replace them with a golf course. All the while, on all continents, trees are disappearing far more rapidly than they are being replaced, and far more rapidly than was estimated just ten years ago – one and a half times as fast worldwide, four times as fast in nine important Asian and Latin American countries including India and Brazil.

If forests are of value, their destruction is costly. Evidence was presented at the United Nations Conference on Desertification in Nairobi in 1977[43] that those costs are ten to twenty times greater than the investment needed for preservation. Celestial observers must by now be aghast at a terrestrial species that not only destroys its habitat with senseless abandon, but does so at a cost severalfold greater than maintaining it. The admonition in Genesis to 'subdue' the earth now has a sinister meaning.

◆

Humankind has little experience in undertaking comprehensive cooperative activities on a global scale. Happily, one of the earliest examples of broad international cooperation took place in the environmental sector. As early as 1853, meteorologists from several nations gathered in Brussels to confer on means to collect and share meteorological observations taken aboard ships at sea. In 1878, at Utrecht in the Netherlands, the International Meteorological Organization was established to foster increased cooperation for the benefit of maritime navigation and agriculture. In 1951, a full-fledged intergovernmental organization, the World Meteorological Organization (WMO), came into existence. One of the most useful of WMO activities has been the invaluable 'World Weather Watch' which provides for the gathering and broad dissemination of meteorological observations made by surface stations, ships, aircraft, and satellites. Throughout the darkest days of international tension, countries all over the world continued to participate and to benefit from direct satellite transmissions of cloud imagery and real-time data. The precedent is a harbinger of what can be done.

A much more complex, and politically more challenging, endeavour was the thirteen-year-long set of negotiations leading to a Law of the Sea Treaty,[44] which included provisions that extended much beyond the environmental. The success of this latter feat remains limited, however, because of the refusal of the United States to ratify the treaty, notwithstanding its active involvement in the negotiations from beginning to end. Unfortunately, a number of other countries have followed the u.s. lead. (The u.s. attitude is a vivid projection of national hypocrisy: those parts of the treaty the United States favours, it regards as customary international law, and expects all countries to abide by them; those parts the United States does not like, it contends are novel and non-binding without express consent. The signal sent out by this sort of picking and choosing makes a mockery of the rule of law and opens broad exceptions damaging to all nations, large and small.)

Even the mammoth undertaking demanded by the Law of the Sea negotiations pales in comparison to what is required if the international community is to be able to protect the peoples of the world from major environmental despoliation. Calls have been heard for a 'Law of the Atmosphere' treaty. Sadly, Mostafa Tolba, the executive director of the u.n. Environment Programme, is likely correct when he observes that the lengthy time frame that would be required to negotiate such a treaty in the face of so many intransigent nations would reduce considerably its worth. All the while, the need for some form of international agreement, and the likely tensions if one is not reached, are increasingly apparent. Gleick has written that 'of all the pressing large-scale environmental problems facing society, global climatic changes appear to have the greatest potential for provoking disputes, worsening tensions, and altering relations between developed and developing countries.'[45]

One of the reasons, of course, for governmental indecision and inaction is that information is incomplete, costs are unknown, and benefits will not accrue within the life span of governments now in power. Nevertheless, there is clear and mounting evidence in country after country that the popular will is in favour of some kind of decisive intervention. A UNEP environment-related survey carried out in fifteen countries worldwide found that in only one of the countries surveyed (Saudi Arabia) did respondents feel that their environments had not worsened in the previous ten years. In all countries surveyed, and by large margins, respondents placed a higher priority on the reduction of health risks associated with the environment than they did on increasing their standard of living. Of the Latin Americans surveyed, for example, fully 85 per cent said that, if offered a choice, they would choose a lower standard of living with fewer health risks than a higher standard of living with more risks.

Less certain is whether the publics in the industrialized countries are yet aware of just how imbalanced is cause and effect in these matters on the global template. It is the industrialized North that has been responsible so far for the major share of carbon emissions, for the greatest percentage of toxic effluents wasted into rivers and streams. It is the industrialized North that has benefited historically – and still benefits – from its greedy assumption that it enjoys 'drawing rights' on the atmosphere, waters, and soil of this planet of a kind and extent that it is far from willing to share with the developing South. Without the full involvement and cooperation of both North and South, however, success in limiting or reversing environmental degradation will be limited; in the absence of an agreed dedication to principles of sustainable development, with all of the changes and the sharing of technology that that demands, the global entente so necessary will be unattainable.

Thus for the same reason that the ambitious Law of the Sea Treaty remains becalmed in the cross-currents of national interest, the range of activities now contributing to environmental degradation complicates efforts to sort out and reduce the harm. Yet increasingly, as has been seen in the recent dramatic agreements reached to eliminate the destruction of the ozone layer, the several ingredients of political will, economic wherewithal, and technological competence will combine to forge new partnerships. The incontrovertible evidence of future environmental destruction in the absence of concerted action is compelling.

Already, the planet's natural resources are being consumed at a rate well in excess of replacement rates, and the release of harmful substances is far more destructive than had been believed, or can be tolerated. These activities, moreover, are so far overwhelmingly concentrated in the industrialized countries. They will be exacerbated severalfold should the countries of the South continue to emulate the economic growth policies of the North. The poverty-instigated environmental destruction – forest destruction, desertification, water pollution – will not only continue but for some time be aggravated, as efforts are made to industrialize; that is inevitable, given the destructive physical impact and chemical poisoning associated with current industrial practices. And throughout, the multiplier effect of population growth will exacerbate further and more rapidly the present dismal trends. Quickly associated with any increase in environmental degradation will be social revolts; these will make political action necessary even as acceptable political formulae become more difficult to design.

Those environmentally related activities that in some instances must be challenged and in others refined or reversed are as monumental in scope and complex in character as any that have ever challenged human ingenuity. Effective management of these issues requires the kind of single-minded determination that motivated those dedicated to the perpetuation of the Cold War. More important, it demands a quite different quality, a devotion to the attainment of human dignity that springs from a genuine sense of humility far in excess of what is generally found in modern societies of the North. The activities to be altered, after all, are in most instances associated with deep-seated human behaviour: the instincts to reproduce, to survive, to enhance well-being; the desire to be economically active, to accumulate material goods, to consume; the impulse of societies to be self-centred and xenophobic.

From the standpoint of governments, there are contradictions and confusions that must be recognized and overcome. In the absence of uncontested scientific evidence and of accurate predictions of social and economic cost – an impediment that will continue for some time to come – leadership of a rare quality is necessary. Entirely new concepts of cost accounting are needed. Governments must be able to reveal to their electorates the real costs associated with natural resource exploitation or destruction, be able to compare the long-term cost of governmental inactivity with the short-term cost of prevention or avoidance, and be able to demand from varying economic sectors and actors an equitable measure of compensation for their environmentally stressful operations.

Statesmen must possess both the conviction to act decisively and the skills to persuade their citizenry that major alterations in lifestyle are absolutely necessary. Change is always a challenge. Yet as the Chinese proverb stated, 'If one doesn't change course, one generally ends up where one is going.' As humankind approaches the next century, we must realize that to end up where we are going will be catastrophic. What was once a mutuality of vulnerability on a North–South axis could unquestionably become a mutuality of human and environmental degradation.

V

The Demographics

The human condition has never been static. In their ceaseless quest for the betterment of circumstance, human beings have formed settlements, migrated great distances, created large farming and industrial enterprises, engaged in bloody wars, pursued magnificent human goals. The constant factor has been one of dynamism, including the propagation of the species.

In the face of oppressive conditions of either human or natural origin, or in an effort to relieve the pressures of burgeoning populations, entire societies have often moved. In doing so they displaced local inhabitants in some instances and opened up previously uninhabited territories in others, introducing new cultures and new technologies into the regions in which they settled.

Never before, however, have the numbers of impoverished and displaced persons been so large as they now are. And never before have the several factors of degraded natural habitat, absence of economic opportunity, and awareness of disparity been so prevalent. The world is poised at the beginning of a period of immense turmoil and upheaval as increasing numbers of desperate, alienated, and persecuted people seek by whatever means is available to them to improve their own welfare. To deny them that improvement and to buttress the privileged behind economic and physical barriers are practices that are at once inhumane and impractical. The human species finds itself in an age where all must benefit or all will suffer.

◆

The human species is peripatetic. Were this not so, the North American continent would be uninhabited. The first migrations to this continent came from Asia, across the land-bridge of the Bering Sea, some twenty to twenty-five thousand years ago. These peoples formed the original stock of the 'indigenous' tribes of Indians and Inuit who were to spread east and south. Their numbers grew to an estimated 350,000 by the time that the next immigrants arrived early in the sixteenth century. These visitors came from the opposite direction, from Europe, and in the first instance engaged primarily in exploratory activities as had the Vikings six centuries earlier in Newfoundland. The first permanent settlement efforts on the continent were those of Jacques Cartier in 1541–3. Migration in significant numbers began only in the eighteenth century into what is now the United States, and later into Canada. In the process, the customs and the traditions of the long-time occupants of the continent were seldom respected, their land claims – even today – denied or ignored, their character and dignity as individuals diminished and destroyed.

The great waves of immigrants that were to occupy the Canadian half of the North American continent came in two periods: 1861–81 and, especially, 1903–13. Their origins in the first interval were overwhelmingly from Britain; in the second, primarily from Eastern Europe. Together with the descendants of the earliest settlers, including Canadians of French descent who numbered 2.45 million by 1921, the Canadian population was overwhelmingly Caucasian. Not in Canada, as in the United States, was there any significant fraction of persons of African stock; in Canada there had not been any form of plantation agriculture and therefore no economic temptation to import slaves, as had been the practice of the sugar-cane and cotton growers of the Caribbean and the American south respectively.

Canada's special labour requirements later in the nineteenth century were met by indentured labourers, not slaves; they came from Asia, not Africa. They were transported to Vancouver to perform the heavy and dangerous tasks necessary in the construction of the Canadian Pacific Railway. Their assimilation into Canadian society was painful and desperately slow. Their later endeavours to find employment in the mines and forests of British Columbia were met with hostility and resistance. Discriminatory behaviour was rampant; legislative enactments to bar non-white workers on the premise of 'safety' were several times declared unconstitutional by the courts.[1] In the prairies, individual Chinese chose to open small businesses, but for many years faced community-sponsored barriers of outrageously racial character. As recently as 1914, the Supreme Court of Canada upheld the constitutional validity of a Saskatchewan statute that prohibited white women from employment in any business owned or managed by Orientals. The legislation was interpreted by the court as a bona fide attempt to protect the morals of Saskatchewan women.[2]

Nor have the acts of the federal government always been of a compassionate kind. In 1914, the first action of the newly commissioned warship HMCS *Rainbow* was to escort out of Canadian waters and to steer to the open sea the *Komagatu Maru* with 376 Indians on board, would-be immigrants to Canada who had been kept moored in Vancouver harbour for several weeks, denied permission to come ashore. Two decades later, the passenger ship *St. Louis*, loaded with European Jews fleeing from the savagery of Hitler, was turned away from the Canadian shore and the asylum it represented.

Yet in the period 1966–86, Canada welcomed 1.5 million immigrants of non-European origin, primarily from Asia and the Caribbean, a pattern of activity that has changed profoundly the complexion and the character of Canadian society. Whereas only twenty years ago nearly four-fifths of all immigrants to Canada came from Europe or from countries settled by Europeans, now more than two-thirds originate from the developing countries of the South. The preferred place of settlement of the majority of these arrivals has been in the largest cities – Toronto, Montreal, and Vancouver. In the result, the ethnic composition of these communities has changed considerably. Some 14 per cent of the current population of Toronto originated in developing countries.[3]

Massive and unprecedented flows of this kind are accompanied by a cascade of sociological issues and implications. The Canadian microcosm is relatively tiny (Canada's 1989 population of 26.5 million represents only one-half of 1 per cent of the world total) but is important because Canada is only one of three countries in the North that continues to accept significant numbers of immigrants from the South. (The two others are the United States and Australia.) Even should present volumes and patterns of immigration continue, however, it must be recognized that this is a very small proportion of the persons migrating from points within developing countries. Much the greater number of those on the move remain in their own country or their own region.

The circumstances that motivate migrants are little different today from what they were at any time in the past: want of personal security, of a means of sustenance, of hope for a better future, or any combination of those factors. In some instances these circumstances are of human origin, as in cases of warfare or persecution; in others, they arise from natural disasters. In centuries past, one of the principal motivations was the insistence of religious orthodoxy. Today, although less widespread, the vivid images of religious conflict found in Northern Ireland, in Lebanon, in Kashmir, or (in other forms) in the West Bank are grim reminders that heavenly inspired dictates remain a potent force for inhumane conduct. Elsewhere, ethnic rivalries arise out of a combination of cultural and religious distinctions, as in Sri Lanka, in Tibet, and in several African countries. And in all too many places, dissent, whether of religious or political origin, prompts discrimination, harassment, and sometimes more. An ugly human characteristic remains, as has always been the case, the insistence of the dominant community upon both conformity and subservience from the minority. Even in the absence of economic or political competition, the bully instinct survives. It is ugly and demeaning, whether practised on a personal, a commercial, or a national level. The only difference among these is the extent of the havoc wrought by the self-righteous, generally always with exclamations of high moral purpose ranging from defence of the truth to defence of the realm.

Ancient as is the practice of migration (as distinct from nomadism) never has the number of those on the move been as high as it is today. This is a reflection, in part, of swelling populations as well as of human hostilities and natural disasters. It is also a reflection of the increasing extent to which the natural environment has been made inhospitable.

It is estimated that up to 60 million people in the world are at this moment in a transitory state, part of vast involuntary migratory patterns of persons displaced by war, civil strife, environmental catastrophe, starvation, political repression, or economic hardship. Less than a quarter of that number fall within the definition of 'political' refugees as used by the United Nations: persons seeking asylum because of a well-founded fear of persecution. Among the others, there may well be many who are fearful, but whose apprehension cannot be 'well-founded.' There are as well still others whose fear is of want. These persons fall into the modern – and unprotected – categories of economic and environmental refugees. The several hundred thousand migrant workers who fled Kuwait and Iraq in the summer of 1990 illustrate how volatile can be the situation and how quickly an immense burden can descend on immediately neighbouring countries as it did in this case upon Jordan, Egypt, and Turkey.

The numbers of all these categories are crude at best. Inaccuracy and incompleteness are common. Many such persons are unregistered, undocumented, and find themselves beyond the reach of national or international relief programs. The incontestably large volume of persons fleeing unendurable circumstances, a volume that is almost entirely located within the developing countries of the South, has far-reaching implications for international stability. In some instances the threat to stability comes from population surges across tribal or political boundaries in numbers that Canadians find difficult to comprehend. The number of displaced persons at the time of the partition of the Indian subcontinent into India and Pakistan in 1947, following cessation of British colonial rule, is estimated to have been 15 million.[4] In 1971, on the severance of Pakistan and the emergence of the east wing as the independent nation of Bangladesh, 10 million persons fled temporarily into India. The civil war in Afghanistan created 5 million refugees. The civil war in Sudan caused 2 million displaced persons. These numbers are to be compared with the grand total of 'Displaced Persons' in Europe following the Second World War. That number was 8 million.

The decade of the 1980s may well be recorded as one of the most brutal in this or any other century. It was a decade of wars, almost all of them civil wars. And it was a decade that continued the trend, beginning with the Second World War and so disturbingly evident in the Vietnam War, for civilian casualties to outnumber military casualties. In the First World War, the death toll was 12.5 million military, 7 million civilian. In the Second World War, it became 18.6 million military, 19.6 million civilian. No one is ever likely to learn the full figures for Vietnam or Afghanistan, although the estimates for the former are 1.1 million military and 1.2 million civilian. The decade just past has seen the lengthy slaughter of the Iraq-Iran War as well as bloody civil wars – many of them surrogate conflicts supported or sponsored by superpower champions – in Afghanistan, Angola, Cambodia, El Salvador, Ethiopia, Guatemala, Lebanon, Mozambique, Nicaragua, Peru, Philippines, Sri

Lanka, and Sudan. It is estimated that in all these wars the death count exceeded 4 million. Of these, 1.3 million were military; twice as many – 2.7 million – were civilian. Ruth Leger Sivard, the tireless accountant of the world's conscience, reports in her superb 1989 edition of *World Military and Social Expenditures* that the twentieth century 'has already had more war deaths than the 18th and 19th centuries combined.'[5] She adds that since the Second World War, 'on an average yearly basis the death toll has been five times greater than in the 19th century, eight times greater than in all the 18th.' These are the tragic consequences of empires reluctant to relax their grip, of ideologically motivated revolutions and equally ideological resistance to them. When civilians are killed at twice the rate of the soldiers, one understands the endeavours of the civilians to get out of the way.

Migratory surges of large dimension are now a characteristic of many developing regions; they are unlikely to diminish in the near future even though, happily, the number of wars gives some evidence of receding. In its most recent report, the United States Committee for Refugees estimates that more than 15 million people are at this time displaced for *political* reasons, many of them living in temporary and often vile conditions in encampments established to maintain – and confine – them.[6] 'Temporary' is, of course, a relative term. In the more than forty years since displaced Palestinians were confined in camps in Gaza, an entire generation has been born and grown to maturity in circumstances that have created a festering attitude of hopelessness, bitterness, and hatred. It is an unlikely portent for a peaceful resettlement.

Of this category of political refugees, the group of highest visibility within Canada has been described as 'boat people,' those unfortunates who have fled the carnage and repression in the countries of Indo-China. In the period 1975–89, more than one hundred thousand persons of this category were granted immigrant status within Canada.

Is it possible to calculate the cost of misery of these proportions, of the forced departure from one's homeland? Several methods could be employed, all of them conjectural but none without some validity. The easiest, perhaps, is to estimate the cost of several millions of persons living in a state of economic neuterdom, as so many now do, in refugee camps of one kind or another. The out-of-pocket cost to the governments extending hospitality, and to the international organizations (principally affiliates of the United Nations) that bear the expenses associated with the provision of shelter, food, health care, and rudimentary social services, can be estimated, even if not accurately. If the displaced persons are not accepted by the host government but are illegal immigrants, then the not inconsiderable cost of enforced confinement must be calculated. The cost to various levels of government in the United States of maintaining illegal border crossers in detention facilities, for example, is an issue of increasing concern. In Canada, each refugee claimant detained on arrival costs the government some Can. $150.00 per day. (Following detainment, pending determination of their status, maintenance costs are generally borne by church groups, NGOs, and local communities.)

A cost that can be determined still less accurately, but nevertheless justifiably, is what economists call 'opportunity cost' – the potential benefits *not* realized because of the economic inactivity of these persons. Even the most conservative calculation produces figures of immense size. If one assumes that only one out of every four of those millions of persons now in refugee camps or detention centres is of working age, and further that each one of those is possessed of such limited skills that he or she is capable of contributing only some U.S. $500 of value per year to the local economy, one finds that the world is forgoing each year billions of dollars worth of economic activity. When one realizes that more than sixty countries in the world have GNPs less than U.S. $2 billion, it is clear that this loss is not an incidental sum.

A further form of cost is political. This cost is not so much calculable as it is describable. How long can a nation maintain within its boundaries a sizeable number of dissatisfied, restive individuals without fear for its own security, perhaps its own social stability? The effect of these outsiders can take several forms. One, certainly, is the resentment that builds up within the local community at what is often seen as the unfair occupation of land and the consumption of resources by outsiders, in circumstances often perceived as being at the expense of locals. Another is the perverse influence, real or imagined, of scheming, unemployed dissidents within the refugee community upon the surrounding nationals. The possibility is not merely theoretical. Camp boundaries are not hermetically sealed. Information, sometimes a limited amount of commerce, and attitudes flow back and forth, influencing communities at either end. If the numbers are large, the environment appropriate, and the time period long, the combination can be volatile. Isolation and authoritarian restraint are not viable as long-term responses. Much more effective, but certainly requiring more daring, was the wise decision of the Jordanian government to open the gates of the camps accommodating Palestinians displaced from the West Bank by occupying Israelis. These people in many instances gradually assimilated into the broad Jordanian society, contributing immensely with their high education levels, their dynamism, and their economic skills. (The long-term effects of the policy still pose risks, however. The acts of the Jordanian government to force the removal from Jordan of Palestinian guerrillas in 1970 and 1971 have left lingering resentments inside and outside the country. The numbers of Palestinians remaining in Jordan are so large that they now actually outnumber the ethnically distinct Jordanians. Their active opposition to Israel's West Bank practices and their perception of the inconsistency of United States policies in the region fuelled an emotional outpouring of support for Iraq following its 1990 invasion of Kuwait.)

Another category of cost is measurable in social and human terms. Here, however, the calculations become difficult and judgmental. What is the loss to society of generations of unfulfilled individuals? What value is to be attached to these absent contributions – the stories not written, the songs not composed, the scientific discoveries not made, the care and compassion for one's community not extended? Within these encampments, common sense and statistical certainty tell us that there are large numbers of individuals possessed of superior natural talents, many more who are desirous of functioning as generous members of society. Clustered in unnatural conditions with little opportunity for the assumption of normal responsibilities, let alone the inspiration for creative activity, there is little likelihood that even a small fraction of these people will be able to realize their human capacity and natural gifts to make contributions commensurate with their talent. Nor, of course, are such losses sustained only by the immediate communities. Brilliance normally casts its light considerable distances; decency by its very nature evokes positive responses over a broad spectrum.

There is still another human cost: the cost to the self-esteem of those persons, particularly in the industrialized countries, who are aware of these circumstances, and who have some means (no matter how limited) of remedying them, yet who have failed to do so. What is the loss in self-respect, in the quality of the human spirit, of those who could make a difference but who have not? What has been the cost to the human race of the barbaric incarceration for twenty-seven years of Nelson Mendela? What of the cost caused by the imprisonment of those many other Nelson Mendelas worldwide not so well known?

If this cost exercise is extended to those in the developing countries who are not physically displaced and detained elsewhere, but who are denied by circumstance any meaningful opportunity to participate economically, politically, or socially in their own communities, the calculations assume truly frightening proportions. Yet it is not unrealistic to measure cost and loss on this basis. The numbers are bewildering. The United Nations estimates that more than 1 billion persons worldwide now live in conditions of absolute poverty, unable to be economically self-sufficient, let alone be economic contributors. It should be no surprise that dissidents, populists, radical activists, and anarchists emerge from these ranks. Governments in the South are aware of these circumstances and are aware, too, of their own limited ability to control or direct them. It is most often we in the North who assume naïvely that injustices and deprivations of this kind are without cost, and are containable. We are naïve if we fail to realize that when an economy fails to meet basic needs, then political tensions rise, ethnic, social, and regional conflict is exacerbated in competition for scarce resources, and nation-building efforts fall into disarray. In these circumstances the dominant groups often react to any signs of protest or anger on the part of the public by establishing repressive political regimes, most frequently under military control. This prompts a reaction to state repression that generates in turn organized civil insurgency in an escalating cycle of violent conflict. Northern observers sigh and note with puzzlement the emergence of still another developing country hot spot before turning their attention to more compelling issues like the latest sports scores.

◆

In centuries past, the departure of persons for other regions was, as today, sometimes voluntary, sometimes forced. The experience of England in the seventeenth and eighteenth centuries reveals that the two were not unrelated. Each was a reflection of a different facet of the English society of the period; each reveals the political power of the then dominant element, described most simply as property-owning adherents of the established church. Daniel Defoe's celebrated pamphlet, *The Shortest Way with the Dissenters*, published in 1702, was a savage satire of the extremist – but establishmentarian – Tory legislation to force religious orthodoxy. It was to escape pressures of this kind that some of the Puritans had already fled to America. 'This lande growes wearye of her Inhabitants,' wrote John Winthrop on the eve of the departure of the *Mayflower*.[7] The same land-owning element of English society moved Parliament to continue the passage of 'enclosure' acts, legislation that permitted the fencing of land and the exclusion of peasants whose wherewithal had been augmented through such menial pursuits as gleaning and the grazing of cattle. From 1750 to 1800, enclosure by private acts of Parliament increased dramatically. No longer required as field labourers because of the advent of mechanized farming, rural dwellers in large numbers had little alternative but to migrate to the large cities in search of employment. There, in the London of that period, as in the Lagos or Bombay or Rio de Janeiro of today, homeless and unemployed wretches presented an immense challenge to local authorities. In the England of that period many of them were arrested as vagrants and transported abroad, often to Australia.

In these ways Parliament responded to the challenges posed by heterodoxy and by the unemployed. In these ways a nation adjusted to the structural changes demanded by industrialization and the mechanization of agriculture. People surplus to the new economic realities were expelled in order to maintain the advantages enjoyed by those able to wield power. The produce of the newly efficient factories found ready markets in the overseas colonies.

How different is the world of today, and how absent are any of those eighteenth-century options as developing country governments face their own challenges of industrialization, of structural adjustment, of surplus population, of a privileged minority resisting any encroachments on their status. In the 1990s there are no guaranteed markets to fund the transformation of societies. In the 1990s, the very governments that practised the wholesale transplant of unwanted human beings are among the most outraged at evidence of similar policies in the developing countries. In any event, there simply exist no longer large tracts of unoccupied land suitable for human habitation. The western plains of North America have long since been fully settled, as have the arable tracts of Australia. Such countries as the Soviet Union, which engaged during the Stalinist era in practices of forced resettlement, now recognize and are suffering from the social and political hazards that those policies created. As the world approaches the twenty-first century, there are no longer available any easy or automatic safety-valves. The countries now suffering most from overpopulation must seek solutions quite different from those seized by the European powers in centuries past.

Few of them have been successful. In the result, the oppressed and the uprooted turn themselves to the only option open to them: migration. The modern equivalent of transportation is flight. Flight from the intense, widespread and irresistible circumstances that make the continuance of life untenable. Flight, not choice, is the correct description because it is not a human instinct to abandon home and roots and depart for somewhere else unless there is an overwhelming push or pull. Euripides in the fifth century BC stated the case succinctly: 'There is no sorrow above the loss of a native land.'[8] Apart from the peculiar – and limited – circumstances of nomadic tribes, the normal attitude of most human beings is to remain where circumstances, terrain, and associates are all familiar. The fear and uncertainty so often associated with migration is a major deterrent to moving, as is well known even to major employers in a country as secure and transparent as Canada. When those who flee undertake the hazards of travel (as in the case of the 'boat people' of Vietnam) in addition to the risks of alighting in unknown and often hostile circumstance, the motivating force can be assumed to be very powerful.

That powerful force in today's world is in many instances environmental in origin. There may as well be war or persecution or a major economic element – as in the case of food shortages, for example – but the underlying cause again and again is environmental: drought, flood, landslide or erosion, desertification – all factors that reduce dramatically food production and distribution. These are the major contributors to the diminishment of food stocks. Another, of course, is the simple fact that populations are increasing more rapidly than is food production. Thus more grain (the dominant food staple) is eaten than is grown, a circumstance that is clearly unsustainable. The United Nations Food and Agriculture Organization (FAO) reported in late March 1990 that world cereal stocks had fallen for the third successive year. Since 1987, reserves have dropped from 450 million tonnes to 293 million tonnes. This is the lowest level since 1981, a time when the world's population was considerably lower than it is now. Stocks are equivalent now to 17 per cent of annual consumption, a figure that FAO regards as below the minimum needed for world food security. (The widespread bumper wheat harvests of 1990 will undoubtedly ease that circumstance somewhat.) As with all shortages, the impact is felt unevenly from region to region. Among the countries most in distress according to FAO are Afghanistan, Angola, Ethiopia, Mozambique, and Sudan. In each, the environment as a factor is present but varies in importance with other factors such as insurrection, political mismanagement, or shortage of transportation. The composition of the several factors is of little concern to a famine-stricken populace. It does present a legal question to the international community, however, as it seeks to determine the juridical status of these individuals. 'Refugees' they certainly are in fact, but not necessarily in law.

The word 'refugee' itself is descriptive of human tragedy. It is as well a legal definition, one that has evolved considerably over the years, yet one that continues to deny the protection of international covenants to persons fleeing from environmental circumstance. The United Nations 1951 Convention Relating to the Status of Refugees, amended by a 1967 Protocol, defines refugees as people who have fled their country of origin because of a well-founded fear of being persecuted 'for reasons of race, religion, nationality, membership of a particular group or political opinion.' This definition, valid so far as it goes, is a reflection of the circumstances existing in Europe following the Second World War, but is scarcely broad enough to capture the range of reasons that prompt people of the developing countries to migrate today. For reasons of necessity, therefore, the United Nations High Commissioner for Refugees has extended his help to include 'whole groups fleeing from dangerous circumstances.'[9] This definition seeks to include those in flight for reasons other than political, but in practical application does little to address the plight of persons affected by the pervasive and complex interaction of poverty-environment-population. Refugee status is simply not accorded by the United Nations or its members to persons fleeing intolerable circumstances of either economic or natural origin.

Even the adjective 'natural' is often inaccurate because there is so often a human cause. Whatever the human-natural mix, however, both the severity and the frequency of disasters are increasing. 'Disaster' fatalities were six times higher in the 1970s than in the previous decade. Disturbingly, the average loss of life in disasters is considerably higher in developing countries than in industrialized countries.[10] There are a number of reasons why this is so, including the obvious ability of well-organized societies to warn their members of impending events, and the likelihood that in those societies persons are able to understand and respond adequately to the warnings. Additional factors, of a negative nature, are poverty, ill health, population concentration, and ineffectual governments, all of which are more likely to be found in the South.

The major cause of involuntary migration for environmental reasons, however, is much more prosaic. It may be defined simply as land degradation. People forced to move for this reason now form 'the single largest class of displaced persons in the world,' and the *permanently* displaced form the largest number among them. The processes that are creating these refugees are likely to continue into the future unless very substantial changes are made in land use and unless populations are stabilized. 'The vision of tens of millions of persons forced to abandon their homelands is a frightening prospect, one without precedent and likely to rival most past and current wars in its impact on humanity.'[11] As striking as are the numbers involved is the momentum with which these displaced persons are uprooted as once-fertile land turns to desert in region after region.

Two countries that attract popular attention in Canada because of the plight of their landless, El Salvador and Ethiopia, are examples of areas once capable of sustaining sizeable populations, but no longer. The current inability of each country to support those seeking to grow their own food has in each case led to social upheaval, political instability, and civil war. Soldiers contribute nothing to environmental recovery, and are seldom noted for humanistic responses to human tragedy. This is so whether the military assistance comes from the Soviet Union, as in Ethiopia, or from the United States, as in El Salvador. The evidence mounts that troops trained and armed by the Soviets in one country, and by the Americans in the other, are the authors of horrendous crimes. In El Salvador, forty thousand civilians have been murdered by the military[12] because they were suspected of opposing the regime. This has been done without any meaningful objection from the United States government with its seeming paranoia of anything that might be considered communist. In Ethiopia, the figures are unverifiable, but at least as great, of people killed because they appeared to the Mengistu regime to oppose communism. In both instances the conscience of the international community has been held at arm's length by the two superpowers in a demonstration that proves only that the commitment of each to military-based foreign policies has been at least as immoral as it has so often been ineffective.

One must not assume that there exists in either El Salvador or Ethiopia a predetermination, or an inevitability, of outcomes. Nor must one assume that the present environmental catastrophes are inevitable products of centuries of land misuse. Neither assumption would be correct. If the tragic circumstances are to be halted and gradually reversed, if similar circumstances are to be avoided elsewhere, an understanding of El Salvador and Ethiopia is necessary. The cases are distinct. Each, nevertheless, affects Canada.

El Salvador is located on the isthmus of Central America, a region of immense cultural, biological, physical, and climatic diversity. The isthmus is marked by rugged mountain landscapes and a frequency of geologic activity (earthquakes and volcanic eruptions) as intense as any in the world. Some 95 per cent of the terrain is hilly or mountainous, with fertile volcanic soil in the valleys. Forests once covered 90 per cent of El Salvador. Now, most wood is imported. There remains 'only a single 20 square kilometre plot of cloud forest relatively undisturbed.'[13] The forests have been destroyed as increasing populations, denied access to most of the arable land by the tiny number of occupying landowners, seek ever more desperate means to grow their own food. A century ago, visitors to this country were able to write of 'the generosity of nature, and the abundance of food.'[14] No longer is this possible. The introduction of plantation-type agriculture, with landownership concentrated in a few families, has encroached heavily on what were once communal lands.[15] By the early 1960s, 20 per cent of all arable land was owned by just 145 estates. The trend has increased since. At the same time, the containment of yellow fever and malaria has contributed to rapid increases in population. The population was less than 800,000 in 1900; by 2000 it will be 8.7 million, considerably more than the land can support. With low fertilizer applications and other agricultural inputs, El Salvador could feed only 3.1 million persons according to a 1975 FAO study;[16] with intermediate inputs, it might support 5.6 million, unlikely though it is that these higher applications could be afforded.

El Salvador is now witness to a horrific erosion of natural and human resources. The first prompts the second. And in each instance, the effects reach far beyond the country's borders. In a desperate attempt to raise agricultural production, immense quantities of pesticides are employed (in one recent year this tiny country is reputed to have used 'at least 20 per cent of the world's total parathion production')[17] with predictable consequences, including dangerously high levels of residue chemicals in the food products exported, often to the same countries that manufactured the chemicals in the first place.[18] An example of the hypocrisy of the North can be seen in current United States legislative endeavours to ban not the export of the chemical pesticides, but the import of fruits and vegetables exposed to them.

As many as 1 million Salvadorans have fled their ravaged homeland, most in circumstances that do not permit the compilation of accurate statistics. By the mid-1980s, it was estimated that between 550,000 and 600,000 were illegally present in the United States.[19] In much smaller numbers, Salvadorans have entered Canada as well.

Ethiopia is as distant and as unlike El Salvador as is physically possible. In historic, physical, and climatic circumstances, the contrasts are extreme. In two respects, however, is there a painful similarity: a ravaged topography and a wretched, malnourished populace. Each of these, of course, is related to the raging civil war – as in El Salvador – and each, too, affects Canada.

Ethiopia is a vast country, mountainous, geologically active, with large plateau areas at altitudes from 2,000 to 3,500 metres above sea level. Rainfall is seasonal and capricious; recurring periods of drought feature in Ethiopia's history. Highland temperatures are too cool for the tsetse fly, the carrier of trypanosomiasis, permitting Ethiopia to be home to the largest concentration of livestock in Africa. For much of its modern history, the country has been ruled on a feudal basis. Land tenure was reserved to a minority, food production was backward and sporadic, domestic insurgency and foreign interventions combined to discourage any rational reform or even an effective food distribution system. The limited introduction of market-based agriculture in the later years of the regime of Emperor Haile Selassie tended to displace even greater numbers of peasant farmers. It was the radical land reform program of the Mengistu government, however, that contributed most massively to soil degradation.

Land reform broke up the vast feudal estates and opened up massive areas of the country for cultivation to previously unpossessed peasants. Erosion became more widespread and more serious as forested hilly areas were cleared. The United States Agency for International Development (USAID) estimates that Ethiopia loses 1 billion tons of topsoil annually.[20] Forty per cent of the country was under forest at the beginning of this century; satellite photographs in the mid-1980s reveal that this has been reduced to 2–4 per cent.[21] As in El Salvador, population growth has been rapid. The United Nations Population Fund (UNFPA) estimates that the population of Ethiopia is now 46 million, up from 27.5 million twenty years ago. In the result, the cultivation of ever smaller plots of land has increased; grazing lands have been ploughed under; the practices of terracing, crop rotations, and fallow periods are being abandoned. Food shortages are stupendous. Refugees fleeing from the combined assaults of civil war, totalitarian government practices, and starvation now number more than 1 million. Those that have fled to neighbouring Somalia are stripping areas of that country of all vegetation as they scavenge for food, fuel, and fodder.

No other relief endeavour has attracted as much, and as sustained, reaction from Canadians as has the continuing famine in Ethiopia. Since mid-1984, when television thrust the misery and mayhem of Ethiopia into the homes of Canadians, until 1990 more than $360 million has been dedicated by Canada to the needs of this wretched country. Of that total, more than one-fifth, or Can. $67 million, has been subscribed directly by Canadians to the appeals of non-governmental organizations. The overwhelming bulk of these funds has been for relief and rehabilitation, not for development. Considerable governmental and private energies have been mobilized and dedicated to the easing of the plight of the famished, often in an endeavour to ensure delivery of emergency food supplies. This has met with limited success. The assessment of the Government of Canada was expressed thus to Parliament in April 1990: 'The situation remains bleak and desperate. I am not at all encouraged that donors will be able to bring the situation under manageable control. But neither am I willing to concede defeat and death for millions of Ethiopians.'[22]

Millions have already died, in most instances from starvation and famine-related illnesses. Little wonder that during the 1980s, more applications were received from Ethiopians seeking to emigrate to Canada than from any other African country (ten thousand) as, in the same decade, more applications were received from Salvadorans (twenty thousand) than from any other Latin American country.

Are there any lessons to be learned from these two case studies? Three, I submit. One, that the forceful imposition of foreign and ideologically inspired political systems upon a society is morally reprehensible; neither capitalism nor communism should presume to be more capable of stewarding arable soils than the age-old wisdom of local farmers. Second, that the poverty-driven desperation that leads to environmental degradation inevitably becomes a linked, descending spiral of increasing human and physical despoliation. The use of military force as a countermeasure is futile and reveals only the intellectual bankruptcy of those who encourage it. Third, that those outside powers that introduced either ideology or weaponry into these two states must now bear some of the responsibility to restore both order and terrain. Yet that is not happening. The increasing reluctance of the major industrialized countries to relieve the plight of those displaced by war has been described by Roger P. Winter, director of the U.S. Committee for Refugees: 'the very countries that in a cold-war context created the world's refugee protection system are now its greatest threat.'[23]

◆

There is no single issue which, by itself, heralds all the changes now under way in the world. Because the most pertinent of those issues are the product of human activity, however, and because their impact increases as human numbers grow, the issue of population is certainly central to any examination of the planetary condition. So extraordinary has been the rate of population growth in this century, and so strong is the momentum of growth through the next two decades at least, that the numbers by themselves are not likely to register adequately with even the most knowledgeable reader. A figure is necessary.

On 11 July 1987 the world's population passed the 5 billion mark. In the three years following, a net growth of another 300 million took place.

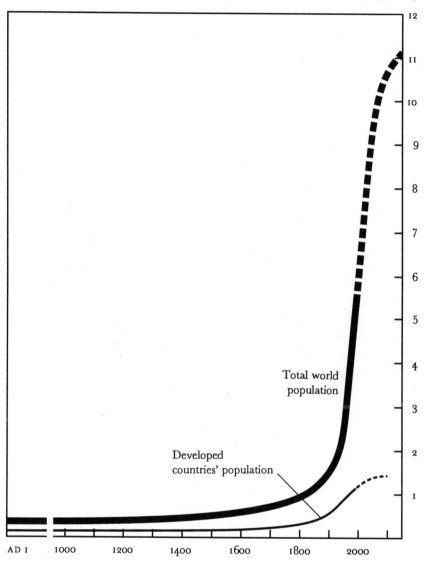

Population
(billions)

Total world
population

Developed
countries' population

PAST AND PROJECTED WORLD POPULATION, AD 1–2150

Source: John D. Durand, 'Historical Estimates of World Population:
An Evaluation,' *Population and Development Review* 3 (3; 1977)

Nor is the rate of growth slowing. The United Nations Population Fund (UNFPA) projects the world population in the year 2000 to be 6.251 billion; in 2025, to be 8.467 billion – 260 million more than earlier predictions.

In August 1984, in Mexico City, the World Population Conference convened its second decennial meeting. That event precipitated a number of studies and analyses of a current and a projected nature. These are now proving to be on the low side. Not for the first time.

From prehistory until about 1000 AD, the world's population did not increase by much. In earliest times, life was so precarious, and food supplies so unreliable, that a rough balance obtained between births and deaths notwithstanding an undoubtedly high fertility rate. The introduction of agricultural practices about 8000 BC lent a greater certainty to food supply but was for a long time largely offset by recurring crises of other natures – plague, war, etc. As the figure shows, population growth was modest for many centuries – from about 300 million at the time of the birth of Christ to some 800 million in the mid-eighteenth century. The doubling period was about 1,500 years. An equally important phenomenon is the fact that the rate of growth was approximately the same in all regions of the world.

From about 1850 onwards, growth accelerated immensely. Mortality decreased with the advent of science and technology. The next doubling period was reduced by 90 per cent; the world required only 150 years to grow from 800 million to 1.7 billion in 1900. That acceleration has continued. By 1950 the figure had reached 2.5 billion. By 1987, 5 billion. Doubling, which once had taken 1,500 years, had now been accomplished in 37.

Growth figures of this magnitude are difficult to digest. They work out to an annual increment of a little more than 100 million persons. One hundred million is about the population of Bangladesh. From now to the turn of the century, then, the world's population will grow by the equivalent of one new Bangladesh every year. That growth will be almost entirely in the South. In the next twenty years, 9,950 births out of every 10,000 in the entire world will take place in the developing countries.

Since 1950, another important distinction has become apparent. The long-standing, roughly parallel, growth rates of countries industrialized and developing ceased. From 1750 to 1850 the two groups were not that far apart: 0.6 per cent annual growth rate for the nations of Europe,

North America, and Japan, 0.4 per cent for Africa, Asia, and Latin America. Each group eased upwards in the next century from 1850 to 1950; 0.9 per cent and 0.6 per cent respectively. From 1950 onwards the change has been startling. Between 1950 and 1970 the growth rates increased and reversed. Accepted projections distribute the population for the year 2000 – 6.25 billion – as 4.95 billion for the developing countries, 1.3 billion for the industrialized countries.

As the developing countries' share of world population grew, their share of production dropped: from 44 per cent in 1800 to 19 per cent a century later and to 17 per cent in 1950. In 1980 the production share had risen to 21 per cent, but the population share was 75 per cent.

Another comparison between North and South is equally salient. The current size of those developing countries now at the threshold of industrialization and in the infancy of self-government is immensely larger than the size of the Northern countries at a comparative moment in their history. India is now 853 million, Indonesia 181 million, Nigeria 113 million, Mexico 89 million. In 1800, by comparison, France was about 30 million, Britain 10 million. In 1850 the United States was about 24 million, Japan 30 million.

The challenges to contemporary developing country governments are thus incomparably greater than were those to the now industrialized countries at an equivalent time in their history. Not only are populations severalfold larger but instant communications reveal to the poor the contrast of living standards with the better off. In all countries, North and South, governmentally imposed curtailments of freedom have followed on population growth; zoning laws, emission standards, and water and land use restrictions are among those well known. Authoritarian measures in countries with populations much greater than Canada's are not, therefore, entirely without precedent. Nor should we be surprised if they increase, as they will, even in the democracies. The challenge to democracies everywhere is to ensure that those restraints be chosen wisely and administered justly. It is a formidable challenge.

North America is home to one of the fastest growing of all national populations. The population of Mexico in 1950 was 25 million. Before this decade concludes, it will be 100 million. At that time more people will be resident in Mexico City alone than occupied the entire country a half-century earlier; as many as the entire population of Canada. Similar growth patterns and demographic shifts can be cited in dozens of developing countries. They represent a wholly new dynamic in international relations, one that is as yet absent in the policy formulation of governments of the North. In its absence, those policies are bankrupt because they are failing to anticipate social upheavals of historically unprecedented scale.

The survival instinct within each human being is a powerful force. In the quest for food, fuel, and shelter, immediate needs are given primacy. The more desperate the need, the more desperate the measures that will be taken. If social structure and economic circumstance combine to deny even a minimum standard of living, environmental havoc and communal disruption are the usual result. If these in turn are so threatening as to diminish any likelihood of a decent life, flight then becomes an instinctive response.

In earlier centuries, families fled religious persecution or economic hardship most often in search of a 'better life,' or a 'new beginning.' Today, entire communities seek refuge elsewhere to survive. Whereas Samuel de Champlain brought thirty-two settlers with him to New France in 1608, and the *Mayflower* carried 102 persons to Massachusetts Bay in 1620, hundreds of thousands have fled Vietnam since 1980. Each day, as many as five thousand persons enter the United States illegally across the Mexican border (less than half of them are apprehended); each day in June 1989, more than five hundred Vietnamese landed in Hong Kong.

Dislocated human beings threaten the stability of the communities in which they land, as they reflect the instability of the societies from which they have fled. These surges represent an immense and growing threat to a peaceful world: corrosive in influence, debilitating in impact, unpredictable in outcome. This issue may well be the largest, yet least recognized, international challenge of this and coming decades. It bears little resemblance to movements of the past and its understanding and management will not be derived from earlier precedents.

It is difficult for anyone from an industrialized country – save, perhaps, members of North American aboriginal communities – even to comprehend the agony and the hopelessness of those people in developing countries whose circumstances are described by the World Bank as 'absolute poverty.' The Bank's definition of that phrase is so shocking as to remove it from the personal experience of virtually every single person in Canada. To exist in absolute poverty is to be so calorie deficient that one lacks the energy needed to work. This is not a definition of idleness, or indifference, or absence of opportunity. It is a definition of reality: because of insufficient food, one is too weak to put in an effective day's work. At present in the developing countries of the South, in the aggregate, one out of four persons falls into that category – more than 1 billion persons too weak effectively to help themselves.

Not since the Great Depression of the 1930s have circumstances in North America been so desperate that there were large numbers of persons migrating in search of work – and food. In Canada and the United States, elaborate safety nets have been designed and put in place to ensure that those tragedies need not recur. In these countries, the unemployed and economically deprived are in greatest number able to find food and necessities because the social economy is able to provide it. Far the greatest percentage of those in need of this kind of assistance are physically able to work. They lack not strength, but jobs.

When one seeks to remain above the threshold of survival, one is reduced to the most basic biological functions. In two fundamental respects, however, humans are distinct from other creatures with which we share this planet. For one, we are more dependent on water – for drinking, for food preparation, for bathing, for washing clothes. Second, humans require cooked food, and for this they need fuel. These two dependencies create the pattern of activity most common in the poorest regions of the world: the carrying of water and the carrying of tree branches or animal dung. These are labours almost inconceivable today in the countries of the North. They are not the simple carriage of a pail of water to a house from the pump in the farmyard, or the movement of firewood from the lee of a building into the interior stove. They are arduous trips several kilometres long. So lengthy are they that the circle of denuded landscape around many African villages can be accurately described: it has a radius of 7 kilometres. That is the distance that a person can reasonably walk in quest of firewood and return in a single day. In many places, nothing of a woody nature remains inside such a circle.

There is a second distinction as well. It is women and children, almost exclusively, that act as beasts of burden carrying water on their heads or their backs. And although the practice is not quite as pervasive, women and children nevertheless carry far more than their share of firewood. This form of gender discrimination is an issue that only the developing countries themselves can address. Yet it must be addressed as one of the major inequities, most widespread, found in rural sectors of impoverished societies.

Firewood and water, under these circumstances, are not squandered. Indeed, for millions of persons in sub-Saharan Africa, fuel shortages are so acute that supplies permit only one cooked meal a day. In countries dependent on root crops such as cassava or on coarse, unmilled grains such as millet and sorghum, which require much cooking, there does not exist an alternative of uncooked fruit or vegetables. Malnourishment is thus compounded by a lack of both food and cooking fuel. In the result, more is at stake here than the level of unemployment or a healthy diet. Children are stunted both physically and intellectually. In Mexico, a recent government study found that only one in every five children under the age of four was of normal weight or height. Worldwide, 146 million children under age five are underweight for their size. This suggests that some countries are at risk of populating themselves with a generation that will be even less capable than the current one to tackle the challenges of the coming decades. (In contrast, those societies such as Japan and South Korea that have been able to sustain healthy economies and – thus – healthy diets find that the younger generation is taller than the preceding one.)

Diet is not, of course, the sole factor influencing either physical or mental health and growth. Social, as well as nutritional, elements must be taken into account. Nevertheless, the denial or deficiency of key nutrients in the diets of women both before and after conception has been linked clearly with low birth weights and with mental and physical retardation. In the South, an estimated 600 million women of child-bearing age suffer from nutritional anaemia.

We in the North have long been properly concerned about maternal and infant needs in our own communities. We are concerned not simply out of a desire to reduce infant mortality; we are properly dedicated to the rearing of a healthy, competent generation capable of assuming our responsibilities in the age-old cycle of all living creatures. We should be equally concerned about the competence of the coming generation in the South. Those children will be the contemporaries of our children and grandchildren and will outnumber them five to one on a planet increasingly pressed to provide the natural resources of earth, air, and water in adequate measure and wholesome quality. To meet that challenge successfully, the human species will require the full panoply of skills and talents of all societies, both North and South. The health of children in the South is therefore in the interest of the children in the North. That being so, the adults of the North bear a fiduciary relationship and responsibility towards them. It is a responsibility that is shamefully disregarded, as evidence adduced at the September 1990 United Nations Children's Summit clearly revealed.

The statistics cry out. UNICEF, the United Nations agency responsible for children, reported to the Summit that each year in the countries of the South 700,000 children go blind as a result of vitamin A deficiency that can be overcome for pennies a day or simple servings of green vegetables. Hundreds of thousands more are born with brain damage that could have been prevented had their mothers been given access to iodized salt while pregnant. Fourteen and a half million children have died in the past year from preventable causes – treatable diseases and inadequate nutrition. Of that number, 3 million die from measles, whooping cough, and tetanus, all preventable by simple immunization at a cost of a few dollars per child; 2.5 million die from diarrhoeal dehydration. Infant mortality rates, until recently, have eased but are now once more on the rise. In Nigeria, 174 infants die for every thousand live births; in Afghanistan, 162; in Mali, 159. By comparison, the rate in Finland is 5, and in Canada 6.

There is no mystery about these deaths and deprivations. No research is required to reduce them substantially. No magic medicines are needed. No more is necessary than a modest allocation of resources. In North and South, that requires some shift in priorities, some decision about what is most important, about which element in our society most deserves help and public funding. One element common to most countries is military expenditures. In few developing countries is a larger share allocated to any other budgetary item than to the military. In the South, the comparisons are so startling as to be disgusting. There, the ratio of soldiers to inhabitants is 1 to 240; of physicians, 1 to 1,950. Since 1960, developing countries have increased their military expenditures at a rate that is double the rise in per capita income. As a percentage of GNP, developing countries dedicate 1.6 per cent to health care, compared to 5.2 per cent to military expenditures. (The comparable figures for the industrialized countries of the North are 4.6 per cent and 5.5 per cent respectively.) In recent years, over twenty-five developing countries have spent more on military activities than on health and education combined.

A much more sensitive spending comparison, one that generates even more anguish, is the amount expended in the North to extend the life of the very elderly by a few days or weeks, compared with the amount spent in the South to encourage the health of the very young. No category of social expenditure has risen more rapidly in the United States and Canada in recent years than has that of health care. No age group of our societies consumes more of that expenditure, and is more demanding of it, apparently, than the aged. In California, studies are under way that indicate that an increasing percentage of all health care costs is dedicated to the needs of persons in the final few weeks of their lives. Some of these, of course, are accident victims, or the severely ill, but most are better defined as elderly and infirm. If the welfare of our children will be increasingly dependent on the welfare of their peers in the developing countries, the health care claims of the aged in the industrialized countries must be examined and weighed. Particularly will this be necessary as the percentage of aged in our societies increases as it is now doing. Smaller family units and longer life expectancies have transformed the demographies of the countries of the North. In 1900, only 4.7 per cent of Britain's population was over sixty-five years of age. Today, that age group represents 15.1 per cent of the total. Fifty years from now, in the European Community as a whole, 25 per cent of the population will be sixty-five or more.

The contrast with the countries of the South is vivid. In several African countries, for example, more than 40 per cent of the population is under fifteen years of age. Because of the demographic imbalance, by the turn of the century half of all people alive will be under the age of twenty-five. In the developing countries as a whole, where five-sixths of the planet's population will be, *35 per cent will be under fourteen.*

As migration from the rural areas intensifies, the population of the urban centres builds. Throughout the South, dozens of cities are already overcrowded, yet destined to grow even larger. In 1960 there were only three cities in Africa with populations of more than 500,000; today there are twenty-eight. In 1960, of the ten largest cities in the world, only three (Shanghai, Beijing, and Buenos Aires) were in the South. In 2000, only two (Tokyo and New York) will *not* be in the South. The balance of urban concentration is already overwhelmingly in the South. Of the twenty-five cities in the world with a current population of more than 7 million, sixteen are in the South, including the largest, Mexico City; it has 18.1 million inhabitants – two-thirds the population of all Canada. By 2000, forty-five of the sixty largest cities will be in the South, eighteen of them larger than 10 million.

Faced with numbers of this magnitude, the provision of basic services on an equitable basis becomes absolutely impossible. Squalor and depravity increase. Political instability grows. And the future is placed in jeopardy. By the year 2000, 51.2 per cent of the world's population will be urban. And, because of the youthful trend of the population of the South, urban dwellers in increasing percentages will be young. By 2000, there will be 247 million more urban children between the ages of five and nineteen than there were in 1986. Of that number, 233 million will be in the developing countries.

In the absence of economic opportunity, urban youths find themselves on the streets: abandoned, uneducated, unemployed, alienated from any societal norms, without any loyalties except to their own gang, and – increasingly – with easy access to rapid-firing weapons. The Independent Commission on International Humanitarian Issues reported in 1986: 'The fate of the street generation is inseparable from the uncertain fate of cities. Bursting or decaying, they were never built with the needs of children in mind. Today, the notion of man as a measure of all things has long vanished from urban life, and huge urban agglomerations have become increasingly inhuman and unmanageable.'[24] One hundred years after Dickens, the phenomenon of street children has returned in numbers far in excess of anything known to Oliver Twist.

The reaction of young persons facing a future without hope is predictable. Yet governments are not always wise predictors. Current events in Gaza and the occupied territories of the West Bank provide ample evidence. So do the appalling events now unfolding in so many large cities in the South. As has been common in the slums of big cities since long before Dickens, street crime is a means of survival. The common urchin activities of pickpocketing and petty theft have given way in the age of television and machine-pistols, however, to homicide and kidnapping. In countries as geographically disparate as Brazil and India, the kidnapping of wealthy businessmen and farmers or their families is an increasingly common entrepreneurial activity. In Bogota, contract killers fix their price according to the vulnerability of the target; for an unsuspecting creditor or landlord or in-law, the charge may be as low as U.S. $100. These business enterprises may consist of two teenagers, one motor bike, and one assault weapon. As between the motorcycle and the machine-gun, the latter is far and away the cheaper and the easier to buy.

When brutality is commonplace, a community becomes enured to it, and even countenances its covert use in response. In Sao Paulo, street children are hunted down and killed by the armed mercenaries of shopkeepers who are enraged at the incidence of shoplifting. Unwilling, perhaps unable, to distinguish between runaways and robbers, between street children and street youth, police and vigilantes mete out cruel punishment in the service of the privileged. In Rio de Janeiro or in Lagos, the image of the police is as clearly defined as it is in Toronto or Los Angeles. It was vividly described by Michael Harrington in *The Other America*: 'For the middle class, the police protect property, give directions and help old ladies. For the urban poor, the police are those who arrest you.'[25]

Why, in these circumstances, do people continue to migrate to the cities? Simply because life in the city, desperate as it is, violent, overcrowded, and uncertain, is often superior to what is available in the village. Moreover, it offers the promise of social amenities such as hospitals and schools, and the lure of opportunities for employment. Hard-pressed governments are often simply unable to extend into the countryside even the most basic of social services, clean water, or shelter, or able to assure the distribution of food or cooking fuel or the other essential ingredients of a tolerable life. Even less are they able to do so when burdened by heavy foreign debt, and by creditors and the international financial institutions who insist that government expenditures be reduced.

These conditions are the consequences of many factors, often interacting with one another. Certainly, poverty and population growth are major contributors and it is of little benefit to address one without the other. Each must be understood better in the North than it has been to date. Because poverty has been either endured or ignored in Northern societies for generations, the novelty of population growth may have a better chance of impact.

These numbers and these circumstances are not points made in abstract debate. They represent real people in real time. They are not of a kind that will diminish of their own accord. Nor are they of a kind that can be resolved effectively by the developing countries themselves. Indeed, in light of the obvious interest and risk to the countries of the North, they should not.

◆

There are two alternatives to massive involuntary movements of peoples in distress. The first response, the only one that is at once humane, practical, and sustainable, is the creation in situ of an environment that will allow these people to follow their own normal preference: to remain at home and lead a life of dignity. This alternative demands effective developmental policies and wise interventions by the public and private sector actors in both North and South. The second alternative, which is limited in its impact because of the very large numbers of persons at risk, is a process of peaceful, non-forced, international resettlement. The perilous state in which so many now find themselves in the South, and the confusion and frequent hostility toward them so common in the North, are consequences of the ineffective application to date of either alternative.

Perhaps because peaceful resettlements of refugees and others have been the subject of so much attention in recent years, some observers have been tempted to suggest that emigration-immigration policies are of greater moment, and of greater potential, than they actually are. Not by any stretch of the imagination can all those fleeing intolerable circumstances be accommodated satisfactorily elsewhere. (Nor, by any calculation, can the needy of the South be helped adequately through resource transfers from the North.) Only through the first alternative, that of sustainable development by the South, with the full collaboration of the North, can these massive problems – and now resulting displacements – be reduced to reasonable proportions.

Migrants whose very survival may be threatened do not always seek to flee to other countries. The obvious reason is that they are often too impoverished or too lacking in power to be able to move. Those that do move, as in the case of the Afghans, the Indo-Chinese, the Ethiopians, and the Salvadorans, are most likely to seek haven in the most accessible adjacent country. The knowledge of a more distant sanctuary like

Canada or the United States is in most instances as lacking as are the resources necessary to make the journey. For this reason, the build-up of refugees in neighbouring countries is most marked: 5 million Afghans in Pakistan, 300,000 Cambodians in Thailand, 40,000 Ethiopians at one point of time in Djibouti (representing 10 per cent of the entire population of that city).

The 'push' factors that force people out of the familiar and into the unknown, creating the stigma of 'refugee,' vary in strength from one time and place to another. They are generally of a kind, however, that attracts widespread media attention, even if only fleetingly. The categories of 'newsworthy' events are familiar: military activity, including repressive authoritative acts of local governments; power struggles between different tribes or groups (as in Nigeria in the late 1960s, or in Burundi or Liberia more recently); natural disasters of an immediate impact such as volcanic eruptions, flooding, or earthquakes; illegal economic pursuits that bring intense turmoil – commerce in narcotics, contraband, prohibited items such as ivory or skins, or undocumented migrants. Most often poverty and underdevelopment underlie these 'push' factors. In addition to the repression of non-representative, sometimes inhumane governments, many countries of the South are beset by poverty-related circumstances such as national indebtedness, inadequate capital, weak infrastructure, and inadequate or non-existent social security systems. These in turn often combine to reduce even further the quality of life of the poor: they permit or even encourage large-scale, mechanized farming ventures that produce agricultural produce for export at the expense of the small farmer, and the exploitation of non-renewable and timber resources at the expense of the environment – all to produce foreign exchange. A series of causal links then transmits the factors and places at risk not simply the inhabitants of the immediate region but, in time, all inhabitants of the planet. These links include:

1 high fertility rates and population growth, as poor families without any social safety nets rely on large families as a means of economic support;
2 pauperization and marginalization of small farmers, as land is subdivided into ever smaller plots and becomes degraded, or is taken over by large-scale, mechanized farming operations;
3 deforestation, as both the large-scale export enterprises and the

impoverished peasants seek to clear and use all land, leading to environmental degradation and particularly to soil erosion;

4 the concentration in urban slums of large numbers of displaced rural dwellers, as they seek to gain a living in unfamiliar and often perilous circumstances, with consequential pressure on available underground water levels.

Some of those who flee are fortunate enough to find themselves part of large organized resettlement schemes. They are a small minority. Schemes of this kind are themselves a recent − and rare − phenomenon. They depend upon imaginative immigration policies of asylum states and, in the final analysis, a clear understanding by the publics of those countries of the reason for those policies, their extent, and their impact. Even the most tolerant of societies can otherwise react emotionally, especially so in instances that are unexpected, as with the dark-of-the-night arrival in a small coastal community of a boatload of strangers seeking asylum.

Following upon the early years of forceful conquest by European powers of their new frontiers in North America and Australia, and the barbaric, centuries-long practice of African slavery affecting as many as 10 million men, women, and children, the period since the mid-nineteenth century has been witness to a historically unprecedented resettlement of large numbers of families in voluntary, planned, and international circumstances. These transfers were in much the majority of instances from Europe to Australia, New Zealand, Canada, or the United States, with much smaller numbers to some African and Latin American destinations. Happily, for the most part, both sending and receiving nations more or less belonged to a single, interconnected economic and cultural system. (A significant exception, tragically, was southern Africa.) This permitted a rational response to the complementary circumstances of the two categories of countries: the new frontier regions were deficient in both capital and labour to meet their requirements of food and natural resource production, while Europe was home to an exportable surplus of each, but was short in grains, fish, timber, and the like.

These circumstances of complementary imbalance were short-lived. By the third decade of the twentieth century, hastened by the slaughter and destruction of the First World War, the nations of Europe were no longer self-sufficient, let alone in surplus condition, with respect to either manpower or capital. The military and civilian casualties of the European combatants in the First World War approached 20 million, with immense impact on the generation of young men. The once great reserves of investment capital, which had been employed with such skill by Britain in particular to create and maintain its worldwide industrial and commercial dominance, had been wasted through massive expenditures on weaponry and warfare. Industrial capacity and superiority now and for the next half-century moved to North America, particularly the United States. For a brief period of time following the Second World War, the combination of chaos and economic collapse in Western Europe, and the much greater economic prosperity of Australia, Canada, and the United States, led to a repetition of the previous pattern of family flows. By 1965, however, those peculiar circumstances had again concluded. Europe's economic recovery, combined with the consequences of its very low birth rates, had created major labour shortages and attractive job opportunities.

The current pattern of controlled international resettlement is broadly dissimilar to that of the two earlier periods. Australia, Canada, and the United States continue to be the major receiving states, but now most migrants come from developing countries. The most obvious difference, of course, is in the racial and cultural distinctiveness of these new settlers. Not Caucasian, not from Judaic-Christian cultures, sometimes not even speaking European-origin languages, they are clearly distinguishable by skin pigment, by dress, and by social custom. They are not always *apparently* in possession of the skills and abilities that Canadians in particular had always – and often incorrectly – associated with previous immigrants: those primarily used in agricultural or manufacturing activities. Finally, quite unlike the greater number of European immigrants in the late nineteenth and early twentieth century who 'filled up' the great hinterland regions, particularly of western Canada, these new immigrants have settled predominantly in large cities.

Immigration patterns in Australia, Canada, and the United States are remarkably similar. Since 1966, all have recorded rapidly accelerating proportions of immigrant arrivals from developing countries and corresponding decreases in the proportion of immigrants of European origin. (In the case of the United States, this trend began a decade earlier with large numbers of arrivals from Latin America and the Caribbean.) The most striking single feature of these flows has been the Asian component, which accounted for fully one-third of the total inflow to these three countries in the period 1976–80.

Some 600,000 persons from the developing countries enter the four principal receiving states each year. In relation to the total populations of these countries, the numbers are quite small. For Canada, for example, in the period 1976–80, immigrants from the South constituted about one-half of 1 per cent of the Canadian population in any of those years. Cumulatively, over that five-year period, the figure was 2.6 per cent of the 1976 population. Notwithstanding the relatively low proportion of the overall population, however, these immigrants gain attention because of their strikingly visible character.

This transformation of Canadian immigration patterns found its origin in the legislation of 1967 that introduced major changes in the concept and the practice of Canada's immigration program. Before 1967, immigration policy was based on a national preference scheme that favoured applicants of European origin and was vulnerable, in result, to charges of racism. The revisions of 1967 opened the door to persons of all national origins by eliminating the national preferences. In its place, a 'points' system was introduced that calculated scores on the basis of several criteria, including occupation, education, language skills, age. Independent migrants were thus permitted to enter, not on the basis of country of origin, but in response to the absorptive capacity of the Canadian labour market. Special provision was made for the entry of dependent family members. Explicit recognition of the needs of refugees was introduced into the law in 1977 and proclaimed in 1978, and a separate treatment stream resulted. Between 1968 and mid-1990, 3,149,572 immigrants landed in Canada.[26]

The year-by-year numbers are far from startling and, compared to the total Canadian population, reveal a decreasing proportion of arriving immigrants. In the 1950s, before the changes in the immigration laws, annual arrivals represented some 0.8 per cent of the total Canadian population. By the mid-1970s, that figure had halved: 0.4 per cent. Year after year since the turn of the century, the total immigrant inflow into Canada has averaged about 150,000 persons per year. Recent policy statements by the Government of Canada suggest that annual target levels in the period 1991–5 may be in the 250,000 range.

If the total numbers have not changed significantly, the composition of that total is dramatically different. From a level representing two-thirds of all immigrants in 1968, Europeans dropped to less than one-quarter by 1987. Burgeoning European economies were the main reason. The other three-quarters is largely from developing countries and has shown a marked increase in the proportion of Asians. Persons from Asia accounted for only 13 per cent of Canada's total inflow in 1968, but 45 per cent in 1987. Europeans are now in second place at 24 per cent. Caribbean immigrants rank third. Their proportion of the total has grown considerably from 5.5 per cent in 1968 to 10 per cent today. In fourth place are immigrants from Latin America, now accounting for 7–8 per cent of all arrivals, undoubtedly precipitated by unsettled political and unpromising economic circumstances throughout Central and South America. The next largest region of origin is Africa from which numbers have increased from slightly less than 4 per cent in 1968 to slightly more than 10 per cent now.

These variations in national origin reflect the changing structure of the global migration 'system.' For the many years since the demise of slavery and with the minor exception of some flows across the Mediterranean, Africa has not been an active participant. Latin Americans, however, are considerably better acquainted with the United States than they are with Canada, and are aware of large and active Hispanic communities there. The principal sending countries of Asia – India and Hong Kong – as well as those in the Caribbean – Jamaica, Guyana, and Haiti – share one of Canada's official languages and, in Asia at least, represent the increasing international awareness of societies. Not surprisingly, as each community establishes itself in Canada, its growth is assured by arrivals of relatives and of applicants who have been encouraged by the success of those in earlier years. Interesting, and of considerable benefit to Canada, are the high educational levels of immigrants to Canada from the two largest groups – Asia and Europe. Some 10 per cent of the entering Europeans, for example, have had university educations. Though this is high by world standards, it is not exceptional when compared to most of the other groups. More than 22 per cent of the Asian immigrants have university educations; of the Africans, 20 per cent are university educated, as are 10.8 per cent of the Latin Americans. The average for these groups (even including the lower Caribbean figure of 4.3 per cent) is, on an unweighted basis, higher than for the resident Canadian population as a whole: 13.7 per cent compared with 1.9 per cent calculated on those persons in each of the groups aged twenty to forty-four.

The lower educational level of Caribbean arrivals seems to be a reflection of the fact that young women come in large numbers. They are likely to be either unskilled domestic workers, a privileged entry category, or skilled (but not university educated) technical workers, such as nurses and secretaries. Canadian census figures reveal that the Caribbean-born immigrants eventually achieve generally high levels of education, perhaps because many younger immigrants arrive with the express intention of continuing their education.[7]

These immigrant groups have far-reaching impact on the Canadian society and on the Canadian economy. Because Canadian fertility levels are far below those needed for replacement, the overall population would steadily and rapidly decrease unless replenished by fresh arrivals from elsewhere. At present reproductive rates, each succeeding Canadian generation diminishes in size by 15 per cent. That there is not yet negative population growth in Canada is the result of two factors. The first is the current, and highly unusual, large number of persons of child-bearing age, the 'baby-boom' generation; the second is immigration. Without any immigration, the total population of Canada would continue to rise until about the year 2011, when it would peak at some 28 million, thence beginning a period of continuing decline, gradual at first, rapidly thereafter. Even at current levels of immigration of some 150,000 per year (and emigration of 70,000 annually) the Canadian population will eventually age and decline, though at a more gradual rate, stabilizing eventually at about 19 million toward the end of the next century. Canada's future, clearly, is dependent upon continuing flows of immigrants, which, increasingly, are of developing country origin. Canada's demographic face is changing now and will change considerably more in years to come.

Census data reveal that developing country immigrants constituted a tiny proportion of the Canadian population in 1961 (less than 1 per cent), with not much change by 1971 (1.6 per cent). The data from the census of 1981 and of 1986 reveal some rise – to 4.0 per cent and 4.6 per cent respectively – but still quite small in statistical terms. More significant is the proportion of persons from the South in the total of foreign-born

Canadians. By 1986, this had risen to 30 per cent. This proportion will increase considerably in years to come as European sourced emigration continues to decline and as persons of European origin now in Canada continue to age and die. Change will be most noticeable in the largest cities.[28] Straight-line projections indicate that by 2001, 20 per cent of the population of Toronto could be made up of visible minorities. Within ten years the South will be a significant element within Canadian society, most evidently so within the larger cities.

Current Canadian immigration policies permit this country to select immigrants from a large pool of attractive applicants. The selection process identifies people who tend to be well educated and who bring with them both marketable skills and, often, considerable capital. This inflow does much more than provide a base for future population growth and stability; it supplies badly needed labour to the Canadian economy. For more than a century, immigrants have found economic opportunity and have made economic contributions.

Canada is a country of immigrants. The result is a multiethnic population and a pluralistic society. Immigrants perform many of the necessary tasks that Canadians themselves are reluctant to do; others make the kind of cultural contribution that enriches communities; the more entrepreneurial sponsor enterprises that create jobs for others. The instances are so great and the successes so spectacular – at both the national and the local levels – that to list them would be a task of encyclopaedic proportions.

Nonetheless, there remain in some Canadian communities remnants of the view that immigrants are either unemployable (and so add to the burdens of Canadians who support the welfare system through their tax payments) or contribute to the unemployment of Canadians (through their willingness to take jobs for lower wages or to work in deplorable circumstances and environments). These impressions are demonstrably misleading; they require nevertheless sensitive, consistent responses on the part of both government and media. Unfortunately, neither of these elements of Canadian society has been a steady source of calm appraisal in recent years. (In 1987, the Parliament of Canada was summoned back in emergency session from its scheduled summer recess to deal with the issue of illegal immigrants claiming refugee status. The immediate cause of this near-hysteric event was the landing in Canada of 174 persons.)

Unfortunately – and tragically in the long term – provocative, time-to-time incidents push into the background the proud record that Canada established in the years following the Second World War as a compassionate and enlightened haven for distressed communities from elsewhere. In several significant cases, Canada attracted considerable international attention and commendation for its humanitarian stance. Among these were the resettlement of tubercular infected displaced persons from Europe, the acceptance of Asian communities expelled from East Africa, and the welcome offered Tibetan refugees following the Chinese occupation of that country. In more recent years, Canadian government initiatives, encouraged and supported by various citizens' groups within Canada, have arranged the entry of special cases of persons interned in asylum camps located in countries of first refuge. Examples are Vietnamese from camps in Thailand, and Salvadorans from Costa Rica, who were identified as satisfying the independent entry requirements.

When human beings flee their homelands, compelled to overcome all the instinctive reasons for remaining in familiar and natural circumstances, they are sending out an alarm signal to the international community that must be heeded with seriousness and with urgency. Their claim calls attention to societal and environmental degradation in the regions they have vacated, and signals the presence of human agony and turmoil to the sanctuary in which they have alighted.

These alarms are becoming more frequent, and the devastation more widespread. Should the international community continue to respond only to the symptoms, however, and even then inadequately, and not to the deep underlying causes, the occurrences will multiply and the eventual impact upon the industrialized countries of the North will increase horrendously. We in the North who are descendants of Plato and Locke, of Montesquieu and Goethe, deny our rational inheritance should we barricade ourselves behind economic barriers and military perimeters, endeavouring futilely to protect our privileged way of life, ignoring the historic fact that such measures have never been successful in the past. In an age of electronic mass communication, of global environmental change, of massive economic interdependencies, we must act wisely and humanely. The lesson of this final decade of the second millennium of the Christian era is that there remain no longer any assured sanctuaries for anyone – be they the privileged of the North or the wretched of the South; neither are there any guarantees of protection or any avoidance of turmoil and disaster; above all, there exist no excuses for indifference. The human dynamic has placed in jeopardy the future of the entire human species. Effective outcomes must involve the efforts of all.

The Polity

Of all living species, only the human has organized itself in such complicated and hierarchical fashion, only the human has developed such aspirations to acquisitiveness and to the extension of power. Since prehistory humans have used weapons to exercise powers and organized their affairs to include military forces. In synergistic fashion, reliance upon the use of force has encouraged humans to be increasingly competitive, to rely less on cooperation for solving problems and resolving disputes. And in the twentieth century weaponry has taken on a life of its own. It is an immensely valuable item of commerce, a significant portion of the manufacturing sector of many national economies, an influential factor in government policy making, and a source of mystery and secrecy that permeates and degrades democratic societies.

Ironically, resources dedicated to military activity deny their use in solving the social and natural problems that spawn instability and conflict. The world today is a matrix of phenomena that threaten human security in ways far different from the traditional, and far more dangerously. These phenomena are not responsive to military countermeasures, but require the negotiation of a new form of social contract. Traditional concepts of security are increasingly irrelevant.

◆

The introduction of sedentary agriculture marked the beginning of humankind's experience as a civilized species. Coincidentally it introduced the modern concept of war − of aggressive military activity. Nomadic tribes had long clashed, of course, in their hunting and gathering quests but these, by nature, were hit-and-run encounters. Only when a defined piece of territory was permanently occupied, as is necessary for the cultivation of crops, did the need for its defence arise. Only when crops were cultivated and the surplus of food represented by the harvest was stored, did the greed of outsiders encourage them to attack. In the many thousands of years since the appearance of the first fertile wheat hybrid, and its cultivation in the valleys of the Tigris and Euphrates rivers in what is now Iraq and Syria, agricultural practices have changed much, but the tactics and strategies of warfare reveal little that is new. Compared with the recent productive revolution in the biotechnologies, which promise hardier fish and animals, more disease-resistant varieties of cultivated plants, and pharmacological advances, the most modern military applications of science seem unimaginative and repetitive. The major change has been the widespread distribution of weaponry with a consequent reduction in constraints against its use.

To the age-old concept of seizing – or defending – land for enjoyment and benefit, the twentieth-century marriage of the military and science has produced little more than a horrendous increase in destructive capacity. With that destructive potential has come an altogether inhumane strategy and savage doctrines: 'unconditional surrender' (the First World War) and 'total war' (the Second World War). These strategies are partly the result of reliance on new types of weaponry, weapons of mass and indiscriminate destruction. The acceptance of these devices into the armouries of modern states has permitted military commanders to threaten retaliatory vengeance of unprecedented proportions: 'punishment beyond the ability to absorb' is one of the gentlemanly phrases used by senior NATO officers; 'assured destruction' is another such phrase that, in the nuclear age, converted into the accepted NATO doctrine of MAD: 'mutual assured destruction.' A more vivid, and more candid, scenario was the one projected by Saddam Hussein of Iraq warning against opposition to his Persian Gulf aggression. He would turn Kuwait into a 'graveyard' if others intervened, he said, which recalled the earlier advice of U.S. General Curtis LeMay to bomb North Vietnam 'back into the Stone Ages.'[1] This routine incorporation of weapons of mass destruction into military strategy, including the quite accepted practice of targeting nuclear warheads against major centres of population (a practice openly acknowledged by both the United States and the Soviet Union), has changed entirely the long-accepted role of military forces as defenders of civilian populations. It was to bolster that role that the Geneva Red Cross Conventions for the protection of non-combatants were developed, and the Nuremberg Principles incorporated into international law. In the nuclear-chemical (and perhaps biological) age, these agreements are essentially rejected by strategists. Modern generals and think-tank participants have reverted to the ancient strategy, if not yet the practice (Hiroshima and Nagasaki aside), of tearing down the walls of an enemy city, massacring all the inhabitants, and leaving only rubble in their wake. As described by Hannah Arendt, 'today the strategy of deterrence has openly changed the role of the military from that of protector into that of a belated and essentially futile avenger.'[2]

Perversely, the introduction of nuclear weapons since the Second World War has reduced considerably in recent years the likelihood of intentional major war between the two great alliances, while increasing in incalculable fashion the hazards represented by accidental or untoward incidents, and increasing, too, the envy and desire of third parties to acquire these 'ultimate' devices. To a grateful world the words 'deterrence' and 'stability' are now the watchwords of military spokespersons. Seldom is their full meaning examined, however. These terms, essentially, are as misleading and as historically anomalous as their counterpart, 'economic growth.' 'Deterrence,' and reliance upon it, is the justification for ever-greater numbers of ever-more destructive weapons, both nuclear and chemical. 'Stability' has not meant a plateau of weapons procurement but an ever-steepening curve pursued more or less evenly until recent months by both NATO and the Warsaw Pact. An unintended, but surely to be anticipated, result has been the development and acquisition of nuclear and chemical weapons by several other states, few of which have shown much interest in safeguards against their use.

The now likely passage of a full half-century without a major European war is hailed, and properly, as an exceptional accomplishment. Unquestionably, the absence of conflict in Europe is to be applauded. Unquestionably, too, the peculiar military preoccupations of each side were major contributors to this end. Historians will judge, however, whether the same result (the end of the Cold War because of the collapse of the Soviet economy) could have come about equally as effectively and in much less hazardous fashion without nuclear brinksmanship. They will assess as well whether the obsession for modernity of weapons systems and the constant oscillation of catch-up by one side or the other did not postpone considerably the reaching of a mutually satisfactory modus vivendi. And they will consider what influence this Northern preoccupation with devastation has had on countless military commanders and dictators in the South.

In the post–Second World War period (1945–89), it must be emphasized, 126 wars were fought elsewhere than in Europe, all but one of them in or between developing countries. Several of the most serious of these – in Korea, Vietnam, and Afghanistan – involved one or more of the great Atlantic basin ideological adversaries. In that same period as well, global arms expenditures increased, in real terms, four or five times, according to a 1989 United Nations study. Weapons of mass destruction proliferated, and the word 'defensive' was cynically attached to any weapons-system no matter how first-strike in nature. Military procurements became a major sustaining element in the United States economy, and a rash of developing countries, in copycat fashion, vigorously asserted themselves as arms exporters. The developing countries became a major market for weapons manufacturers; sales totalled U.S. $38.4 billion in 1988, declining to U.S. $29.3 billion in 1989. (The Soviet Union, the United States, France, and China have for some years been the leaders of a large and active field of exporting nations.) Despite international efforts to stop it, and United Nations treaties and resolutions to deny its legitimacy, outer space became militarized. Language descriptive of military activity has become so contrived and so misleading as to prompt questions of the intellectual capacity of those who craft it and those who use it. To speak of military 'surgical strikes' is to demean the language; to call an illegal act of aggression 'Just Cause' is belittling and patronizing.

There was likely no more cynicism, and much more honesty of language, in the acts of the armed horsemen who harassed and pillaged the early farmers of the Fertile Crescent. Their motivation was naked greed, unembellished by sophistry and advertising agency tinsel. Nevertheless, had Genghis Khan been confronted by as sudden and as dramatic a series of reversals as has occurred in Eastern Europe in a matter of months in the last half of 1989, one is tempted to believe that his response would have been less timid, more imaginative, and more candid than has been the reaction of the NATO Alliance and a number of individual governments.

The discovery that horses could be ridden, as well as driven in front of carts, was one of the five significant factors of change in warfare. (The other four were archery, gunpowder, the airplane, and the submarine; all others, such as radar, target-acquisition technologies, missiles, and communications systems, are simply brilliant improvements on techniques employed by warriors since antiquity.) Armed horsemen brought movement and struck fear. The marriage of horse and rider, with the resulting increase in strength and speed of attacker, came out of central Asia, from deep in that part of the world we now call the South. When first seen by the Greeks, this strange apparition appeared as a single creature, giving rise to the myth of the centaur. (Many centuries later, it was the turn of Europeans to introduce the horse into a different continent, in South America in the sixteenth century, where it swept away armies such as the Peruvian, which had never before seen this remarkable animal.) The horse was the ideal partner of the nomadic robbers who sought for themselves what they could not grow by stealing produce from the farmer who had no means of escape. Initially, these exploits were thievery rather than warfare, but as they spread and as the influence of the more aggressive of these groups became more permanent through territorial occupation, the military element increased: first in the form of conquering and subduing, then by exercising an armed governorship. In only three generations the transition occurred from thief to statesman. From the loins of Genghis Khan the marauder emerged his grandson Kublai Khan the governor.

It is significant that the younger Khan settled in China for it was in China a thousand years earlier that one of the world's earliest, and still among the most acclaimed, military strategists lived. The brilliant Sun Tzu was the advocate of a limited use of armed force, of inflicting the least possible casualties, and of engaging in force only as a last resort.

In the twenty-three hundred years since Sun Tzu lived and wrote his still-read monograph, the military formula has changed little. The task is to take (or destroy) or to prevent the taking (or destroying) of territory. A more sophisticated variation is to threaten to take (or destroy), and to threaten to respond. In these latter instances the wielding of influence is paramount; the threat to occupy (or destroy) is subordinated to the exercise of influence and assumes the quality of blackmail.

If the formula has not changed, the destructive capacity certainly has. The popular image of the Second World War as the most destructive military exchange in history is correct; naval bombardments, submarine attacks, artillery exchanges, day and night high-explosive and fire bombings, all culminated with the world's first – and so far only – two applications of nuclear weapons. In six years, a cumulative explosive force had been unleashed equivalent to 3 million tons of TNT. The destruction was horrendous. Yet that total pales before the insatiable appetite for destructive capability that is the hallmark of the modern military establishment. This appetite is evident in the bloated size of today's armouries. A single United States *Trident I* submarine carries missiles with an explosive equivalent of 24 million tons of TNT; eight Second World Wars. The United States Navy, ever prudent, is upgrading these weapons to make them even more powerful. The demise of the Cold War and the collapse of much of the rationale for armaments of this power – if in fact there ever was a defensible rationale – are apparently as irrelevant to navy planners as are the teachings of Sun Tzu. And without question, in other 'defence' establishments in other countries – the Soviet Union, China, France, and Britain – there are other admirals and scientists who have lost all sense of proportion in their apparently insatiable lust for doomsday weapons.

How does one explain this kind of imbalance, this irrational belief in the salvation of horrendous destructiveness, this dedication to competition and conflict rather than to cooperation and problem solving? The men and women taking these decisions and offering this advice are not intrinsically evil. Those scientists and technologists in white lab coats working to make nuclear explosive devices even more powerful, chemical weapons even more lethal, are likely to be loving parents, participants in neighbourhood social events, volunteers in local charitable activities. Yet they reveal a troubling schizophrenia evident in many sectors of society in the industrialized countries, a willingness to divorce individual responsibility from state-dictated norms. Yet to survive as social communities, we must feel as well as think.

Father Mathew Fox, the Dominican priest silenced by the Vatican in 1989, argued that a sad result of Cartesian philosophy is the separation of the heart from the mind. He characterized this concentration of attention on the left side of the brain as a lobotomy of the sensory and visceral, a turning away from the instincts that the aboriginal peoples of this planet have relied upon to sustain themselves and their environment for millennia.[3] A different but strikingly similar observation was uttered by the late Richard Feynman, a Nobel Laureate in nuclear physics, in his explanation of his participation in the Manhattan Project: 'You see, what happened to me – what happened to the rest of us – is we started for a good reason, then you're working very hard to accomplish something, and it's pleasure, it's excitement. And you stop thinking you know; you just stop.'[4]

The images of overwhelming military superiority projected by the nations of the North are well understood by military-inclined governments in the South. Iraq is only the most recent of a long series of tragic examples.

◆

One of the most unorthodox campaigns of the Second World War was the lengthy effort to weaken the grip of the Japanese occupying forces in Malaya through the covert supply of arms and other assistance to the underground resistance. Air drops of weapons and ammunition took place over many months. A dedicated unit – 'Force 136' – was given responsibility for the operation. Aircraft and agents flew out of bases in Burma. The recipients of the arms were for the most part Malayans of Chinese origin who had fled into the heavy jungle in the face of the extreme cruelties meted out to persons of Chinese descent by the Japanese invaders.

In the postwar period, those weapons and those veteran jungle fighters fuelled the bitter struggle for Malayan independence against the British colonial power. The heroic partners of Force 136 were now labelled 'Communist Terrorists,' or cTs for short. The 'Emergency' declared by the British government in 1948 was not concluded until 1960, three years after the granting of full independence to the Federation of Malaya. For many years still to come, however, the hard-core remnants of the cTs, operating for the most part from remote bases near the Thai border, posed a significant threat to the stability and legitimacy of the democratically elected Malayan government. These guerrillas were able to sustain themselves for almost three decades because of the huge caches of weapons parachuted in, and buried in the jungle floor, during the Second World War. Weapons intended for use on an identified enemy became a major component in the attempt to destabilize and overthrow a legitimate government many years later.

The Emergency in Malaya (the country changed its name to Malaysia in 1964) had concluded and the CT threat was well under control by the time that the United States decided to intervene in the civil war in Vietnam. Until the withdrawal of U.S. forces from Saigon in 1973, and the subsequent occupation of the entire country by North Vietnamese forces, the flood of arms and armaments into that country by the United States on the one hand and by the Soviet Union on the other likely exceeded any preceding transfers of weaponry, not exempting the Second World War. United States military expenditures in Vietnam are estimated at U.S. $200 billion. Armoured vehicles, aircraft, ships, artillery and missile tubes, land-mines and explosives, and automatic firing weapons poured into the country beyond all count. On the departure of the United States, vast quantities of this weaponry were abandoned. Vietnam, never docilely subservient to Soviet control, had become one of the most heavily armed countries in the entire world. It influenced for many years the balance of power in Southeast Asia. Powerful enough to skirmish on occasion with the People's Liberation Army of China, Vietnam posed a major threat to all the countries of Southeast Asia. It was feared well beyond the Indo-China region. Thailand, Malaysia, Singapore, Indonesia, and the Philippines were all rightly wary of this ideologically militant, territorially aggressive regime. With its massive inventory of weapons it was well placed to support communist insurgents in all of Southeast Asia.

The Soviet invasion of Afghanistan in 1979 not only brought to a sudden conclusion the period of detente between the superpowers, it launched a massive transfer of American 'small' arms into Afghanistan to bolster those elements within that country who opposed the Soviet-supported government. A savage war continued for ten years before the Soviet pull-out in 1989. During that period, Soviet and American weapons in incalculable volumes flooded into Afghanistan. They exist in numbers so in excess of any possible use in that country now or in the future that for some months they have been cascading out, into Pakistan and India. Now, in Sind Province of Pakistan, in the Punjab region and in Kashmir in India, these weapons are in the hands of extremists, insurgents, terrorists, and bandits. The numbers that police are seizing are so large as to be astonishing, yet the numbers still in possession of persons willing to use them are so huge that civil unrest is virtually guaranteed for years to come.

In 1948, following an extended period of political tumult and military acrimony, Costa Rica chose to eliminate its armed forces. Since that time, this tiny Central American nation has been a model of social tranquillity and progress. Freed of the quarrels so associated with politically ambitious military factions, freed, too, of the economic burden of equipping and maintaining armed forces, Costa Rica has introduced imaginative and effective health care, education, housing, and social assistance programs. Costa Rica's immediate neighbours, Nicaragua to the north and Panama to the south, chose not to pursue that course; they became international examples of turbulence. Both have found themselves the focus of external attention and the recipients of vast quantities of modern weapons, as happened in nearby El Salvador and Guatemala. Human rights in these circumstances all but vanish. The civil sector becomes subjugated to military 'necessity.' The productive (mostly agricultural) segment of the economy attracts inadequate support, except for the holdings of the tiny number of ultrarich large-scale landowners. Meanwhile, television conveys to vicarious thrill seekers worldwide the tragicomic image of grown men – and young boys – complete with costumes and grease paint firing deadly weapons not so much at one another as at helpless civilians. Priests are murdered, peasants are tortured, women are mutilated, yet arms and ammunition continue to flow.

Peace has come to Nicaragua, and may yet settle elsewhere in the troubled isthmus. But remnants of militarism will remain for many years. The disarmament of the Nicaraguan Contras, and the destruction of their weapons under international supervision, is a welcome step, as is the gradual demobilization of the Sandinista army. No one can doubt, however, that left undestroyed in that country, and still building up in monstrous numbers elsewhere in Central America, are modern weapons that will challenge the ability of peacekeepers for generations to come. Policemen, aid workers, and small farmers will continue to be the favourite targets of ill-trained, overarmed, undisciplined 'soldiers.'

Hideous as these examples are, there is another that defies any rational explanation: the eight-year-long war between Iran and Iraq. This organized slaughter of hundreds of thousands cost each side billions of dollars and untold human misery in cities that came under rocket attack and in Kurdish villages that were the targets of chemical weapons. Every bit as irrational as was the conflict, however, was the attitude of the rest of the world. The Security Council did not seize hold of the conflict under the mandatory provisions of chapter VII of the charter. Throughout, each of the adversaries had no difficulty in procuring arms and ammunition to permit the conflict to continue. The Soviet Union was not the only hardware source. Israel, China, and several of the NATO countries were willing commercial suppliers. All told, according to the United States Arms Control and Disarmament Agency, the belligerents obtained arms from 28 different countries. One of the results was a supremely confident, arrogant, and heavily armed Iraq with 1 million uniformed combatants, 5,500 battle tanks, 513 combat aircraft, and 51 naval vessels. It became a country of the South determined to use its military might to establish its regional supremacy and its petroleum primacy. Its invasion of Kuwait would have been unthinkable, whatever the historic territorial claims and the contemporary oil production grievances, without a military establishment inflated out of all proportion to either need or likelihood of responsible use.

The easing of tensions in Central Europe has given welcome impetus to conventional (i.e., non-nuclear) arms control negotiations that had remained totally stalled for more than sixteen years until revived recently in a new format. Launched in 1973 under the title 'Mutual and Balanced Force Reductions' (MBFR), reborn in a different manner in 1989 as the Negotiation on Conventional Forces in Europe (CFE), this element of the arms race has not enjoyed the more dramatic press coverage given to the negotiations for nuclear arms limitation. With the return to democratically elected governments in Eastern Europe, however, and the desire to reduce the crushing cost of massive standing armies, CFE is surging forward. A far-reaching treaty was concluded in November 1990, coincident with the 'Charter of Paris for a New Europe.' Soviet troops will be transferred out of Eastern Europe; force levels that had earlier been agreed upon for both Soviet and United States troops in Europe at a 1990 summit meeting in Washington, DC, were confirmed. Warsaw Pact countries have converted their military alliance into a political association. Vast quantities of modern weapons of lethal destructive power are to be removed from active inventories, including some, like U.S. chemical artillery shells that were stored in Germany unknown to the civilians living nearby. What happens to much of this weaponry will be a test of the common sense as well as the good faith of all these states. Should these mammoth armouries pass into the hands of *any* third parties, for *any* reasons, under *any* mechanisms regarding restraints against use, tragedies of incalculable dimensions will unfold.

No longer can one assume that weapons will be used as intended, or not be used at all. In boomerang fashion, projectiles return to their source. Tanks, aircraft, and missiles that are patriotically transferred to freedom-loving 'allies,' or sold like cornflakes in the huge international arms bazaar, have a habit of being used in unexpected fashion. As British soldiers were shot by British manufactured weapons during the Malayan Emergency, the deadly trail of licit and illicit arms transfers forms a menacing web reaching into countries on all continents. HMS *Sheffield* was sunk in the South Atlantic by an Argentine-launched *Exocet* missile obtained from France, just as the USS *Stark* was heavily damaged in the Persian Gulf by an *Exocet* from an Iraqi aircraft in that period so recent when Iraq was an American 'ally.'

The extent and character of military equipment at present in the hands of armed forces worldwide defies any comparison with circumstances of only thirty years ago. In the possession now of governments indifferent to norms of human rights or international standards of non-aggression, in use by factions and groups defiant of any sense of responsibility towards non-combatants, are massive volumes of powerful armaments that find their way with ease to virtually any purchaser anxious to obtain them. In places like Lebanon and Liberia, the warring factions possess and employ inventories of armoured vehicles, missiles, and large-calibre weapons of greater destructive force than were employed in the Second World War. Iraq was in command of an immense modern war machine, obtained almost in its entirety from the industrialized countries of the North. In the hands of Mohawk Indians in communities along both sides of the Canada–United States border are weapons in such numbers that the New York State police, in 1990 testimony to a legislative enquiry, stated it was vastly out-weaponed and was incapable of carrying out its peace officer responsibilities. Available to the mentally unbalanced as well as to dissidents, mercenaries, and fanatics all over the world are arms of a kind that transform these groups from dangerous criminals into lethal armies. At most risk are societies that have deliberately chosen not to pursue militaristic options, that have dedicated available resources to social purposes. In most of the tiny, democratic nations of the Commonwealth Caribbean, for example, a handful of zealots could hold hostage a freely elected government, as happened in the summer of 1990 in Trinidad, because those governments chose to be civilian and open, and because arms supermarkets in Miami were open for business.

Notwithstanding all this evidence, and even in the face of an evaporation of the Cold War, the flow of weapons continues. Whether openly or covertly, the nature of the arms trade past and present ensures that clandestine armouries are available to virtually any purchaser with cash or credit. The plight of the mortally wounded and the maimed and the orphaned, however, remains the same whatever the manufacturer. Bullets of American, French, Soviet, or Chinese origin are all the same: they rip apart human flesh and destroy human hopes. Controls and conditions of sale are variously mocked or evaded by weapons dealers, by narco-traffickers, by hoodlums, by the mentally disturbed, by the National Security Adviser to former United States President Ronald Reagan.

Wherever there are large profits to be made, there are 'businessmen' and adventurers willing to seek them. Sadly as well, the commercial sales agents of NATO governments eagerly assume the role of active vendors. In developing countries around the world, arms trade fairs are a growth industry. There, in the midst of poverty, weapons experts from North and South proudly push their 'defensive' products on local governments incapable of financing elementary schools or local health clinics. Among the most repulsive of images common in today's world is that of the immaculately tailored, overweight, retired military officer from a NATO country seated in a hotel bar in a developing country hotel peddling his deadly weapons to local middlemen anxious for their commissions.

In country after developing country, not least in Africa, expenditures on the defence sector exceed those on most social sectors, often more than on health and education combined. Whereas developing countries as a whole dedicate about the same percentage of their gross national product to military purposes as do industrialized countries (5–6 per cent), the figures vary wildly for industrial and scientific research and development: 2.5 per cent for industrialized countries, 0.2 per cent for developing countries. This combination of support for present military activities and denial of support for an improved economic and social future is bending many developing countries into a downward spiral of

despair and disintegration. Opponents of these policies are often ruth-
lessly repressed by the military élites now in power. For those deprived
of any constitutional process of change, coups d'état may be the only
alternative. (It has been estimated that in sub-Saharan Africa alone, there
have been more than two hundred successful or attempted coups in the
past forty years.) As resistance to military rule increases, the military seize
on this threat to their continuance as justification for increasing the
numbers of persons in uniform, bolstering the support of the ranks
through higher salaries and benefits, and acquiring ever-more sophisticated technologies to be used virtually exclusively for the repression of
democratic activities.

When military commanders do seize the reins of government, it is no
guarantee even of orderliness and tranquillity let alone the protection of
human rights. The frequent inability of the military to govern with even
a modicum of effectiveness is seen in the widespread failure of military
governments to maintain discipline among their soldiers and law and
order among the population. In the southern cone of South America,
military commanders have instructed or allowed their forces to combat
terrorism and oppose communism by such tactics as the rape and torture
of teenage girls, the kidnapping of infants and children, and the 'disappearing' of those believed to oppose the military's way of doing things. In
Nigeria, military governments are seemingly impotent to contain the
flagrant violence and weapons offences that make a taxi trip from Lagos
airport into the city, or an automobile ride in many parts of the country
day or night, an often hazardous undertaking. In the highlands of Vietnam, unemployed demobilized soldiers prey upon bus and truck traffic.

To a world often puzzled by the vagaries of superpower foreign policies, the long-held naïve belief of Soviet and East European strategists
that they were supporting genuine peoples movements in developing
countries by supplying weapons and training terrorists is only slightly
more repulsive than President Reagan's policies of arms transfers and
political support to so many military élites. Surrogate wars are heinous;
policies that advocate them deserve contempt. Sadly, the human saga
reveals that the practice is far from new. For centuries, the rich in some
societies have hired the poor elsewhere to fight and die on their behalf.
President Reagan's promise of financial assistance to the Contras to
overthrow the Sandinista government of Nicaragua was made exactly

400 years after Pope Sixtus V promised financial aid to King Philip II of Spain to send an armada against England.

The dangerous liaison between the industrialized countries of the North and the military cliques in the South who war on their own people stands both as a testament to the self-righteous principles of governments in the North and as a long-term threat to their own vital international interests. The much-vaunted international economy cannot function if airliners, communications links, and industrial facilities continue to be the targets of well-trained and well-equipped fanatic terrorists, if business leaders are the prey of kidnappers. Only through the demilitarization of conflicts, both civil and international, and the suffocation of external sources of weapons will military regimes be forced to focus on the essential economic and social issues, and to begin the slow task of building democratic institutions and processes.

Yet one must not expect that this kind of policy is likely. For one reason, the major Southern importers of arms (the top four in the period 1983–7 were Iraq, Iran, Syria, Vietnam) are not noted as open societies. For another, current United States military policy is directed towards an increase, rather than the reverse, of military intervention. 'Low-intensity conflict' in Third World settings[5] is the new direction. In the meantime the cost and inconvenience of security measures at airports all over the world continues to rise and evidence mounts of the extent of human tragedy as weapons proliferate. In Colombia, for example, homicide is now the leading cause of death for males between fifteen and forty-five.

A sad commentary on the divisions in today's world is the fact that military weapons are acquired by the North with the express aim that they *not* be used, whereas they are acquired by the South with the express intent, for the most part, that they will be used. Until planners in the North grasp this distinction, all communities throughout the world increasingly will be targets. Kuwait is an example as telling in the context of the 1990s as Czechoslovakia, Manchuria, and Ethiopia were in the period of the 1930s. It was Thomas Jefferson who wrote more than two hundred years ago that 'The care of human life and happiness, and not their destruction, is the first and only legitimate object of good government.'[6] In the global village, that object, not commerce in weapons, must become a universal norm. Yet, hypocritically, governments of the North continue to embrace the one in theory and engage in the other in practice. How commonly heard is the sanctimonious statement that 'as a nation, we must maintain our capacity to manufacture our own weapons and ammunition requirements; in order to keep those facilities in place in peacetime, we need to export the surplus products.' What those government spokesmen are saying, even though unconsciously, is 'in our narrow attempt to protect our own citizens from future harm, we are active participants now in the slaughter of innocent people in developing countries.' Thucydides' observation remains apt in these circumstances: 'The strong did what they could, and the weak suffered what they must.'[7]

◆

What gene in the physiology of humans harbours this instinctive capacity for slaughter and destruction, admires and holds in esteem weaponry and militarism, sees beauty and mysticism in warfare, prefers force to peaceful forms of dispute resolution? The visceral determinants of 'manly' behaviour – the physical repulsion of wild beasts, the protection of family and possessions from marauders, the courageous foraging into unknown territories to obtain food – these have become the stuff of myths. The adventurism of Odysseus and his shipmates fuelled the imagination of would-be travellers for millennia, and inspired countless explorations since. Yet hand-in-hand with *The Odyssey*, admirers of a different form of heroism have been equally enchanted with the warlike exploits of Agamemnon and Achilles, of Paris and Hector, as chronicled in the pages of the other Homeric classic, *The Iliad*. These two types of masculine initiative, the one seeking to broaden knowledge and experience, the other bent to dominance and conflict, each of them often permeated with risk and danger, merged in the long ago mists of antiquity. And in those same distant times were joined the apparently most natural, yet least humane, inclination to barbarism with spiritual explanation and support. Long before the appearance of monotheistic religions, an assortment of gods of various shapes and sizes were created to stimulate ferocity, to buoy up heroism, and to justify savage behaviour. Long, too, before that modern manifestation of territorial sovereignty – the nation-state – had come forward, religion as a motivation and justification for warfare was well accepted. With remarkable continuity, those elements of society most dedicated to peace and to scholarship, to creativity and to love, have spawned multitudes of admirers and participants in the practice of war and the use of force.

From the beginnings of recorded history through the most recent of television reports, human inclination to savage practice has revealed no cessation and precious little remorse. Torture, bestiality, and cruelty of the most extreme kind are carried out routinely, and justified either blandly or triumphantly. And all the while the efforts and the intellects of some of the most gifted of humans have been dedicated to sustaining or extolling these practices. Sometimes motivated by economic benefit, sometimes by privilege, sometimes by acceptance or acclaim, often by deeply felt religion, rationalization is sourced in the most unlikely of roots. Some of the most uplifting of sacred music, some of the most moving literature, some of the most delicate artistry are paeans to war. The traditional practice of the Anglican church to mount battle flags in cathedrals dedicated to Christian love rouses no curiosity among the faithful; one worships God in the presence of tokens of apparently equal value: the lamb and the sword. Worldwide, in museums dedicated to the preservation of the finest of human creative accomplishment, visitors pass from galleries displaying magnificent painted or sculpted interpretations of natural beauty to rooms mounting arrays of delicately engraved and jewelled instruments of death and war: scimitars and cutlasses, pistols and musketry. From the most rudimentary of aboriginal tribesmen to the warriors of the twentieth century, there is evidence of a desire to beautify carnage: to decorate spears and arrows, to paint messages and designs on aerial bombs and artillery shells, to dedicate rapturous literature to the most bestial of human behaviour.

In the process, the opponents of militarism have almost always been marginalized. Conscientious objectors and religious pacifists have at best been tolerated, at worst ridiculed and persecuted. In an atmosphere of military glory, dissidents are characterized as subversive. Patriotism of one form or another has been a vehicle melding together elements of religion, politics, and culture. The drama of a youthful soldier-king, selflessly leading his loyal subjects into battle in defence of the realm and the purification of God's covenant, has stirred the hearts and minds of countless generations and been incorrectly applied to wildly differing situations, but always has it acted as a stimulus to selfless camaraderie:

We few, we happy few, we band of brothers;
For he today that sheds his blood with me
Shall be my brother; be he ne'er so vile
This day shall gentle his condition:
And gentlemen in England now a-bed
Shall think themselves accurs'd they were not here
And hold their manhoods cheap whiles any speaks
That fought with us upon Saint Crispin's day.[8]

The sceptical voice has carried much less weight, much less influence, been interpreted often as eccentric:

My friend, I have lived almost 50 years, and I have seen life as it is. Pain, misery, hunger ... cruelty beyond belief. I have heard the singing from taverns and the moans from bundles of filth on the streets. I have been a soldier and seen my comrades fall in battle ... or die more slowly under the lash in Africa. I have held them in my arms at the final moment. These were men who saw life as it is yet they died despairing. No glory, no gallant last words only their eyes filled with confusion whimpering the question why! I do not think they asked why they were dying but why they had lived. When life itself seems lunatic, who knows where madness lies? Too much sanity may be madness. To seek treasure where there is only trash. Perhaps to be practical is madness. And maddest of all, to see life as it is and not as it should be.[9]

The struggle, until recently, has never been evenly balanced, at least in Christendom. From the days of Constantine, the concept of a just war has prevailed and found its way into jurisprudence. Bishops and jurists alike have come forward to defend the bloodiest of aggressive acts and the most penurious of conquests if only the element of 'justice' was detectable. To those seeking it to justify their cause, it was seldom elusive. Not even the relatively recent, but closely reasoned, message of the United States Conference of Catholic Bishops has as yet influenced United States defence policy. In the nuclear age, argue the bishops, the concept of 'just war' is not supportive of 'total war' waged with modern weapons of mass destruction. The presumption today is 'against the use of force as a means of settling disputes.'[10]

To mask and control the normal human revulsion of bloodshed and fear of injury, myths have been created, unnatural norms of conduct designed, and inhuman practices glorified. Muted or ignored have been the horrifying elements: injury and death, deprivation and separation, the visitation of destruction and squalor upon innocent civilians, the destruction of the natural environment by modern chemicals in a throwback to the vicious practice of the Romans at Carthage. In the process, the truly heroic, the selfless, the highest of motivations, the unquestioned propriety of resistance to aggression and oppression – these have become confused and misappropriated. The homage paid to the captain of the USS *Vincennes*, the terror bombing of Dresden, the 'explanations' of the Mai Lae massacre – these are actions and reactions that tarnish, not exalt, the basic strains of decency and honour and courage which are basic to our humane societies. Confusion has arisen, too, and not unexpectedly, from those who gain economically from the requirements of war; the opportunity for profit making has been a compelling attraction to provisioners and armourers, weapons makers and financiers, even as the costs of such enterprises become an intolerable burden on those who pay.

Barbara Tuchman, in *A Distant Mirror*,[11] described eloquently a war that failed because it ran out of economic steam six centuries ago. Engels addressed the direct dependence of military strength upon economic power: 'nothing is more dependent on economic conditions than precisely the army and the navy' he is often said to have observed. In 1989, a harassed Mikhail Gorbachev recognized that linkage when he confessed that the USSR economy was incapable of supporting the giant Soviet war machine. There followed the first meaningful reduction of weaponry since the conclusion of the Second World War. Now, populations that have borne for forty years the massive expenditures necessary to support modern nuclear military establishments are recognizing as for the first time the volume of funding that has been dedicated to this cause, and the cost that has accrued in the form of neglected elements of the civilian economy – schools, highways, health care facilities, etc. The prospect of a 'peace dividend' is now influencing increasingly the negotiations toward the structure of the new Europe. With wisdom and foresight, governments of both North and South may now identify the most important of their priorities, acknowledge the wisdom of Jefferson's words, and declare similar dividends for the benefit of the peoples of the developing countries and, not incidentally, for the strengthening of democratic processes in them. To assume that that will happen without intense resistance from the military-industrial constituencies, however, is naïve to an extreme. The image of courageous, selfless, patriotic servicemen and women will be exploited shamelessly by those with vested interests in bloated military establishments of a size and kind far in excess of the justifiable, necessary, and prudent requirements of any community.

◆

The cost of war in terms of human suffering is so immense as to be incalculable. It is a cost that often applies as much to victor as to vanquished. There are other costs, however, insidious costs, that are prompted by the 'use-of-force' school of thought. These are the erosion of human values, derogation of human dignity, weakening of the democratic process. All, usually, in the name of defence of the realm and its honourable values.

The first of these costs can be measured in the dedication of economic and human resources to the production of destructive devices and the maintenance of standing armies. The proportion of Gross National Product identifiably related to 'war' or 'military' or 'defence' has varied considerably from region to region and from time to time. Nor have these types of expenditures necessarily been non-remunerative. At the apex of the Elizabethan dominance of the oceans, the value of the resources and riches obtained by the plundering English sea captains was far greater than the not-inconsiderable investment in the means of plunder. The more modern return on defence expenditures has been of much less public benefit. In the mid-to-late twentieth century the proliferation of high-cost defence industries has produced an unprecedented economic return to investors. Whether those investments and those returns benefit proportionately the broader community is increasingly suspect. The Palme Commission argued that a heavy commitment of national resources to military purposes 'requires economic and social sacrifice. The supply of scientific labour and equipment is limited ... Resources used for defence are not available for purposes of civilian innovation, economic growth, social or medical progress ... As in the case of military spending and employment, military research should only be justified on grounds of security: its economic costs will always be greater than its economic benefits.'[12]

More recently, financial analysts have concluded that a major distinguishing feature between the high-achievement, research and development–based Japanese economy and the less-competitive, export-deficit United States economy is the proportion of economic activity in the latter dedicated to defence and defence-related measures. In Japan, the percentage of GDP that fell into this defence category in 1988 was 1.0 per cent; in the United States it was 6.0 per cent. The Palme Commission had anticipated that kind of comparison. Indeed, it was a pioneer in the methodical economic analysis of military expenditures in countries North and South. It concluded: 'Military spending is a charge on the economic future of all countries, the richest and the poorest, those who import and those who export arms, the East and the West ... The economic benefits of military spending are trivial in comparison with its economic costs.'[13]

Quite apart from the factor of dynamism is the danger inherent in a single-industry economic dependency, and the distorting influence on legislators and administrations of an immensely powerful defence lobby dependent on government contracts. The United States Congress has become exceedingly vulnerable to the pork-barrelling tactics of this sector of the industrial economy. Defence industries of one form or another are located in the overwhelming majority of the 435 congressional electoral districts. In the result, quid pro quo voting patterns are the subject of frequent newspaper criticisms. So important to this or that community are the economic and other benefit factors that equipment procurements cannot be said to be decided only on military need.

The late American economist Arthur Burns was cited by the Palme Commission as having anticipated this very kind of non-security justification for security-related expenditures. In 1968 he wrote: 'We need to recognize that the scale of defense expenditures has, to a significant degree, become a self-reinforcing process. Its momentum derives not only from the energy of military planners, contractors, scientists and engineers. To some degree it is abetted also by the practical interests and anxieties of ordinary citizens.'[14]

This mutually beneficial and highly influential combination of defence producers and defence consumers was anticipated also by the late President Dwight D. Eisenhower. Warning against the unhealthy outcome of a 'military-industrial complex,' President Eisenhower said:

> In the council of government we must guard against the acquisition of unwanted influence, whether sought or unsought, by the military-industrial complex. The potential for the disastrous rise of misplaced power exists and will persist. We must never let the weight of this combination endanger our liberties or democratic processes. We should take nothing for granted. Only an alert and knowledgeable citizenry can compel the proper meshing of the huge industrial and military machinery of defence with our peaceful methods and goals so that security and liberty may prosper together.'[15]

How entirely different was the attitude of another Republican president, Ronald Reagan, only twenty years later. Whereas Eisenhower was one of the most experienced military commanders of the Second World War and, of all U.S. presidents, far and away more familiar with military matters than any other since Ulysses S. Grant a century earlier, Ronald Reagan's military experience was gained in Hollywood film studios. Eisenhower was openly sceptical of the value of armaments. The Reagan administration had a different view. President Reagan's first science adviser, Dr George Keyworth, told the American Association for the Advancement of Science in Washington in June 1981 that 'It is no longer within our economic capability, nor perhaps even desirable, to aspire to primacy across the spectrum of scientific disciplines.'[16] That being so, priorities must be identified. Dr Keyworth's conclusion: 'Military might second to none' must be the aim of scientific research in the United States.

There is no military-industrial complex in Canada, nor is military research the government's highest priority. Nevertheless, the influence of the defence industry is not to be underestimated. The huge advertisements that appear in Canadian newspapers on the eve of large defence procurement programs illustrate the belief of defence contractors in the extent of public interest in this or that item of expensive gadgetry. Quite clearly, that interest centres much more on the economic impact in given communities of a large defence contract than on the need for the items or the respective merits of the competing bidders. More worrisome is the ideological message usually contained in the ads, implying that the defence of freedom demands these programs. Quite separately from the realities of Soviet expansionist policies or aggressive stances, the defence contractors nurture − both directly and through their elected representatives − the public fear of communism and communist intransigence. The Cold War has been a bonanza to the high-tech sector and, in the process, has contributed much to the value-added end of the Canadian economy. Without question as well, there has been some spillover into the civilian sector. The extent and the efficiency of that transfer process is questionable, however, as the Palme Commission pointed out.

A tragic consequence of the primacy of defence industries in countries of the North is the effort of economic planners in countries of the South to replicate the pattern. The developing countries understandably are tempted to design their own economies on the basis of what they perceive to be successful Northern models. A number of them have succeeded in their bid to enter the field of arms manufacture. Success in this sector at once reduces their need to import the items manufactured and eases their entry into an often highly profitable export market. These countries then participate in the same trade-off so criticized by the Palme Commission: while gaining in the experience of advanced industrial manufacturing, they forfeit the opportunity to dedicate the same resources and energies to civilian needs. The list of arms-manufacturing countries in the South is long and growing. Brazil, Israel, India, Argentina, South Korea, Taiwan, Egypt, Chile, Indonesia, and Mexico have the greatest productive capacities of all non-communist regimes according to the U.S. Arms Control and Disarmament Agency.[17] Their industries are often government owned. The temptation to encourage their profitability through large government contracts is often difficult to resist. And so this, too, adds momentum to the military spending.

One should not underestimate the importance of defence-related manufacturing to the economies of these countries. It has been calculated that the value of conventional arms manufactured in developing countries has increased from a couple of million dollars in 1950 (a date, admittedly, that preceded the independence of most colonial states) to something more than U.S. $1.6 billion in 1984.[18] An Israeli study by the Jaffee Centre for Strategic Studies at Tel Aviv University found in the mid-1980s that Israeli arms exports accounted for 20 per cent of the country's manufactured exports, and 10 per cent of all Israeli exports.

North–South arms transfers often take place under the mantle of official foreign aid programs. In 1986, 67 per cent of all United States official aid to developing countries, valued at U.S. $20.2 billion, fell into the 'security' as distinct from the 'development' category. In 1988, the share dropped to 63 per cent, and in 1990 to 61 per cent. The three largest recipient countries in recent years have been Israel, Egypt, and the Philippines. Grants and credits for the purchase of defence equipment, services, and training have been the largest single element in the entire United States aid programs throughout the eighties.[19]

There is reciprocal interest in this kind of transfer. The recipient armed forces increase their armouries of modern equipment. The United States manufacturers increase their sales to a solvent purchaser (the United States government) while placing their products in foreign markets where they may be used to gain a foothold for future commercial sales. The United States armed forces gain the advantage in a number of instances of lower per-copy prices for the equipment that they are buying for their own use. This latter advantage encourages the United States Air Force, for example, to encourage those commercial sales and to act as a vigorous travelling sales representative for the manufacturers of the fighter aircraft. Each F-16 sold abroad extends the assembly run at the United States production factories and, under the sales contracts with the Pentagon, reduces the price of every airplane purchased by the United States government.

Thus do governments and armed forces of the North influence foreign policies and budget performances in the South. They use a judicious combination of military camaraderie (the pilot-to-pilot argument that 'you are entitled to the finest airplane; we fly the F-16 because it's the best and you should insist on nothing less'), expense-paid trips for foreign commanders and cabinet ministers to tour production facilities, and sharing of intelligence and advice about the size and nature of the regional military threat facing those opposed to communism. France sells Mirage 2000s to India while the United States sells F-16s to Pakistan; in the Middle East, Britain sells Tornados to Saudi Arabia, France sells Mirages to Iraq, and the Soviet Union sells MIG-29s to Syria. All, of course, in the name of stability.

In the result:

1 The developing countries increase their dependence on the North for training, spare parts, modernization, and financing.

2 Development proponents – those advocating greater priority for schools, health care, the agricultural sector, and basic infrastructure – take second place to military planners.

3 Because of the limited supply in all developing countries of investment capital, skilled labour, and government funds, military expenditures not only have a diversionary effect; they are inflationary as well. Military demands compete in inelastic economies.

4 Social and political events within a developing country and its environs attract tendentious interpretations by increasingly apprehensive local advisers, often concluding with assessment of an 'enhanced risk' and a recommendation for even greater defence expenditures and greater military preparedness.

And so continues the self-reinforcing spiral of cost.

It is this willingness to interpret events in military terms that prompts the United States and some at least of its NATO allies to encourage relatively impoverished countries to acquire sophisticated military equipment that they do not require, often cannot adequately maintain or operate, and certainly cannot afford, often on the gratuitous advice that 'others' in the region are acquiring similar arms and by so doing constitute an increasing and viable threat. In all-too-many instances, the threat that is actually enhanced takes the form of aggrieved junior military officers who choose to challenge the legitimacy and the authority of civilian governments through an attempted coup d'état. The sad state of the South is that no fewer than seventy-two countries have at some point since 1959 been under the control of military governments. In 1988, sixty-four had military governments. Although the recent return to civilian government throughout Latin America is a welcome event, it must be measured against the fact that the proportion of all developing countries under military rule *increased* from 26 per cent in 1969 to 52 per cent in 1987. One is hard-pressed to think of a single one of them that has not been the recipient of military equipment, training, or advice from one or other of the superpowers or their allies. The sophistry of the arguments of Jeanne

Kirkpatrick, who endeavours to distinguish dictatorial from authoritarian governments (the latter being less reprehensible, and therefore supportable by the United States), is not generally appreciated by the impoverished masses living in military-governed countries falling into either category.

The Soviet Union has been far from disengaged in this kind of behaviour. Weapons and weapon-related items account for about one-fifth of all exports from the Soviet Union.[20] A major variation from the United States practice is the Soviet policy of selling weapons in preference to giving them away as development aid. Arms have been a major foreign exchange earner for the USSR.

What prompted the 125 wars involving Third World countries in the period 1945–89? Beneath the veneer of the ubiquitous accusations of communist expansionism or imperialist revanchement could be found in most cases either age-old boundary contests, tribal rivalries, or basic economic and social injustices. In some instances these factors combined; in others they were used by international communism as a pretext for intervention. Whatever the cause, however, because these wars are now fought with weaponry of greater fire-power than anything available in the past, the number of casualties has been astronomical. Ruth Leger Sivard counted twenty-seven individual wars under way in 1987, 'the highest number since 1700,' and calculated that the total death toll in them was some 2.2 million.[21] The absence of effective training and discipline of military personnel may be one reason why the civilian death count represents some 75 per cent of all killed, but it does not account for and certainly should not excuse the excessive numbers of civilian casualties in such wars as Vietnam and Panama. It will be some time yet before the final figures are determined for the Panama invasion, but the preliminary counts show some seventy-five military deaths (of which twenty-three were U.S.) and more than two hundred civilian deaths. (Some human rights groups contend the latter figure is much too low.) In Vietnam, the most widely accepted estimate of civilian deaths is some 1.2 million, slightly higher than all military deaths (of which 56,231 were American). Worldwide, in the period 1945–89, total war deaths have been 21.809 million, of which 13.319 million have been civilians and 6.810 million military. It is a distressing total, and a shameful civilian-military balance. It signals that weapon-supplying countries place a low value on human life, on international norms, and on peaceful mechanisms for dispute settlement. One of the results is that violence becomes more widespread and gains the status of an accepted practice. Should governments of the North from time to time express their revulsion – as in the case of Cambodia – their moral indignation is tainted with their previous participation in arms transfers.

The ironic but predictable consequence of huge military build-ups, with mountains of weapons supplied by major supplier countries both communist and non-communist, is the immense supply of arms and ammunition, most of it in the form of deadly rapid-firing assault rifles (M-16s and Kalishnokovs or their several imitators) now in place all over the world. Political terrorists, common gangsters, or individual opportunists are so heavily armed that the challenge to peace officers is overwhelming. This contribution from North to South will increasingly threaten the stability and tranquillity of developing countries and threaten, too, the interests of the North. The vulnerability of industrial installations, of expatriate business executives, and of international airlines shows little sign of easing. The protective cost of reducing these risks has created a new growth industry: security guards. In Canada alone, the cost of airport security now exceeds $100 million annually.

The world is perilously close to resembling medieval Europe, a time and place when every distinct interest group employed its own private army. As the ability of individual developing countries to govern effectively diminishes, as the market in the industrialized countries for narcotics grows increasingly, as the interest of weapons manufacturers to find new outlets is spurred by East–West detente, as the likelihood for economic equity diminishes, the political stability of the developing countries appears in many instances to be disturbingly remote. That instability, inexorably, affects the stability, the welfare, and the interests of the industrialized countries as, directly and indirectly, the violence and the terrorism spill across boundaries. The usual Northern response of still more weaponry is as immoral as it is bankrupt of results.

◆

Mystery has always been an important part of human experience, and was commonplace to the ancients. Conception, birth, and death; weather and the seasons; fire; the sun, the moon, and the stars; gravity – these and many other phenomena were beyond the understanding of early humans, as many natural phenomena today are still not clearly interpreted. The human species early on manifested its distinctiveness by its craving for some explanation of mysterious events or elements, by seeking actively a better understanding of the components and circumstances so influential in the human environment.

'Why?' is a question posed exclusively by humans. The formulation of a response has prompted two distinct forms of human activity. The first took the form of religion, and, in similar fashion but for different reasons, the early craft guilds. The adherents of each of these forms of organization husbanded mystery and, in many instances, profited from it. 'Stewards of the mysteries of God,' St Paul called his associates. Although without an advocate as articulate as Paul, the guilds for their part nevertheless guarded the secrets of their crafts with near-religious fervour for the benefit of their proprietor brethren. The second and quite different response to mystery has functioned in opposite fashion: the transparent and deliberate pursuit and dissemination of knowledge. This activity has traditionally taken the form of institutions of scholarship – of research and teaching. Somewhat ironically, before the founding and spread of universities, the seats of learning were often located in religious orders, for here in many instances were found the few persons able to read, write, and count. In those instances the mysteries were compartmentalized.

There has never been an easy relationship between the guardians of secrecy and the advocates of openness. Knowledge has always been understood to be an element of power. It should not, therefore, be unexpected that tension exists between those who are privy to mysteries and those who wish to become so. It is, after all, in the interests of the specialist neither to reveal nor to demean the secrets of his craft. In *Measure for Measure*, when Abhorson the Executioner is told by his superior to accept the assistance of a clown in the performance of his duty, he is appalled. 'Fie upon him! he will discredit our mystery.'[22]

The most powerful recent proponents of mystery and secrecy have been business and government. The techniques they have employed, however, are polar opposites. Business manages mystery by revealing it for profit; government endeavours all too often to deny access. The business management concept most frequently takes the form of copyright and patents, which are the endeavour of societies to recognize the proprietary interests of those who have made intellectual and financial investment in an outcome, and to promise to them an appropriate reward should these outcomes enjoy a market value. The system provides an orderly and beneficial revelation of mysteries. Properly employed, patents ensure that technologies of use to humankind are disseminated and employed for the general public benefit, not hidden and denied to the owners of less-advantageous processes or devices. Since the Industrial Revolution, this system has by and large worked well and has seldom been challenged per se.

In recent years, however, dramatic scientific advances in such fields as the biotechnologies and electronics, often achieved at great expense by employees or contractors of large business enterprises, have led to the sequestering of knowledge on a scale and to an extent quite unprecedented. The developing countries of the South could benefit from this knowledge, yet are effectively denied access to it because they cannot buy or obtain it by licence. As a result, this kind of protection of mystery is increasingly a cause of North–South tension. One example is the patents that have recently been issued for some forms of biological life. They raise the prospect of an increase in the dependence of developing countries as they seek agricultural genetic species, and of the possible diminishment of biodiversity, especially in plant forms. The issue of patents in instances of this kind, and the related practice of 'plant breeders rights,' now involve half a dozen international organizations seeking some balance between private gain and public benefit. This particular element of mystery is now gaining much more attention of scholars, publics, and governments than it has previously received.

The second modern repository of mystery – government – has never demonstrated persuasively the merit of its continuing claim for secrecy. Here, in democracies and dictatorships alike, secrecy is a naked instrument of power. In democracies, where governments claim their legitimacy on the trust and confidence extended to them by the majority of the electorate, the deceitful misuse of that confidence and the breach of that trust are, unfortunately, increasingly evident. The most dramatic single example of this type of conduct was that of President Richard Nixon, whose acts were described by Theodore H. White as a 'Breach of Faith.'[23] A quite different, and incalculably more common, departure of governments from the openness and trust expected of them takes the form of the abuse of secrecy – secrecy that binds every public official in most modern democracies at pain of criminal prosecution not to disclose ever so many categories of information: details of budgets in the making, many of the costs associated with governance, the policy deliberations of ministers, the household practices of Her Majesty the Queen, or anything that could conceivably be interpreted as of value to anyone outside government. No single activity of government is more commonplace than the protection of secrets. No word has been more demeaned than 'secret,' which now applies to virtually anything. Nothing motivates ministers to be more assiduous in their conduct, nothing so denies to the public the information it requires to form reasoned judgments, nothing contributes more to a diminishment of the publics' confidence in their governors, nothing is likely more dangerous to the health of democratic institutions and the freedom of individuals.

This debilitating practice called secrecy is in its present form a recent phenomenon. It is in large measure a product of the penchant of the military to protect its intelligence, and of the indecent partnership entered into between scientists and soldiers to create the mysteries of the nuclear age. It acts as a screen for scoundrels in the North, and a refuge for repressive dictators in the South. It is perhaps the most insidious product of those elements in society who regard the use of force as a more precious resource than the rule of law. It may well prove to be a major weakness in the ability of the societies of the North to respond effectively to the requirements of the coming century.

The extent to which democratic process and confidence in government in the NATO countries have been weakened by security obsessions can only be conjectured. Any historic assessment of the damage done to the public purse and the public good by irresponsible or stupid defence-related decisions will catalogue a sad and lengthy list of indictments – of neglected safety measures in nuclear weapons plants, of far-reaching and long-lasting environmental damage and hazards, of abuses of power and flagrantly corrupt procurement practices, of denial of relevant information to political authorities, of purposefully engineered 'provocative' practices to alarm potential adversaries and activate defensive mechanisms, of contrived hysteria about the menace of communism. When evidence of such practices has been uncovered, the curiously inept responses of those exposed have been all-too-often voiced in terms of the necessity to defend liberty against the threats of those who seek to weaken and destroy our open societies!

These same self-serving descriptions of the state of the world have produced in the North a very uneven and inaccurate awareness of events not only in the Soviet Union but as well in the developing countries of the South. One of the most enduring has been the practice of fomenting fear and hatred of the 'mysterious' Soviet Union.[24] George Kennan, perhaps the world's most respected observer of the USSR, the author of the famous 'X' article in *Foreign Affairs* in 1947 and the architect of the successful American containment policies so effective during the Stalin period and immediately thereafter, described thus Ronald Reagan's nuclear weapons policies and his simplistic musings about the 'evil empire' USSR: it is 'predicated on such wild and implausible scenarios, involves so fantastic a view of the monstrosity of our Soviet adversaries, omits so many obviously relevant considerations, and reflects so childish a conception of the way great governments are motivated and behave, that I find myself thinking there must be something of great importance that I have missed.'[25] Nevertheless, President Reagan's exploitation of mystery contributed to his unprecedented popularity while in office. And in lock-step, the countries of the North followed. In democratic societies that depend for their legitimacy upon a transparent trust between governors and governed, that require for their sustained health the informed and understanding support of the electorate, the inflated spectre of the communist menace has permitted a nuclear conspiracy of secrecy and deception to become a structural element. The result is degrading and debilitating of the very social and political ideals these governments claim to serve, has perpetrated monstrous lies and cover-ups, has endangered the physical and environmental health of those working in or living near weapons factories, and has contributed to the serious jeopardy in which the non-competitive economies of some countries now find themselves.

Assumptions that circumstances in distant societies are threatening or unworthy, and deserving of extraordinary response, are not of recent origin. They form part of the xenophobic-ethnocentric balance that communities employ to bolster their own sense of cohesion, importance, and permanence. Countering these tendencies is a slow process, requiring a number of positive steps of which openness is the key. Among them are the encouragement of broader access to factual information through both educational and journalistic channels, practices that are the opposite of government secrecy. An additional important step would be the official discouragement of xenophobic statements. All these, however, in many instances require an abandonment of the now current assumptions that much public business is of such a sensitive nature that it must not be disclosed to the very public in whose name it is conducted. This fosters a conspiratorial attitude to government that is mimicked in dozens of developing countries and that erodes both confidence and legitimacy.

A clandestine style of governance is one attribute of the 'command' or pyramidical structure of government practised since the era of John Locke and that now reveals the need for thorough overhaul in the age of massive and quickly dispersed information. It is this sort of structure that allows government leaders to intervene in the command process of the military forces, weakening the important distinction between civilian and military, and in turn contributing to a strengthening of the secrecy syndrome. The best-known practitioner of this process this century was undoubtedly Prime Minister Winston Churchill, who even adopted the code name 'Former Naval Person.' There are other, more recent, examples that flowered during the period of the Cold War.

Issues of legitimacy of government, and of effectiveness of governance, need much more attention. In developing countries in particular, the structural weaknesses of the institutions of governance form a major impediment to improvements in the social and economic sectors. Support to the military does nothing to overcome those frailties. If governments in the South are not reflective of the will of the electorate; if they are not able to honour their international commitments, including the protection of the lives and property of foreigners within their jurisdiction; if they are not able successfully to ensure the lawful conduct of their own citizens and constrain them from the production and trafficking of narcotic substances (or the laundering of the proceeds); if they are not able to contain terrorism – then these defaults have an effect on the future form of democracy as well as on the coherence of the international community.

Countries of all political persuasions and attitudes both North and South are now immensely dependent upon predictable and well-functioning international activity. The global trends of commerce and industry emphasize the importance to all national actors of well-functioning governments. Yet these same governments, with increasing frequency, are ineffective, to a considerable extent because they no longer enjoy the confidence of the governed. One of the reasons for this, without question, is the long-standing practice of those governments of being less than candid and forthcoming with respect to matters of considerable concern to their citizenry. If electorates are to be responsible in the exercise of their franchise, and if governments are in fact as well as in appearance to be responsible, people must have the ability to monitor as well as to judge. It follows that if democracy and human rights are a legitimate aspiration for all peoples everywhere, as we in much of the North have long argued, then it is in our interest to ensure that we project a wholesome model, that we not advocate one policy and practise another, whether this be in the form of our own institutions or in the military support of dictatorships elsewhere. Mystery and myth are not the proper ends of good government. Yet so long as governments North or South view the world through the lens of military values, and respond to turbulence with military means, then so long will they subscribe to the democratically destructive practices of mystery and secrecy.

◆

Security is an elusive concept. At a personal level, philosophers and sages since antiquity have encouraged its abhorrence on the grounds that absolute security encourages indolence.[26] At a national level, a distinction may be drawn between need, which is real, and compulsion, which is self-destructive. In his famous essay *Common Sense*, published in February 1776, Thom. Paine reflected that 'the inability of moral virtue to govern the world' rendered necessary civil government of which the design and end was 'freedom and security.' A century later, however, the American poet James Russell Lowell warned against imbalance: 'He who is firmly seated in authority soon learns to think security, and not progress, the highest lesson of statecraft.'[27]

Two centuries following Paine, it may be argued that Lowell's warnings reflect perceptibly the state of the world today. The industrialized countries of the North have for decades been so preoccupied with their own national security – most often defined in terms not much changed since Clausewitz[28] – that they have failed to heed the appalling social and economic shortcomings in the developing countries. In the result, the countries of the North are quite unappreciative of the new planetary balances. Their classical concepts of national security have become largely irrelevant. Sadly, traditional military preoccupations have diverted attention from the real risks that now prevail. Many of these emanate from the South, are of threat to the North, yet are far different from the classical definitions of security.

The Second World War, and the Cold War that followed, featured the industrialized states in the principal roles. The countries of the South were either of marginal importance or, later, troublesome sideshows for the superpower adversaries and their Atlantic basin allies. Throughout this latter period of half a century, issues were examined most frequently through a military prism, and prescriptive policies more often than not centred on the military ingredient. Societies that had themselves been born in revolution, and that traced their vitality and their dedication to justice back to the spontaneity of radical change – primarily the United States and France – became inflexible proponents of the status quo, relinquishing with reluctance their influence on overseas possessions, defending stoutly the entrenched interests of landowners and élites no matter how inequitable their interests.

With the sudden easing of East–West tensions in 1989–90, instability and conflict in the developing countries, once interpreted in Cold War terms or viewed with indifference, became by default the main event. Nor should the new-found attraction have been entirely surprising. There was now, after all, a new motivation for interest. Military establishments in the North, facing public pressure for their reduction and dismantlement, were arguing for their continuance in terms of 'Third World' dangers. Military contractors were now boasting of the prowess of their counter-insurgency weaponry and products. President Bush, in a speech delivered a day following the Iraqi invasion of Kuwait, described American security in military terms: 'Even in a world where democracy and freedom have made great gains, threats remain. Terrorism. Hostage-taking. Renegade regimes and unpredictable rulers – new sources of instability – all require a strong and engaged America.'[29] In response to these threats, the president promised a strong military capability. He said nothing about the circumstances that gave rise to the instability, or the reason why he

regarded the sources as 'new.' To the credit of the United States, however, and to the applause of all who seek a functioning, effective, and
pluralistic international security system, the Security Council was fully
engaged from the outset in the Persian Gulf crisis. The joint pronouncements of international cooperation by Presidents Bush and
Gorbachev at their Helsinki meeting on 9 September 1990 could not have
been anticipated even a year earlier. Slowly, and certainly not without
resistance within the military establishments of each of the United States
and the USSR, the once-familiar element of competitiveness rather than
cooperation, the instinctive superpower characteristic for so long, appears
to be ebbing. The ingredients of supremacy and superficiality of diagnosis,
once characteristic of so many incidents of crisis proportion, are perhaps
losing their dominance in the process of decision making.

Yet hand in hand with this cautious evolution, there is no sign of a
redirection of emphasis and investment away from military spending and
towards genuine problem solving. This, notwithstanding that military
forces anywhere have yet to demonstrate how they could make a positive
contribution to increasing agricultural production, to reducing fertility
rates, to restoring the wholesomeness of the environment, or to solving
the debt crisis. Neither, unless one leaps at the improbable, are there
military solutions to ill-performing economies, to incompetent governments, to infectious diseases, or to discrimination against women or
human rights abuses. Neither nuclear ballistic missiles nor rapid-
deployment paratroops have the slightest effect on educational de-
ficiencies in children or on malnutrition in adults. Acts of aggression by
countries such as Iraq must of course be met decisively but all the while
these other issues, singly and in combination, are the ones that will
determine increasingly in the future the security of the industrialized
countries of the North. These are the issues, reflected all too often in
immense disparities in living standards, that underlie a good deal of
Middle East instability. Flagrant breaches of international law and
resistance to Security Council resolutions are not unknown elsewhere in
the region; these combine to guarantee unrest. *All* ingredients must be
recognized; *all* must be given effective treatment – which is to say that the
precepts of Hans Morgenthau are not entirely invalid.

Without question the 'tendency to dominate' that Morgenthau claimed
to be 'an element of all human associations'[30] remains evident in coun-

tries North and South, as does the importance of political power within and among states, as Thom. Paine deemed necessary. What is no longer valid, however, is Morgenthau's thesis that 'armed strength as a threat or a potentiality is the most important material factor making for the political power of a nation.'[31] Today, the several other factors cited by Morgenthau are in sum more than the match of armed strength as the determinant of political power: natural resources, industrial capacity, national character, quality of government. In question now is the assumption that military power is the dominant element in international relations. In the past two decades, countries that have eschewed both political and military power in their preference for economic performance have not only become exceedingly influential but have created for their citizens a standard and quality of life envied and applauded by the military superpowers. To criticize Japan, as it is popular in some quarters to do, on the ground that its economic success results from a failure to accept its share of defence responsibilities is not entirely fair and far from accurate.

Although much of the emphasis given by so many countries to the quantity and quality of their armed forces is based upon the genuine fear (real or perceived) of potential enemies within and without, a major part of the emphasis, whether admitted or not, stems still from the belief that military strength enhances the international status of a state, gives to it the stature of a 'power.' Notwithstanding any number of examples that indicate clearly that military strength does not lead to effective influence of a political or economic kind, the myth persists. It emanates, of course, from military establishments and military observers (veterans groups, arms manufacturers, military publications, and the like) all with vested, and altogether legitimate, interests in their own points of view. In a world rife with overwhelmingly important problems of a non-military nature, however, military prowess of the traditional kind should not be the norm, much less the normative, criterion for national reputations and influence.

The military competence now needed in so many countries North and South is not the ability to engage in brutal wars of either conventional or unorthodox nature; required now is the ability of national armed forces to demonstrate that they are competent to discharge the range of honourable, constructive, challenging roles that are supportive of democratic processes and social stability, not competitive with either of them. Needed especially in the post–Cold War era are units structured, trained, and equipped to participate with units from other national sources in United Nations–sanctioned activities. Unless the countries of the North begin to revise their strategies and their values in this fashion, it is sheer fantasy to assume that many of the countries of the South will take the initiative. As the 1990s begin, the 1980s vocabulary of Ronald Reagan must be abandoned: the mindless categorization of countries as 'allies' and 'friends' with the former ranking above the latter. As this century concludes, the requirements of a stable, functioning international community are for the most part not of a traditional military nature. Countries willing and able to dedicate their resources to the real determinants of security should be applauded, not derided by politicians or journalists with minds still locked in a 1950s misunderstanding of the nature of human needs and human demands.

At least one of the superpower leaders acknowledged this basic change in his address to the Conference on Security and Cooperation in Europe (CSCE) in Paris in November 1990. Said President Gorbachev of the USSR: 'Concern over the survival of the human race is no longer centered almost exclusively on the removal of the threat of nuclear war, as it was only a short time ago. It is increasingly focused on peaceful global problems, among them those of environment, energy, food and water supply, social ills, crime, mass poverty, foreign debt.'[32] President Gorbachev's remarks echo the statement made by Prime Minister Pierre Elliott Trudeau to the first CSCE at Helsinki in July 1975:

> Whatever stability this conference anticipates in Europe will be shortlived if we do not seize the opportunity now offered to us to create elsewhere the conditions necessary to permit standards of living to be raised, to permit the economies of tropical countries to be improved, stabilized and made sufficient, to ensure that rural development is encouraged and food production is increased, to provide hope for a better future to the hundreds of millions of people outside of Europe now existing at the subsistence level.[33]

As environmental degradation increasingly diminishes the future health of all living organisms, scientific resources and government leadership must be dedicated to the design of alternative lifestyles. As impoverished people seek a means of livelihood that offers them a modicum of human dignity, new and more effective forms of social organization and economic productivity are required. And as disenchanted, disenfranchised, disregarded youth turn to criminal activities or terrorism, efforts must be turned to a cessation of weapons transfers, to the provision of jobs, and to effective police work.

In so many developing countries where public officials are paid wages at levels less than the poverty level, the likelihood that some of those persons are amenable to bribery and corruption should not be surprising. (The practice, after all, is scarcely unknown in the high-wage societies of the North.) With corruption, there disappears the confidence in even-handedness that is so necessary for an effective and legal governmental regime. The answer is not the imposition of military force but the provision of salary scales and training to permit law-enforcement agencies to regain their own sense of pride and the respect of their communities. In the twelve-year-long struggle with the Communist Terrorists in Malaya, the brunt of the responsibility was taken by the police, not by the army. In the now celebrated contest in that country for the hearts and minds of vulnerable villagers – a contest repeated since, and more often than not lost, in dozens of other locales worldwide including Vietnam and El Salvador – the key determinant is confidence on the part of the people that the authorities can be trusted to protect them and their interests. Armies, foreign armies especially, are much less able to create the necessary bonding than are local police forces responsible to local, elected governments at both national and municipal levels.

From the perspective of the countries of the North, the stability that they seek for the pursuit of their economic and other interests is simply no longer attainable through the barrel of a gun, if it ever was. Nor is it attainable should massive inequity and degrading poverty be dominant features of societies in the South. One of the most alarming manifestations of poverty to have emerged for centuries – AIDS – is an example of the barrenness of security policies based upon military power. It serves as an example of the vulnerability of all peoples everywhere to the new forms of threats, and the need to fashion new attitudes and new responses distinct from the now irrelevant and ineffective concepts of 'security.'

AIDS was estimated by the World Health Organization in 1990 to have afflicted more than 260,000 persons worldwide. The HIV virus, which at present advances in virtually 100 per cent of cases to full-blown AIDS, is present in an estimated 5–10 million additional people. No other disease has ever so mystified modern biomedical researchers and clinicians, none has ever aroused such immense hysteria and alarm, none has had the potential to be so destructive of communities and age groups. AIDS was unknown in the early 1980s. Like the hole in the ozone layer, it had not been predicted. A decade later, it is spreading with alarming speed through many regions of the world. Because the virus remains dormant for years in the human body, detection is difficult and isolation of no benefit. Far and away the most effective response to AIDS is prevention. There is as yet no cure, not even effective forms of treatment, and no likelihood of a vaccine for years to come. Crisis management is not the answer; crisis avoidance is. Avoidance, however, demands understanding, the ability to function and to communicate, the means to offer alternatives to risky behavioural practices; in short, the kind of sensitive, anticipatory, enduring, socially oriented policies and activities that are the antithesis of most military-type responses.

The origin of AIDS is not so important as is an understanding of the architecture of the virus and its function. Important, too, however, is the fact that AIDS, like all infectious diseases, is transmitted worldwide. With unprecedented speed, the epidemiology of this affliction has spread around the globe and could easily reach into every community, no matter how remote, in every continent. In Bangkok, HIV infection among intravenous drug users rose from less than 1 per cent in 1987 to 50 per cent by early 1990. In New York and in New Jersey, HIV/AIDS is now the leading cause of death among black women between the ages of fifteen and forty-four; HIV seroprevalence in women of child-bearing age in those states 'predicts much higher mortality in the coming years.'[34] In central Africa, the rate of transmission is so high that fears are expressed for the survival of an entire generation of young men and women. Paediatric AIDS, the result of HIV infection of the foetus by virally affected mothers, is rapidly becoming a major public health issue in Europe and North America.

AIDS is far from the only infectious disease deserving attention. Although not so dramatic, the incidence of malaria is much higher and increasingly reaches into Northern communities as infected travellers return home. It remains the leading cause of morbidity and mortality in many countries of the South and could quite readily appear and spread in those many countries of the North in which the particular vector mosquitoes are present. The same risk attaches to other mosquito-borne diseases such as yellow fever and dengue. Several viral diseases once thought to be restricted to tropical climates are now being reported in Europe and North America. Still other viruses, previously unknown, are spreading from animal hosts to humans for reasons not yet fully understood.

These kinds of perils have nothing to do with traditional interpretations of national security. Their only linkage to military activity is the fact that funds needed for research and treatment are given a much lower priority by governments both North and South than the insatiable demands of military commanders. The use of arms has never, at any time, anywhere, resolved the underlying social problems that stimulated unrest and violence. Medical research and field applications, however, have eliminated completely one of humankind's most dastardly enemies, smallpox, and are capable of similar triumphs over any number of other maladies. Yet in our blind response to the seductive siren-song of weapons manufacturers and defence strategists, we continue to allow our governments to pour funds into military procurement programs out of all proportion to their effective application, while denying them to the tried and true (and relatively inexpensive) campaigns to provide clean water, health education, immunization, and family planning.

◆

The era of state security based primarily upon military preparedness is now over, even though many governments North and South are unprepared to admit it. The real risks facing all peoples, including those in the industrialized countries of the North, have been masked for decades by incorrect assumptions. The error in diagnosis made by the West in the years following the Second World War was described recently in forceful terms by McGeorge Bundy, former special assistant for national security to President John F. Kennedy, discussing the outbreak of hostilities in Korea in 1950: 'There came a mistaken intensification of the belief that all Communist actions everywhere were part of a single, implacably aggressive, worldwide war against freedom itself.'[35]

That image of a monolithic, irrepressible military machine wholly in charge in the communist countries of Eastern Europe, and indomitable internationally, flooded our minds and shaped our attitudes. So suffocating, all-powerful, and infinite were these regimes deemed to be that the phrase 'Better dead than Red' gained popularity, even plausibility in certain Western societies. Intelligence estimates routinely warned of missile-gaps, of military superiority in conventional terms, of invincible secret-police and bureaucratic structures, of the effectiveness of infiltration elsewhere – of the continuing threat to democracies and the need for military responses. So ingrained became these images that successive revelations of the inaccuracies in the intelligence of the inefficiencies of the Soviet Union and its allies, of the ineptness of Soviet involvement in developing countries, were all swept aside as meaningless. The impression had become dominant, and reality was rejected. Then, quite unpredictably, the impression was shattered. Evidence of the powerlessness of even the most determined and well armed of authoritarian regimes suddenly filled TV screens worldwide with the events of Wenceslas Square and downtown Bucharest and Brandenburg Gate.

Now, new attitudes must be shaped, new realities accepted, with respect not only to the Soviet Union and communism, but to all the circumstances of global dimensions, including the plight of the developing countries and the common plight of all members of the human species. One reality is the fact that national security no longer begins and ends with the state. Many other actors, from individuals to international agencies to large commercial enterprises, are playing increasingly significant roles. Economics, environment, health, food, water, migrants – these are the powerful elements that now determine security. In their management, factors such as persuasion, rule making, dispute resolution, rational anticipation, and compassion for the elements of human dignity are all far more important than Clausewitz's simplistic determination. Military responses of a traditional kind are seldom even effective in instances where military intervention is invited, as illustrated by the madcap adventures of United States forces attacking Cuban construction gangs in Grenada or Stealth bombers missing targets by hundreds of metres in Panama. Nor, because of the interwoven political, human, and economic elements found in situations such as the Persian Gulf, can decisive military force be brought to bear without massive human agony extending far beyond the combatants.

A tragedy of unprecedented proportions is building and all the while the sycophantic attention of the North's television and press skitters in mindless automatism from Managua to Panama City to Kuwait.

Relentlessly, the determinants of global warming are accumulating, the population of the planet is continuing to grow, the social and economic miasma of billions of people is worsening, the demand for narcotic substances in the North is increasing, the incidents of violence are escalating, the disparity in living standards between rich and poor is widening ever more dangerously. The abilities of governments to govern are decreasing ever more in North and South as members of society withdraw their confidence from traditional structures and processes. These processes are deemed by journalists as not newsworthy because they cannot be transferred to ninety seconds of videotape. Northern governments, which set their priorities in response to television and newspaper agendas, continue to focus on the superficial.

Barbara Ward warned of the momentum of unheeded events in 1966: 'In the last few decades, mankind has been overcome by the most fateful change in its entire history. Modern science and technology have created so close a network of communication, transport, economic interdependence – and potential nuclear destruction – that planet earth, on its journey through infinity, has acquired the intimacy, the fellowship, and the vulnerability of a spaceship. In such a close community, there must be rules for survival.'[36] We are now living in our unanticipated future, surprised by unimaginable events such as ozone holes over the poles or the speed of AIDS or the bankruptcy of entire countries. We are challenged by the momentum of natural forces that we have ignored for decades while tempted by military rhetoric to overlook them and vent our frustration in atavistic and self-defeating demonstrations of armed might.

A new outlook is needed, one more subtle and all embracing than in the past. A new form of social contract is required, one based on scientific reality and tempered by humanitarian constants. That contract must be one that emphasizes fairness not privilege, law not force, stewardship not exploitation, tolerance not extremism – a social contract far more demanding of human endeavour and far more challenging than the centuries-old structures and processes that lineal thinkers have declared modern simply by the insertion of electronic components and the attachment of nuclear bombs.

More compelling now than at any time in the long journey of the human species is the need to become in fact and in law a community; more available now than at any previous time is the knowledge necessary to design that community and to make it function effectively. We are all now, as Bill Moyers has said, pilgrims 'on a journey that makes strangers obsolete and friendship imperative.'[37]

Time Past / Time Now

Overwhelming change has rarely if ever been willingly accepted by any community or society. Yet human history has never witnessed the assemblage of so many constituent ingredients signalling change as are present today, ingredients which for the most part are products of the scientific and technological era of the past century. Well within the realm of possibility now – as never before – are the options of devastating environmental degradation or nuclear holocaust on the one hand, and of sustainable equitable responses to virtually all of humankind's wants and needs on the other.

Never before have the deteriorating tendencies gained momentum so rapidly or been of such planetary dimension. Never before has the contest between privilege and powerlessness been so vivid or its outcome so unavoidable. And never before have the elementary principles of decency, dignity, fairness, and equity been more attractive or potentially more productive.

There is a logic to the integrity of all biological species and processes that cannot be defied and must no longer be challenged, certainly not on North–South lines. In the information age, in the nuclear age, in the population age, there is no alternative to change. Without attitudinal change, however, humankind will be victims, not beneficiaries – we in the North as well as those in the South.

◆

Hinges of history have never been evident to those poised upon them.

Time Past/Time Now, from Al Purdy; *The Collected Poems of Al Purdy* (Toronto: McClelland and Stewart 1986)[1]

The natural evolution of a fertile hybrid wheat in the valleys of the Tigris and Euphrates rivers was to change the lifestyle of the great majority of all human beings, concluding the long period of nomadic wanderings and permitting the beginning of settled agriculture. So miraculous must have seemed this variety of non-self-propagating cereal grain to those dwelling in the region, however, so fixed were the customs of the period, that generations passed before new farming techniques were derived and disseminated. Columbus's accounts of the New World did not stimulate an immediate mass exodus from a Europe stultified by religious orthodoxy and inflexible land tenure. His first accounts were met with the same incredulousness that greeted Marco Polo on his return from China. James Watts's steam engine did not instantly industrialize England. In a time of horseback communication, and stagecoach transportation, news of novelty travelled slowly. Applications of steam-generated power required many decades of adaptation before there was widespread evidence of change. As with all new technologies since, utilization was initially intermittent and seemingly random.

In all history, the people most likely to have felt the immediacy of change were the inhabitants of communities first visited by outsiders. In those instances where the outsiders were of European origin, and the communities were located in the South, the impact was vivid and close to instantaneous. Whether welcomed, tolerated, or resisted, the newcomers often revealed themselves as barbarous. The Spanish conquistadors, for example, systematically eliminated entirely every community of Carib Indians in the Caribbean region, often in bestial fashion, but always for the glorification of the Christian church. This was an extreme example: there was no endeavour, as in Mexico and Peru, to convert the Indians. Instead, a cold-blooded campaign of genocide directed to the aboriginal peoples. Not so much change, here, as extinction of a culture and a people.

Elsewhere, change must often have appeared in more diminutive guise, halting, uncertain, of uneven application, seldom ever with an apocalyptic crescendo to announce its arrival. The hinge much more likely appeared as a disjuncture, an anomaly in the expected cycle of events. Peter Drucker employed a metaphor of that sort when he described the present as the 'Age of Discontinuity,'[2] an age when assumptions about linear progressions are no longer valid, when outcomes can no longer be assumed. Discontinuous as events may be, subject to reversal and variance, remission and advance, there has accumulated nevertheless enough evidence in recent years for humankind to acknowledge that ours is the first generation ever to be aware of several profound truths. It is up to us, therefore, to ensure that those truths are neither ignored nor misinterpreted, for to do either would be the ultimate heresy.

Truth number one relates to the environment. Our generation is not, of course, the first to be aware that this planet is the only one in the solar system that possesses the peculiar combination of circumstances needed to support human life. What we have been the first to learn, however, is that that combination, while robust, is much more delicately balanced, much more vulnerable to human interference, than had been earlier believed; that careless and short-sighted behaviour can upset the balance, can degrade and destroy the vital life-support systems essential to our well-being as a species. We have learned, too, that the degradation of some of those systems, if allowed to continue too long, will become irreversible, no matter what is done to stem the effect. Ours is the first generation in all history to possess this knowledge. It is knowledge that should encourage us to live prudently. Should we fail to do so, we will diminish directly the welfare of our descendants.

Truth number two. We have known since our early days in school that the human species is alone among all biological life in its ability to record its own history, to keep track of its accomplishments and its failures, its triumphs and its tragedies. As our schooling continued, we learned just how extensive has been failure, how frequently has humankind repeated its errors, how often our species refused to admit its misdeeds. We have learned as well, however, and ours is the first generation to possess the empirical evidence to prove it, that human error measured in nuclear terms can be so far reaching in its consequences, so devastating in its many effects, that for the first time in human experience there will be no second chance, no opportunity for a cover-up or a clean-up. A nuclear error, if committed, is potentially irremedial. This knowledge should force us to demand responsibility from governments. Should we fail to do so, we will be held hostage to the ambitions of nuclear adventurers.

Truth number three. We have had some sense in years gone by that human beings were capable of attending to most of their needs if only the necessary resources could be assembled. We have learned in the past decade or so that recent advances in science and technology have been so extensive that inadequate knowledge is no longer a barrier to the significant enhancement of human welfare worldwide. When resources are properly deployed, and political decisions wisely taken, humankind's oldest scourges can be overcome. Disease, malnourishment, illiteracy, and other enemies of human dignity can be reduced and often eliminated. Ours is the first generation to realize that human misery will henceforth be the result of human indifference, and nothing else. It is knowledge that is possessed by the wretched as well as by the privileged. That knowledge and that realization will inspire us to act humanely. Should we fail to do so, we will become prisoners of our own callous consciences; become hostage, as well, to worldwide outbreaks of resentment.

These three truths distinguish our generation from every previous one since the beginning of time. These, in the original sense of the word, are 'awful' truths for they demand solemn respect. They should humble each one of us. Humbleness alone is inadequate as a response to knowledge of this magnitude, however. Something more is necessary. That something has to be resolve to use our knowledge wisely. Should we not do so, ours will be the first generation to possess still another truth: that we have *consciously* passed on to our children a world less wholesome, less humane, less stable, and less promising than the one that we inherited. And we will know, too, that it is our greed, our arrogance, and our indifference that are responsible. It is a testament that will be borne most particularly by those now living in the industrialized countries of the North, for we are possessed not only of these truths but possessed as well of the means to ensure a beneficial planetary disposition of the knowledge that underlies them. To fail this challenge is to commit succeeding generations to the perilous condition of refugees, seeking sanctuary in a world which offers none – not from economic hazard, not from environmental degradation, nor social instability or political upheaval.

At no time in the past has an entire generation dared dream that continuously rising standards of living were possible, as is assumed today by so many in the North. At no time in the past could there have been such indifference on the part of some that, for the vast majority, not even basic survival is assured. Never in the imperfect tapestry of human activity has there been such an extraordinary – and indefensible – contrast between those few whose lives are so comfortable as to permit indolence and obesity, and those many whose existence is so wretched as to query even the concept of a just God. Should the quest of the few continue unabated for additional extravagances, the agony of the many will prove uncontainable. As each element is driven by self-centred interests – the rich for greater luxuries and the poor for simple survival – the resulting disequilibria will surely favour the poor.

This juncture in the human pageant demands that we abandon a number of deeply instilled practices and attitudes. Equally, it demands that we design and adopt several others that are novel, or at least unprecedented. This will not happen smoothly or in the absence of disruption. Major change never has. Nor will all participate willingly. That is why adjustments of this magnitude must originate in the governed. Governments, dependent on popularity, will never have the political courage to inaugurate the necessary steps. Governments may or may not understand, as Professor Paul Freund so vividly pointed out, that 'history is a tension between heritage and heresy,' but governments in the industrialized democracies have seldom shown the willingness and accepted the responsibility to be a structural part of that 'tension.' With few exceptions, massive, rapid governmental initiative has taken place only in circumstances of, or surrounding, war. This is a reflection of the fact that democratic societies are generally reluctant to acknowledge that their governments are possessed of the knowledge, or should be equipped with the means, to permit broad response to novel events. Electorates do not encourage unorthodox governmental policies. This may be wise, but it places great responsibility on the populace to become informed and to assume the role of activist in order to break the grip of inertia, to accept that the equilibrium of the past no longer functions in our favour. The responsibility is all the greater in a period of widespread assumption that change is generally benign and that adjustment can be both simple and successful, requiring little involvement and no discomfort. In historic terms, that assumption is incorrect.

◆

In many parts of the world, over long periods of time, societies neither experienced nor envisaged change. The rhythms of life and death were well known and in large part dictated by natural, or seasonal, phenomena. For lengthy periods there was no reason to anticipate any betterment, or any worsening, of circumstance that had been familiar for many years past. The constraints of geography (present) and communications (absent) ensured that life was lived locally. In some societies, the extent of this sameness has been so limitless as to be almost unimaginable to a late-twentieth-century Canadian. An example is the Bakhtiari, a nomadic grouping that has altered little its pattern of life in what is now Iran since the retreat of the last ice age some twelve thousand years ago. The group carries with it all its possessions as it crosses six perilous mountain ranges annually in its outward quest for fresh pastures, then crosses the same six ranges again on return, packing and unpacking each day of the year. Of them, Bronowski wrote: 'There is no room for innovation, because there is not time, on the move, between evening and morning, coming and going all their lives, to develop a new device or a new thought – not even a new tune. The only habits that survive are the old habits. The only ambition of the son is to be like the father.'[3]

Repetitiveness and dreariness have been the norm for most persons in most parts of the world, relieved only recently and largely only in the North. In his autobiography, Harold Eeman, a well-to-do Belgian, described the daily toil of the men who worked the barge paths near Ghent as the nineteenth century turned to the twentieth. The barges were 'hauled by slow, heavy men in corduroys, harnessed and sweating like horses, leaning forward against the broad leather strap until their dangling hands nearly touched the ground. In this manner, their blond hair, limp with sweat, hanging like a curtain in front of their faces, these barge-slaves toiled along the tow-paths of canals and rivers, from one end of Europe to another, blind to all that lay around them, their vision limited to the narrow strip of the soil on which they trod and under which, some day, they would at last find rest.'[4]

That is an image of a past so different from the present that it is one with which no present-day North American can associate. Yet we seem equally oblivious to the extent of the changes that have taken place in our lifetimes, at least to the sense of the pace of change in today's world. With some prompting, educated adults in 1990 can reel off an extraordinary list of technological innovations encountered in a single lifetime, yet be curiously aloof to their effect, and certainly void of any wonder about them. For persons alive today, living comfortably within their biblical life span of three score and ten, the incidence of new processes, new gadgets, and new knowledge, all introduced since their births, is so overwhelming as to deny comparison with any previous period of history: penicillin, radar, television, the electron microscope, antihistamines, jet aircraft, stereophonic sound, oral contraceptives, laser xerography, nuclear weapons, human heart transplants, transistors, ballpoint pens, nylon, VCRs, earth-orbiting satellites, colour motion pictures, antibiotics, a range of vitamins, FM, polyethylene plastic, helicopters, cortisone, pacemakers, computers, cellular telephones – the list goes on and on. For those persons able to benefit from this cornucopia, the very richness of scientific and technological accomplishment can give rise to assumptions that all problems are soluble, all desires are attainable, all human conduct is defensible. These assumptions are not only naïve but dangerous, for they tend to permit individual responsibility to be abdicated and delegated to others, to place impossible expectations on technology, and to give the impression that all applications of knowledge are wise. These assumptions assume as well an equality of access that simply does not exist.

Without question, the extent of scientific discovery in the next seventy years will be at least the equal of the past seventy. The new knowledge about to be generated will permit many human afflictions to be overcome, many leisure-time pursuits to be introduced, many human requirements to be met. None of these brilliant accomplishments, however, will contribute to the daily welfare of the billions of less-well-to-do persons, much less ensure the continuance of the human species, without more: without a realization that we live on a hinge of history and that time is no longer on our side.

Realizations of this magnitude are admittedly rare, but certainly not unprecedented. What a wrenching intellectual and emotional experience it must have been for humans to accept that the world was spherical and not flat; what confusion must have followed an early community's first exposure to people from somewhere else (as has happened within our lifetime to several tribes in the interiors of South Pacific islands, giving rise to peculiar and irrational responses such as 'cargo cults'); what profound uncertainty has overtaken major religious communities when articles of faith have been challenged and then abandoned. On one occasion or another, the human species – or significant segments of it – through history has been required to re-examine some of the most basic tenets of its reality as new knowledge comes to its attention. The response in some circumstances has been political, as with the emergence of the nation-state. In others it has been social, as in the adjustment to Darwin's revelations about the origin of the species. What is quite clear, however, is that those societies which did not adjust to the new realities – to Galileo's confirmation of the theories of Copernicus, to Newton's laws of motion, to Locke's and Rousseau's views of the organization of society – have not flourished, and have in some instances floundered.

Not all segments of even a close-knit society move at an even pace. Quite understandably, some schools of thought or belief are unwilling to accept what is said to be new, regarding it as unproved, or voguish, or even heretical. Not even within scientific circles can there ever be expected to be unanimity of opinion with respect to new theories. Planck and Einstein and Heisenberg have all been dead for many years, yet there is still not full acceptance of the implications of their work, and so the study of the theories of particle waves, of chaos, and of uncertainty all continue, just as physicians took some time to accept the 'truth' of Harvey's explanation of the circulation of blood. Sometimes reluctance to change is rooted in deeply held religious convictions, as it continues to be with respect to acceptance or rejection of the creation myth. Resistance of that kind is not easily overcome; the Roman Catholic church pardoned Galileo only in recent years – three centuries following his inquisition – and released his *Dialogue* from the Index of Prohibited Books only shortly before. This phenomenon of slow acceptance is likely universal; certainly it is assumed to be so. What begs equal acceptance and acknowledgment is the consequence of such tardiness. Today, as in the sixteenth century, reluctance to accept and to adjust must be understood to carry with it widespread implications. The striking coincidence of Newton's birth in England in the same year as Galileo's commitment to house arrest in Rome, and the subsequent shift of scientific accomplishment north from the Mediterranean, is one example from the past. Today, when interest on developing country debt accumulates by U.S.$274 million per *day*, when population is increasing by nine thousand persons every single *hour*, when net deposits of carbon into the atmosphere increase at the rate of 11,000 metric tonnes per *minute* – in these circumstances, the passage of time does not favour those who prevaricate. Nor, within the single atmosphere which envelops this planet and all humankind, can it be safely assumed that communities on one continent can respond to a different metronome than those on another.

It would be of immense help to modern societies, and especially to their governments, to understand how human beings in the past accommodated themselves to some of the key hinges of history; how the realities came to be accepted; how the necessary adjustments were made; how in the process of change essential values were identified and preserved; how long these adjustments took. We turn to historians for information of this kind, especially to social historians, but the information we gain is seldom entirely adequate. This, of course, is because circumstances never replicate themselves exactly, and because of intrinsic shortcomings in the descriptive material available to us.

The accounts of historians, as they themselves will quickly acknowledge, are unlikely to be any more accurate, any less subjective, or any more balanced than is the work of any other record-keeper. What makes these works so worthy, however, is the fact that, from Herodotus onwards, the more candid of historians have revealed frankly their own biases and their own shortcomings. It is this candour, of course, that gives to the work of these witnesses their utility. They confess their attitudes. More often than not, in contrast, the observations of participants in the events being recorded are neither candid nor accurate. Scholars in future years, for example, will not likely regard either Nancy Reagan or Kurt Waldheim as the most balanced of chroniclers of the events in which they were so deeply engaged, notwithstanding their intimate knowledge of detail.

The misuse of history – or its misinterpretation – should not automatically be blamed on the record-keepers. Much more often the fault rests with the reader than with the writer. Here is where selectivity and tendentiousness enter with widespread effect. Someone who believes, for example, that military activity has been central to the fate of nations is likely to give greater heed to the writings of military historians and less to those whose interests are economic or social. Such selectivity is exacerbated frequently by the absence of adequately documented material. Not always available, even for those who seek them, are perspectives from all geographic or temporal points of view, nor are the observations of commentators knowledgeable in all disciplines.

Those omissions don't change the events but they surely affect their consequences. In the result we are all myopic as we form opinions. The human tendency all too often is to assume awareness – if not knowledge – far beyond what we should recognize honestly as our limits of comprehension. The solution, in this age of ever-increasing specialization, demands that we admit ignorance, that we confess an absence of understanding. The exercise of common sense commences with the posing of basic questions.

So should begin the quest of a reader seeking a more satisfactory sense of what is happening today in the developing regions of the world. The quick answers, which appear frequently on TV screens, are all too often reflections of ignorance or prejudice, are potentially of more harm than help. Indeed, if one considers them for more than a moment, they are an insult to intelligence. Yet they persist. And they multiply. Can one seriously believe that a mother in a tropical country is so indifferent to her children's health that she would not willingly improve their diet were she able? Are we to assume that a developing country businessman prefers unproductive, costly manufacturing and distribution techniques? Is it valid even to suggest that governments of newly independent countries will not choose socially advantageous policies if given the option? Are we to assume that corruption is so prevalent as to be the norm in developing countries but so rare as to be unusual in industrialized societies? Perhaps most important of all, can we reasonably assume that democratically elected governments in countries of the South with deteriorating standards of living should be able to function effectively, to respect civil rights, to contain fanaticism, to protect the environment? Such an assumption may well prove to be the ultimate in naïvety; that in circumstances of dropping incomes, inadequate nutrition, poor health, personal insecurity, questionable education, and no hope for betterment – that in these circumstances democracy and moderation will prevail.

Countries of the South are not by any means free of villains or fools or irresponsible citizens, but I daresay the ratio to population is no greater than in the industrialized countries. Yet in our arrogance or in our laziness, we in the North succumb to the temptation of believing that standards of living in the South are low because values are low, that human pathos and wretchedness is more often than not linked to human moral weakness and human character flaws. This self-flattering assumption on the part of the relatively well-to-do is not of course unknown within our own societies, where the rich patronize the poor and explain income disparity on the basis of alleged hard work or superior intellect or desire to achieve; where aboriginal peoples are denied the dignity they deserve because they are perceived to be 'different.' To rebut such assumptions should be easy. Many of the present pillars of society in countries such as Canada are the direct descendants of vagrants swept off the streets of London, or of penniless refugees fleeing persecution. Given economic, social, and political opportunity, they prospered. And so did their new country as a result. Cultural distinctions surely contribute to differences in attitude and activity, but not to attributes or competence.

Given equality of opportunity, the youth of the South will in time perform meritoriously and competitively with the youth of the North. Without the disincentives which the North too often now places in the way of the South, many of the countries there will burgeon and prosper. Our failure to accept those truths reflects more than simply our assumptions or our ignorance. It leads to our own future detriment as societies and as individuals. It is why attitudinal change must be pursued with vigour even though its acceptance will be neither immediate nor universal. Can there be a more ignominious image of human weakness than that of youth in the North dying of drug abuse and youth in the South dying of starvation? No one can deny that each excess demands our involvement, even as that involvement demands a change in the personal expectations of those in the North.

◆

Efforts by the privileged to retain their advantage are likely as old as human association. Never before in history, however, has the entrenchment of privilege assumed global dimensions involving national actors. And never before has the accumulated inertia of the disadvantaged been so powerful as to threaten the well-being of the privileged across national frontiers. Whatever equilibrium has been maintained in the past is rapidly dissipating. The North–South relationship is now in a state of profound disequilibrium. Fortunately, the distorting screen of the East–West struggle has been lifted and the extent of global disparity can be viewed in human rather than ideological terms. Our response, therefore, need no longer be ideological but may be human as well. As it must be.

Within societies, the abuse of privilege by a few has often given way to a revolt by the many. These uprisings, of course, have not always been successful. Even less frequently have their outcomes led to an effective easing of affliction. Yet in those instances where a genuine sharing of power did ensue, the 'reformed' societies flourished as a result of the release of previously untapped energies. Human initiative seized the opportunities made available. The resulting social and economic changes benefited all strata of society, including the more well to do, for they permitted a strengthening of political stability and an easing of the increasingly untenable circumstances which had prevailed before. The replacement of uncertainty and repression by openness and opportunity has been the key in many instances to vitality and to the responsible exercise of freedom.

One of the enduring definitions of this kind of struggle was pronounced by Abraham Lincoln in 1861 during the classic civil confrontation in the United States, one dedicated to the preservation of the Union but waged on the most basic issue of equity – slavery. The Union, stated Lincoln, was endeavouring to preserve a form of government 'whose leading object is to elevate the condition of men – to lift artificial weights from all shoulders – to clear the paths of laudable pursuit for all – to afford all an unfettered start, and a fair chance, in the race of life.'[5] Not guarantees of success, not permanent safety nets against failure, simply the removal of artificial impediments and the provision of a 'fair chance.'

That, in brief, is the need today of many of the developing countries of the South. Should the need not be addressed, and reasonably resolved, 'laudable pursuit' increasingly, and inevitably, will be denied not just to the nations of the South but to those of the North as well because of the interdependence which now ties all societies one to the other. It is necessary therefore that circumstances in the South be viewed in their entirety, that assessments be carried out fairly, and that symptoms be distinguished from cause. The conclusion of the Cold War gives promise that this is possible.

Much earlier than had been anticipated, the first opportunity for East–West cooperation in a developing country setting presented itself in August 1990 with the Iraqi invasion of Kuwait. In a region of the world long regarded by both the United States and the Soviet Union as of considerable strategic importance, one that for years had been the cockpit of instability and rivalry, there was committed an act so flagrantly in violation of the United Nations Charter that the international community chose to identify it as such. Unlike the long, sorry record of disregard or apologia for aggressive acts, human rights violations, denial of Security Council resolutions, and loss of innocent human lives during the era of the Cold War, the nations of the North for the first time chose to acknowledge in concert the illegality of aggressive acts. In doing so, they strengthened the concept of community.

Here was one of those rare moments to look forward, of the kind seized by Prime Minister Churchill and President Roosevelt on board HMS *Prince of Wales*, anchored in Placentia Bay, Newfoundland, in August 1941 (see chapter II). There, in the depths of the Second World War, they chose to act as statesmen, not simply as wartime commanders-in-chief. They exercised rare statesmanship at a moment when none would have been critical had their goals been more immediate, their aims more modest. These two individuals, served by wise advisers, chose to distinguish their cause from that of their enemies. By doing so, they ennobled it. They issued not simply a pledge to meet violence with violence, armed aggression with armed resistance, but a vision of a future marked by political peace and social justice. In the waters off Newfoundland, Churchill and Roosevelt released the Atlantic Charter, the principles of which illuminated the cause of the wartime allies, attracted the understanding of many in neutral nations, and shaped the sinews of the United Nations Organization which emerged at San Francisco four years later. At a moment when the military survival of their forces occupied them, they chose to speak of renunciation of force, of political self-determination, of economic collaboration, of a system of general security, of disarmament. The immediate reaction of national leaders to the Persian Gulf crisis was considerably less statesmanlike.

Much emphasis was given, and with constructive results, to the effective functioning of the Security Council. A dramatic build-up in Saudi Arabia ensued. Much less attention was paid to the extent of human suffering: hundreds of thousands of refugees streamed out of the region; economies near and far were deeply afflicted – some by billions of dollars of lost trade and investments. Forced out of Kuwait and Iraq were not only businessmen from Northern countries but as well countless technicians and labourers from the South – from places as far distant as the Philippines. Given virtually no attention was the question of how Iraq had become so militarily powerful during the long Iraq-Iran war. This latter issue deserves much consideration for it reveals with a vengeance the short-sightedness of the North in its episodic responses to events in the South.

Throughout the eight years of that appallingly bloody war, featuring child soldiers, poison gas attacks, and hundreds of thousands of civilian casualties, the industrialized countries of the North demonstrated little interest in concluding the hostilities. Instead, and notwithstanding that Iraq was the initial aggressor, they transferred weapons in immense quantities to Iraq to offset Iran's initial military advantage. The non-democratic character of the Iraqi government fazed the arms vendors not a whit. Led by the Soviet Union, they gave the impression that their interest was best served through massive weapons transfers. Thus did the industrialized countries signal to the rest of the world their priorities and their values throughout the long years of this bloody conflict. By August 1990, Iraq had come to be possessed of weaponry and other military assets far greater than those of any other country in the region with the single exception of Israel, and obviously far in excess of the requirements of any peaceful state.

Iran had much earlier become a powerful military force. It, too, had acquired its weapons from the North, principally from the United States. And they came in circumstances that undoubtedly contributed to the overthrow of the shah and to a subsequent sequence of unhappy events, including hostage taking. The externally sourced gadgetry that flooded into Iran in the 1960s and 1970s was not all of military significance but in their application these items were all instruments of rapid and far-reaching change. Their arrival, and their accompaniment by large numbers of external technicians, led to the very result they were intended to deny – revolution and instability. These earlier events dissuaded Northern policy makers not a bit, however, as they responded to the Iraqi aggression. Massive weapons transfers to the current ally was the automatic reaction. With the same uncritical reflex as had been demonstrated in each of Iran and Iraq, and with tragic results, weapons were showered upon the Gulf states, this time accompanied by large numbers of foreign forces. The Saudi arms market was a tempting one. Initial sales contracts from the United States alone are likely to exceed u.s. $20 billion in value. This, according to the *New York Times*, would be the largest single arms sale in history.[6] In years to come, without question, the world will be required to observe the results of such a policy as this third state in the region is converted into a military powder-keg.

The social fabric of the Middle East is neither uniform nor amenable

to sweeping alteration. Old customs and old attitudes are well entrenched. For that reason the Iranian experience demands re-examina-
tion as errors repeat themselves. The Bakhtiari nomads to which
reference was made earlier in this chapter live in the Zagros Mountains
in the Northwest of Iran. In Professor Paul Freund's terms, they represent heritage. At the other end of the Iranian fabric, twelve thousand
years more modern, heresy in the 1970s took the form of F-14 military jets
and Phoenix missile systems. The strain imposed by their rapid introduction into a society influenced so heavily by ancient heritage proved
unbearable. Rupture and anarchy were the immediate consequences.
Confusion and oscillating tendencies continue still, as they do elsewhere
in a region wracked with competing influences.

Why did the introduction of modern technologies and modern systems,
intended in one way or another to be instruments of development, prove
to be so stressful and lead to rupture? For two decades before the revolution of 1979, it had been widely accepted that the *absence* of development
was destabilizing, that the disparity between rich and poor across national
lines or within them could not be tolerated indefinitely and could be eased
only by development. Pope Paul VI had so implied when he stated that
'the new name for peace is development.'[7] Willy Brandt had identified
development as 'the greatest challenge to mankind for the remainder of
this century.'[8] Was, then, the situation in Iran an anomalous one? Was the
loss of stability occasioned by the absence or the presence of development?
It is important to know which lest the errors continue. The answer is 'no'
and 'yes.' 'No' to the suggestion that development was the cause; 'yes' to
the proposal that the *form* of developmental effort was.

Four major ingredients contributed to the widespread unrest in Iran,
cumulatively more pervasive and influential than hostility towards the
shah's repressive and autocratic methods and measures. Each of the four
was development-related.

1 Development emphasis was placed on industrialization, much of it of
   a military or military-related nature, to the almost total neglect of
   agriculture.
2 The benefits of the developmental process fell unevenly among the
   several social groups in Iran, increasing rather than decreasing economic disparity.

3 Inadequate preparation had been made for the social impact of rapid economic change.
4 The presence in large numbers of foreigners, many of them seemingly in influential positions, gave to the majority of Iranians the impression that their country had passed into the control of outsiders.

Together these factors resulted in immense popular disaffection. Fuelled by this volatile mixture, religion proved to be a powerful vehicle for change. The country headed back towards heritage even at the immediate expense of many legal and economic reforms.

'Development' in these circumstances assumes an unexpected, even sinister, profile. Revealed immediately is the fallacy in categorizing most official financial transfers to developing countries as 'developmental assistance,' even though a good portion of the transfers may take the form of war materials – items of destruction, not development. Exposed as well is the fact that much of such assistance may be of little or no help at all to the average citizen in the country receiving it. To rural dwellers, a modern hospital in the capital city is unlikely to respond to needs. In the absence of a system of effective taxation and income distribution, even the most profitable of industrial enterprises established with development assistance can contribute only to a deepening, not a lessening, of economic disparity. Still less is there likelihood of a smooth and even absorption of foreign-funded change when the regime in power is not only authoritarian but is representative of only one fraction of the populace. That was the case in Iran in the 1970s, and of Iraq in the 1980s. It is the case in Saudi Arabia today.

There is not likely any single, overwhelmingly important criterion of development, the presence or absence of which determines for observers and participants alike how a country is doing. In the absence of such a universal marker, one must be cautious and exercise a good deal of common sense and local knowledge. 'Gross National Product per capita,' the most often-used benchmark, can be misleading, for it is the aggregate of country-wide statistics and can camouflage wide disparities between one region and another, or between different groupings. It can fail as well to reveal the frailty of a number of non-economic circumstances which may be every bit as important as income: circumstances of health, literacy, or access to clean drinking water, for example.

As one endeavours to assess the success or otherwise of developmental efforts, the choice of criteria and the method of application can vary widely. So, too, can the results which emerge. A country possessed of an immensely valuable natural resource, as is Saudi Arabia, especially if it dedicates a good portion of its income to such facilities as schools and hospitals, can give the statistical impression of 'development,' of having 'developed.' Yet within that society may be found major disparities of income, of status, of education. Absent as well may be many of the criteria often associated with development: the ability to generate original technologies, the capacity to conduct scientific research, the willingness to participate actively and constructively in the international community, an openness to intellectual ferment and debate including political debate. Another kind of disparity may be found within even the richest, the 'most developed' of the industrialized countries, including the United States. Even here there are geographic regions, some of them rural, some of them located in the urban core of large metropolitan cities, where unemployment rates are so high, educational levels so low, infant morbidity and mortality so extensive, and poverty so pervasive that many of the criteria for 'underdevelopment' apply. In those instances, the claim is sometimes made that the people so afflicted – often members of one or another visible minority – live in 'developing country' circumstances. The argument is then advanced that development assistance flowing overseas should more appropriately be directed within the country.

There is not, nor should there be, any automatic or universal response to such a plea. If the goal of 'development' is human dignity, then a broad range of criteria should be considered essential. Of these, the most important, it can be argued, is a narrowing of the broad disparities which now exist between the very poor and the very wealthy, both within any one society and among societies. That being so, a definition of the word 'development' must include the concept of equity; hand in hand with economic vitality there must be social fairness. Social fairness, in turn, demands that there be accountability for human activity in order to moderate the all-too-widespread tendency for the rich to live at the expense of the poor, or of the environment, or of a stable social order, or of a well-functioning economy. It was the obvious absence of such accountability that led to the hostility broadly felt throughout the Middle

East towards the extravagant wealth of the Kuwaiti ruling family regime – and, still, of some other regimes in the region.

There is no universal, guaranteed, formula to reach the goal of social fairness. Arguments of Marxist design have proved so bankrupt in application that few would any longer advocate a communist economic system to address the issues of inequity. A simplistic sharing of wealth is as ineffective in many respects as is its absolute opposite, the unregulated capitalist economy. Each system fails in many instances to provide the incentive necessary for those with low incomes to improve their circumstances, as each fails to curb the excesses of those at the other end who have gained positions of privilege. The necessary ingredient of individual opportunity is in each of such systems often much less evident in practice than is either touted or desirable. This, because opportunity, by its nature, depends on a well-designed social, as well as economic, system.

So important to the long-term health of a society is the moderation of extreme disparity that philosophers and economists alike have long argued forcefully for its alleviation. On grounds both moral and disturbingly practical, Chateaubriand observed two centuries ago: 'Try to convince the poor man, once he has learned to read and ceased to believe, once he has become as well informed as yourself, try to convince him that he must submit to every sort of privation, while his neighbour possesses a thousand times what he needs; in the last result you would have to kill him.'9 His contemporary, Adam Smith, the ethicist as well as pragmatist, understood this argument and so argued for equitable disposition of wealth.

Perhaps the single common ingredient absolutely essential to the effective address of the disparity problem is fairness, the criterion chosen by Lincoln. So stated, it is evident how frail are many of the structures and processes now in place and intended to counter or dampen the frustration and the anger of those seeking a better life. Resentment against the perceived exploitation of resources; bitterness against the dilution of cultural identity; rage against indifference, deceit, and double standards on the part of the privileged: these are powerful forces. They should not be expected to diminish in those countries where they are most evident – the South – unless the expectations of the peoples living there are in some measure met. A minimum first step by those in the North is simply taking seriously the concerns of the common people in those countries; a second is the application by the countries of the North of the same standards of conduct they routinely employ among themselves. How seldom are either practised, however, and how cumulative become the resentments as a result.

By what possible standard of measurement can the North justify activities of the following kind?

1 The insistent penetration from the North of tobacco and tobacco products into developing countries when these substances are known to be dangerous to human health, and at a time when their use is declining in the North. (The global incidence of tobacco-caused mortality is already in the millions each year and is projected by WHO to increase considerably in years to come, particularly in the developing countries.)

2 The conscious export to tropical countries of pharmaceutical products or food supplements that are, in some instances, banned in the North, are outdated (and therefore impotent), are thermosensitive (and therefore subject to chemical disintegration when stored in non-refrigerated circumstances), or are subject to flagrant misuse by misinformed consumers.

3 The promotion of the use of toxic herbicides and pesticides, and their packaging with inappropriate or ineffective warning labels, in societies where illiteracy is known to be pervasive.

4 The supply of weaponry, restrainment apparatus, and techniques for their use to regimes known to abuse systematically the human rights of their own populations.

5 The refusal to make available family planning information and technical assistance to countries whose attitudes toward abortion differ from that of militant protest groups in the North.

6 The continuance of ineffective practices to reduce narcotic demand in the North while all the while insisting on ever-more interventionist measures in the South to diminish and interdict production.

7 The interpretation and application of international legal norms in fashions which are discriminatory, arbitrary, or inconsistent with acceptable standards.

8 The use of import quotas and other non-tariff barriers when the cost to the developing countries of the South is out of all proportion to the general level of benefit to the North.

9 The unwillingness to consider 'on principle' mechanisms of debt reduction for the benefit of the countries of the South even as similar techniques 'on principle' are employed within the North in dealing with bank failures here.

10 The shipment to the South of toxic industrial wastes for storage and disposal in order to escape stringent safeguards and costly public health conditions in the countries of origin.

11 The dumping in developing countries of highly subsidized agricultural produce, flagrantly weakening the already frail price incentives for local food producers.

Cumulatively, these practices have led to the description of the North as a 'predatory' economy, even as 'predatory' societies. These are the practices by which the South judges the North, not the simple and often only marginally effective flow of official development assistance. These are the practices which will influence social and economic development, political stability, and environmental wholesomeness much more than the shipment of food aid or the provision of foreign technical experts. Developing country societies for the most part seek only opportunity, and desire it on the same basis as the countries of the North. Are we in the North so lacking in self-confidence that we are not willing to extend to them the same rules of the game that we employ? Are we so afflicted by narcissism that we are unwilling to assess, or be moved by, the impact in the South of decisions taken in the North?

Pause for a moment to consider the benefits to the Middle East – and to long-term stability in the world – had the direct incremental costs of the military build-up in the Persian Gulf been dedicated to *real* development purposes; had the tens of billions of dollars in military concentration and weapons acquisitions been used for irrigation and water enhancement schemes, for indigenous scientific research, for health care delivery, for education. These, not wars, are the solutions to the tensions in the region.

As the Cold War concludes, and the military threat to individual nations in the North assumes differing forms, there will re-emerge the advocacy of those long practised in perceiving international circumstance in military terms. They will argue for the re-equipping and the redirection of military forces. Forgotten will be the military origins of the tragedies of Iran and Iraq, overlooked will be the massive misuse of foreign weaponry in countries all over the world, untabulated will be much more pressing non-military opportunities to use Northern resources in pursuit of Northern – as well as Southern – interests. It will not be easy on either military or economic grounds to convince governments not to accept the old and familiar arguments. The willingness of politicians to drape themselves in the flag of patriotism when public opinion polls encourage them to do so, and the continued truth of Keynes's puzzled conclusion that only war conditions are sufficient to prompt governments to organize expenditure on a massive scale, combine to emphasize how necessary is a forceful expression of public opinion to ensure that the world's new realities are met in the form of new responses.

That expression of opinion must take the form of an insistence on fairness and its most common application, the rule of law. Since the days of the ancients, it has been well understood that advocates of peaceful resolution of conflict and the use of legal norms are likely to be drowned out in the cacophony of war. (Cicero wrote: 'Laws are silent amidst the clash of arms.')[10] At no other time, however, is it more necessary for them to be heeded. Especially is that required of a generation that has created nuclear and other weapons of mass destruction, and which adamantly refuses to constrain their use. To pass the armaments dilemma in its present volatile state to the next generation would be an unprecedented demonstration of arrogance compounded by indifference. It would be the least benevolent of any possible testamentary disposition: the power to end life for no apparent reason.

◆

In years to come, thoughtful Canadians may well regard the summer of 1990 as the beginning of a new era, one not yet understood, one potentially very troubling, one which demanded reconsideration of past attitudes and past behaviour. In a period of a few weeks, this door to the future opened without warning, revealing to Canadians in their bewilderment images of societies of which they had been a part, yet which clearly they did not understand. We were forced to ask ourselves where lay responsibility for untoward events suddenly so obvious: linguistic tensions and native grievances in Canada, historic and economic disputes in countries bordering the Persian Gulf. Inescapably, troubling issues of equity and orderliness, of good faith and reciprocity, projected themselves into the public consciousness. To what degree had we been indifferent to fairness, had we disregarded decency, had we refused to embrace pluralism and cooperation?

Quietly yet pervasively, questions were posed and discussions ensued of a kind not often encountered in the brevity of a Canadian summer. Governments and publics alike were caught wholly unprepared. In vain did one wait for an articulate description of community, for even the simplest pronouncement of those fundamentals of a caring, principled society, of what was at issue in either the Persian Gulf or between the Mohawk people and their neighbours on the banks of the St Lawrence River.

For several weeks prior to the Iraqi invasion and occupation of Kuwait, Canadians had been mesmerized by a quite different occupation, one within two Mohawk Indian communities along this historic water route to the heart of the continent. It began with the expropriation by a nearby Quebec town of a parcel of land claimed by the Mohawks as belonging to the Kanesatake peoples since time immemorial. In response native roadblocks had been set up, initially to emphasize the seriousness of the claim to the disputed lands and those nearby, later to increase the pressure for a satisfactory settlement by blocking access to a major bridge linking Montreal with a populous south-shore suburb. When an ill-conceived police assault was thrown back, and one policeman killed, anger intensified, noise levels escalated, and emotion overwhelmed reasoned debate. What began as an irresponsible seizure of an Indian burial ground in order to enlarge a local golf course was now a symbol of native determination to lend legitimacy to land claims and other grievances from coast to coast. Thousands of frustrated commuters engaged in angry racist demonstrations; sympathetic Indian bands blocked rail-lines elsewhere; Mohawk 'warriors' in camouflage and masks with deadly assault weapons illegal in Canada dominated television and newspapers. A frantic Quebec government called on the Canadian Armed Forces to restore order. Worldwide, the image was projected of an embattled indigenous people confronted by the military might of the majority population. At the height of this impasse, Iraqi troops rolled into Kuwait.

Thus did events precipitate and force Canadians to face the very basis of their communities – one Canadian, the other global. The opportunity presented itself for thoughtful interpretations and constructive applications of the constitutional underpinnings of those societies: within Canada, to understand and define 'community'; internationally, to enhance the effective functions of the United Nations. Instead, as the Canadian Armed Forces were sent into action, in one instance to assault native Canadians and in the other to pursue an unclear mission in the Persian Gulf, Canadians were given a glimpse of what could be their future in the absence of a well-formulated social contract: a future riven with hostility and dependent on the application of force. They observed in the events surrounding both Kuwait and Kanesatake the consequences of indifference to poverty on the part of the privileged when coupled with the unfettered access to weaponry by all who seek to be armed. They saw the ease with which political leaders and newspaper editorialists took refuge in inflammatory language and simplistic explanations. The final decade of the twentieth century had begun with examples of jingoism and bravado, indifference and incompetence, of a kind that would not have been out of place in the Dark Ages.

Thus does the volume of human events cascade onto our consciousness. Not calmly and predictably, not in measured and temperate tones. Suddenly, explosively, dangerously. Yet all too slowly have we come to understand that instinctive responses are unlikely to be either humane or rational. In the absence of involvement and commitment, outcomes can be unpredictable and damaging. In the summer of 1990, Canadians watched with dismay displays of mob violence on the perimeter of Montreal, and military aggression on the shores of the Persian Gulf. They gained the impression that in this warehouse of weapons we call the world, built as it is on the foundations of wretchedness and desperation, the sole policy option attractive to leaders is to act as military policemen. In the space of a few weeks, it became evident that the privileged of the world, wherever they may be, are not invulnerable to the backlash of the dispossessed. It became evident as well that the distress of the unprivileged cannot indefinitely be countered by either indifference or might. Canadians began asking themselves questions of a kind not often raised: Has the human race, in five thousand years of recorded history, learned only to huff and puff, to swagger about in greasepaint and battledress? Are we willing to be revealed by history as a generation that was so indifferent to human squalor and human suffering, so insensitive to human rights and human dignity, that it employed its resources not to relieve inequity but only to counter with force breaches of the peace as they inevitably, and predictably, occur?

This hinge of history on which we endeavour to maintain our balance has posed the clearest of questions: Is the normative model of national conduct and international behaviour to be militaristic? Is power and prestige and preference to be that of unilateral interpretations of law, of equity as a privilege rather than a right? Are human dignity, human decency, human understanding optional qualities, unlikely goals? What weight is to be given social justice, environmental wholesomeness, peaceful resolution of conflict, cultural achievement?

One can express either sadness or outrage at the value systems of the countries of the North that place priority on consumption, that express indifference to violence, that seemingly shun sharing and denigrate compassion. In circumstances, however, where the health and welfare of even the most privileged are now at risk because of rampant infectious disease, potential environmental disasters, ominously aggrieved minorities, and uncertain economic indicators – circumstances which increasingly reduce the quality of life of children and grandchildren now alive, circumstances which in most instances are both predictable and preventable – in these instances one must question more than the value system of this generation. In question is its rationality.

Increasingly, the response to challenge is to blame others: the Japanese for manufacturing better cars, immigrants for changing the appearance of our neighbourhoods, native Canadians for reminding us of the historic injustices they have suffered. As the incidence of AIDS increases, religious bigots find scriptural ecstasy in denouncing homosexuality. As burgeoning populations in Asia demand such basics as household electricity and refrigeration, we thunder warnings about the danger which such improvements bring to the temperature of *our* global atmosphere. As developing countries face increasing economic deprivation and social instability, we preach sermons about the morality of paying debts and maintaining law and order. Our sense of propriety seems limited to protecting *our* jobs and *our* standards of living.

Whether recognized as such or not, these attitudes are images of defeat, of withdrawal. 'Deepen the moat, draw up the bridges, double the guard on the battlements.' We are saying in essence that privilege must be defended against the hordes of wretched who would presume to share. We are admitting the failure of our self-confidence to deal successfully with the most fundamental of problems – the sustenance of humanism.

In the messy, interdependent and unprecedented period of time in which our lives have been set, the intellectual resources of the entire human species must be mustered. The wisdom, the tolerance, the insights, and the skills of every segment of human society can contribute to a functioning, sustainable international community. Yet in society after society, indefensible discriminatory barriers continue to be erected, effectively denying the participation of women, of aborigines, of minority groups. In an information age, governments crave secrecy, and politicians thrive on imagery rather than substance. In an era of perilous international circumstance, we venerate hypocrisy and demonstrate that universality and consistency are still far distant in practice though never before more immediately necessary. In a period of enchantment about a global economy and about the genius of the market, we forget that the abdication of political leadership in favour of the uninhibited jungle of the market is the extreme escape from social responsibility. We forget, too, that development was never originally an exclusively economic concept, bereft of artistic, cultural, and philosophic ingredients.

On the eve of the twenty-first century, there are old lessons to be relearned and new lessons to be thought through. Of the former, none is more basic than that all human life is of value. Of the latter, one of the most difficult to accept is that wars can no longer be won. Taken together, those lessons emphasize our dependence upon one another, the mutuality of our vulnerability to peril, the irrelevance of concepts of racialism and nationalism, the benefits that will accrue when we accept that in distinctiveness there are riches, that among strangers will be found angels.[11]

Are we able, as humans, to respond adequately and in time to these and the other lessons of our age? I don't doubt that we are, but in order to do so we must add a measure of honesty to the humanism so lacking. Not our religious persuasion, our credit ratings, or our biological lineage guarantees that we in the North are the repositories of universal revealed truth. Pluralism, consultation, coherence, consensus, compassion, co-operation – these age-old qualities demand respect and active support. These are the qualities that will create within us an awareness that frustration and indignation are powerful forces; that these forces, when fuelled by economic deprivation and armed by modern weapons, can explode and vent outrageously. These are the qualities that will contribute as well to our realization that for years to come there will be a contest between the advocates of moderation on the one hand and those demanding extremist solutions on the other. In such contests, pendulums tend to swing through wide arcs and dark spaces. They demand some modulating mechanism.

Perhaps, in the final analysis, on this hinge of history, that is the role of all persons of good intent: to modulate the excesses which now threaten our planet and our species; to demonstrate that as individuals we support the simple precepts of justice and decency; to recognize within ourselves that our self-worth rests on an ethical base, one we dare not abandon; to confess that we are human beings, as are billions of others; to demand of our governments the same modulation, the same demonstration, the same recognition, even the same confession. It is the easiest of roles, yet the most difficult. It is central to every religious faith. It has never been more necessary. It is called variously humility, love, understanding. On the eve of the twenty-first century its name is realism.

APPENDIX I

The International Development
Research Centre

The International Development Research Centre (IDRC) was created by an act
of Parliament of Canada in 1970 with a mandate to assist the developing
countries in utilizing science and technology for the benefit of their populations.
The centre's funding is drawn almost entirely from public revenues as appro-
priated by Parliament; it is to Parliament that the centre is accountable. IDRC's
policies are set for it by an independent, international Board of Governors
consisting for the most part of distinguished scientists and developmental experts.
The bare majority of governors (11) are Canadian; the balance are drawn from
ten different countries, seven of which are developing countries. Among those
serving on the Board have been Nobel Laureates and others regarded by their
peers as deserving of highest commendation.

The centre functions in largest part through the funding of scientific research
projects that are identified, designed, conducted, and managed by developing
country scientists in their own countries. It seeks in this fashion to ensure that the
research undertaken and the solutions applied are appropriate for the circumstances of those countries, and that the experience and competence gained
through the research activity benefit local researchers and remain in the country.
In discharge of its statutory mandate to engage in research as well as to
encourage and support research, IDRC from time to time initiates scholarly
investigations.

IDRC is organized in a fashion which permits it to respond effectively and
promptly to the research requirements of the developing countries. The principal calls upon its resources fall into the disciplinary sectors of agriculture, food

and nutrition sciences; health sciences; information sciences; the social sciences; earth and engineering sciences. Interdisciplinary activities are encouraged, and much emphasis is placed on sound environmental policies and practices as well as on balanced gender participation and benefit. While the centre's headquarters are located in Ottawa, the bulk of its international staff function from regional offices located in Cairo, Dakar, Nairobi, Montevideo, New Delhi, and Singapore.

Over the years, IDRC has been the recipient of numerous international honours and awards. Among them is the 'XXIst Century Award' given it in 1988 by the international honours science society Sigma Xi. The accompanying citation reads in part: "IDRC is uniquely responsive to the needs and priorities of developing countries. Its perceptive, imaginative and generous *modus operandi* has profound implications for the stability and well-being of the interdependent world of the 21st Century.'

APPENDIX II

Abbreviations

AIDS	Acquired immune deficiency syndrome
CFCS	Chlorofluorocarbons
CFE	Negotiation on Conventional Forces in Europe
CO_2	Carbon dioxide
FAO	United Nations Food and Agriculture Organization
GATT	General Agreement on Tariffs and Trade
GCMS	General circulation models
GDP	Gross domestic product
GNP	Gross national product
HIV	Human immunodeficiency virus
IDRC	International Development Research Centre
IFIS	International financial institutions
IMF	International Monetary Fund
LIBOR	London Inter-Bank Offered Rate
MBFR	Mutual and Balanced Force Reductions
MFA	Multi-Fibre Arrangement
NATO	North Atlantic Treaty Organization
NICS	Newly industrialized countries
ODA	Official development assistance
OECD	Organization for Economic Cooperation and Development
OPEC	Organization of Petroleum Exporting Countries
UNCTAD	United Nations Conference on Trade and Development
UNDP	United Nations Development Program

UNFPA   United Nations Population Fund
UNICEF   United Nations Children's Fund
USAID   United States Agency for International Development
USCR   United States Committee for Refugees
WHO   United Nations World Health Organization
WMO   World Meteorological Organization

Notes

CHAPTER I

1 Francis Bacon, *Novum Organum*
2 Brandt Commission, *North-South: A Programme for Survival*, The Report of the Independent Commission on International Development Issues under the Chairmanship of Willy Brandt (London: Pan Books 1980)
3 Brundtland Commission, *Our Common Future*, The Report of the World Commission on Environment and Development under the Chairmanship of Prime Minister Gro Harlem Brundtland (New York: Oxford University Press 1987)
4 Saburo Okita, 'The Emerging Prospects for Development and the World Economy' (Third Raul Prebisch Lecture to the General Assembly of UNCTAD, Geneva, 9 July 1987), in S. Okita, *Japan in the World Economy of the 1980s* (Tokyo: University of Tokyo Press 1989)
5 François Mitterand, interview with James Reston, *New York Times*, 4 June 1981

CHAPTER II

1 Robert Ardrey, *The Territorial Imperative* (New York: Athenium 1970)
2 Konrad Lorenz, *On Aggression* (San Diego: Harcourt Brace Jovanovich 1974)
3 Aristotle, *Politics*, i.2.1253a; René Descartes, *Discourse on Method*
4 Senator Daniel Moynihan, *New York Review of Books*, 28 June 1990, 3
5 John H. Finley, Jr., *Four Stages of Greek Thought* (London: Oxford University Press 1966)
6 Gilbert Murray, *Hellenism and the Modern World* (London: George Allen and Unwin 1953), 28
7 See, in this respect, William S. Hass, *The Destiny of the Mind* (London: Faber and Faber 1956).

8 J. Bronowski, *The Ascent of Man* (Boston/Toronto: Little Brown 1973), 217-18
9 As quoted in T.W. Wallbank, A.M. Taylor, N.M. Bailkey, G.F. Jewsbury, C.J. Lewis, and N.J. Hackett, *Civilization Past and Present*, vol. 1 (London: Scott Foresman 1981), 138
10 'Oh, East is East, and West is West, and never the twain shall meet ... ' Rudyard Kipling, 'The Ballad of East and West'
11 Peter C. Newman, *Company of Adventurers* (Toronto: Viking 1985), 90
12 Daniel J. Boorstin, *The Discoverers* (New York: Random House 1983), 177
13 John Maynard Keynes, 'Economic Possibilities for Our Grandchildren,' in *The Collected Works of John Maynard Keynes: Essays in Persuasion*, vol. IX (London: Macmillan, St. Martin's Press 1972), 324
14 See A.G. Gardiner, *The Life of George Cadbury* (London: Cassell 1932), 225-7
15 Winston S. Churchill, *The Grand Alliance* (Boston: Houghton Mifflin 1950), 443
16 This was signed at Washington, DC, by the United States, the United Kingdom, the USSR, and the People's Republic of China, and later adhered to by Australia, Belgium, Canada, Costa Rica, Cuba, Czechoslovakia, Dominican Republic, El Salvador, Greece, Guatemala, Haiti, Honduras, India, Luxembourg, the Netherlands, New Zealand, Nicaragua, Norway, Panama, Poland, South Africa, and Yugoslavia.
17 George Gordon, Lord Bryon, 'Childe Harold's Pilgrimage,' canto III, line 313

CHAPTER III

1 World Bank, *World Development Report, 1988* (New York: Oxford University Press 1988)
2 IMF, *World Economic Outlook*, May 1990, 152, 144
3 *World Bank News*, IX, No. 4 (25 January 1990), 3
4 *Latin American Commodities Report*, 15 May 1990
5 The Multi-Fibre Arrangement of 1 January 1974 involves cotton, wool, and artificial fibres. For purposes of monitoring and regulating, there are 72 categories of textiles and garments. For historic reasons, sisal can be one of the fibres constrained.
6 Fernand Braudel, 'The Perspective of the World,' in *Civilization and Capitalism, 15th–18th Century*, vol. III (London: Collins/Fontana Press 1984), 535
7 Visit to Brazil of the Executive Committee of the Inter-American Dialogue
8 Peter F. Drucker, 'The Changed World Economy,' *Foreign Affairs* 64 (1986), 791
9 Robert Hormats, 'The World Economy under Stress,' *Foreign Affairs* 64 (1986), 457
10 UNCTAD, *Trade and Development Report, 1986*, p. VI
11 IMF *International Financial Statistics, Supplement on Trade Statistics, 1988*, p. xiii
12 Norman S. Fieleke, *The International Economy under Stress* (Cambridge, Mass.: Ballinger Publishing Company 1988)
13 IMF, *International Financial Statistics, 1988*
14 Drucker, 'The Changed World Economy,' 782
15 Brandt Commission, *North–South: A Programme for Survival* (London: Pan Books 1980)

16 IMF, *World Economic Outlook*, October 1989, 99
17 Ibid., 102
18 House of Commons, Canada, Standing Committee on External Affairs and International Trade, *Securing Our Global Future: Canada's Stake in the Unfinished Business of Third World Debt*, June 1990, 1
19 Ibid
20 Bahram Nowzad, 'Lessons of the Debt Decade: Will We Learn?' *Finance and Development*, March 1990, 12
21 J.W. Sewell and S.K. Tucker, *Growth, Exports and Jobs in a Changing Economy: Agenda 1988* (Washington, DC, Overseas Development Council 1988) 10
22 Globe and Mail, 23 January 1988, B1
23 OECD, *Development Cooperation*, 1988, 114
24 Gerald Helleiner, 'The Sub-Saharan Africa Debt Problem: Issues for International Policy,' University of Toronto, 1989 (Mimeo.)
25 Offsetting the large inflows of bank credit in 1981 were large repayments of 'trade' credits. The reduction of these latter during the decade has moderated the impact of reduced bank credits.
26 Nigel Harris, *The End of the Third World* (Middlesex, England: Penguin Books 1987), 143
27 *Securing Our Global Future*, 49
28 Wladimir Andreff, 'The International Centralization of Capital and the Re-ordering of World Capitalism,' *Capital and Class*, Spring 1984
29 IMF, *World Economic Outlook*, October 1989
30 F. Frebel, J. Heinrichs, and O. Kreye, *The New International Division of Labour* (Cambridge: Cambridge University Press 1980), part III
31 David Gordon, 'The Global Economy: New Edifice or Crumbling Foundations?' *New Left Review* 158 (March–April 1988)
32 *Committee for Development Planning: Report on the Twenty-Sixth Session*, Supplement No. 7 (New York: United Nations Economic and Social Council 1990)
33 World Bank, *World Development Report, 1987*, 214–15
34 Robert W. Cox, *Production, Power and World Order* (New York: Columbia University Press 1987), vol. 1, 244–53
35 World Bank, *World Development Report, 1987*, 204–5

CHAPTER IV

1 'Second Treatise,' in P. Laslett, ed., *Two Treatises on Government* (Cambridge: Cambridge University Press 1967), 315
2 *The Seven Lamps of Architecture*, 1849, cap. VI, sec. 9, in E.T. Cook and A.D.O. Wedderburn, eds, *The Works of John Ruskin* (London: Geo. Allen 1903)
3 Henry David Thoreau, 'Walking' (1862), in *Excursions* (Riverside, Cambridge: H.O. Houghton 1863), 161–214
4 *The Biosphere*, A Scientific American Book (San Francisco: W.H. Freeman & Co. 1970), 1

5 National Research Council, *Petroleum in the Marine Environment* (Washington, DC 1975)
6 National Research Council, *Oil in the Sea: Inputs, Fates, and Effects* (Washington, DC 1985)
7 *North–South: A Program for Survival*, The Report of the Independent Commission on International Development Issues under the Chairmanship of Willy Brandt (London: Pan Books 1980), 114
8 *Our Common Future*, The Report of the World Commission on Environment and Development under the Chairmanship of Prime Minister Gro Harlem Brundtland (New York: Oxford University Press 1987), 2
9 *The Changing Atmosphere – Implications for Global Security*, Conference Proceedings (Geneva: Secretariat of the World Meteorological Organization 1989), 292
10 World Resources Institute, *World Resources Report* 1990–91, 102–3
11 Y. Kaufman, C. Tucker, and I. Fung, *Remote Sensing of Biomass Burning in the Tropics* (NASA/GSFC/GISS Code 640, 1989)
12 Alfred, Lord Tennyson, 'Ulysses,' lines 20–21 (written 1833, published 1842)
13 James Whitcomb Riley, *Wet Weather Talk* (1883)
14 *The Changing Atmosphere*, 292
15 International Council of Scientific Unions, Scientific Committee on Problems of the Environment, *Environmental Consequences of Nuclear War* (Paris 1989)
16 This calculation reflects the World Resources Institute figure of CO_2 emissions in Canada: 4.3 metric tons per capita. Were all greenhouse gases included, the figures would have been larger still.
17 F. Pearce, 'Felled Trees Double Blow to Global Warming,' *New Scientist*, 16 September 1989, 25
18 United Nations Environmental Programme, *Environmental Effects Panel Report, pursuant to Article 6 of the Montreal Protocol on Substances that Deplete the Ozone Layer* (Nairobi 1989), 11–24
19 Ibid
20 United Nations Environment Programme, *The Ozone Layer* (UNEP/GEMS Environment Library No. 2; Nairobi 1987)
21 L.D. Grant, *Health Effects Issues Associated with Regional and Global Air Pollution Problems*, Toronto Conference Proceedings (Geneva: World Meteorological Organization 1988), 243–70
22 Mintzer, 'Cooling Down a Warming World: Chlorofluorocarbons, the Greenhouse Effect, and the Montreal Protocol,' *International Environmental Affairs* 112 (1; 1989), 12–25
23 CFCs and halons are synthetic chemicals used in a variety of industrial and domestic applications – refrigerants, foam-blowing agents, aerosols, fire extinguishers, solvents, and more.
24 George C. Marshall Institute, Washington, DC, *Scientific Perspectives on the Greenhouse Problem* (1989)
25 B. Singh, 'The Implications for Climate Change for Natural Resources in Quebec,' *Climate Change Digest* 88-08 (Ottawa: Environment Canada 1988)
26 E.E. Wheaton, T. Singh, R. Dempster, K.O. Higginbotham, J.P. Thorpe, G.C.

Van Kooten, and J.S. Taylor, *An Exploration and Assessment of the Implications of Climatic Change for the Boreal Forest and Forestry Economics of the Prairie Provinces and Northwest Territories: Phase One,* Technical Report No. 211 (Saskatoon, Sask.: Saskatchewan Research Council 1987)

27 B. Smit, 'Implications of Climatic Change for Agriculture in Ontario,' *Climate Change Digest* 87-02 (Ottawa: Environment Canada 1987)

28 G.D.V. Williams, R.A. Fautley, K.H. Jones, R.B. Stewart, and E.E. Wheaton, 'Estimating Effects of Climatic Change on Agriculture in Saskatchewan,' *Climate Change Digest* 88-06 (Ottawa: Environment Canada 1988)

29 L.M. Arthur, 'The Implication of Climatic Change for Agriculture in the Prairie Provinces,' *Climate Change Digest* 88-01 (Ottawa: Environment Canada 1988)

30 Smit, 'Implications of Climatic Change'

31 T. Mendis, 'The Greenhouse Effect; A Plus for Manitoba?' *Conservation Comment* (Manitoba Natural Resources No. 127, Winnipeg), August 1989

32 B. Smit, 'Climate Warming and Canada's Comparative Position in Agriculture,' *Climate Change Digest* 89-01 (Ottawa: Environment Canada 1989)

33 M. Sanderson, 'Implications of Climatic Change for Navigation and Power Generation in the Great Lakes,' *Climate Change Digest* 87-03 (Ottawa: Environment Canada 1987)

34 Ibid.

35 Martec, Ltd., 'Effects of a One Metre Rise in Mean Sea-Level at Saint John, New Brunswick, and the Lower Reaches of the Saint John River,' *Climate Change Digest* 87-04 (Ottawa: Environment Canada 1987); P. Lane and Assoc., 'Preliminary Study of the Possible Impacts of a One Metre Rise in Sea Level at Charlottetown, P.E.I.,' ibid. 88-02

36 D. Ireland, *Effects of Climatic Change on World Industry, Trade and Investment: A Discussion Paper* (Halifax: Institute for Research on Public Policy 1989)

37 S. Wells and A. Edwards, 'Gone with the Waves,' *New Scientist* 124 (1989), 47–51

38 J.D. Milliman et al, 'Environmental and Economic Implications of Rising Sea Levels and Subsiding Deltas: The Nile and Bengal Examples,' *Ambio* 18 (1989), 340–5

39 John Terborgh, *Where Have All the Birds Gone? Essays on the Biology and Conservation of Birds that Migrate to the American Tropics* (Princeton: Princeton University Press 1989), 159

40 Canada is the world's third largest producer of industrial roundwood, and accounts for 60 per cent of all newsprint, 52 per cent of all softwood lumber, and 33 per cent of all wood pulp traded on world markets (1989 FAO Yearbook, Rome).

41 Statistics Canada, *Imports: Merchandise Trade – 1988* (Ottawa: Supply and Services, Canada, 1989)

42 Rachel Carson, *Silent Spring* (Boston: Houghton Mifflin 1962)

43 *United Nations Conference on Desertification,* Nairobi, 1977 (New York: United Nations 1978)

44 'United Nations Convention on the Law of the Sea,' *International Legal Materials* 21 (1982), 1261

45 P.H. Gleick, 'Climate Change and International Politics: Problems Facing Developing Countries,' *Ambio* 18 (1989), 333-9

CHAPTER V

1 Ivan L. Head, 'The Stranger in Our Midst: A Sketch of the Legal Status of the Alien in Canada,' *Canadian Yearbook of International Law* 1964: 107
2 '*Quong Wing v The King*,' *Supreme Court Reports* 49 (1914), 440
3 T.R. Balakrishnan, 'Immigration and the Changing Ethnic Mosaic of Canadian Cities,' University of Western Ontario, 1988 (Mimeo.)
4 On the occasion of the cessation of British colonial rule and the creation of the independent nations of India and Pakistan, see F. Robinson, ed., *The Cambridge Encyclopedia of India, Pakistan, Bangladesh, Sri Lanka, Nepal, Bhutan, and the Maldives* (Cambridge: Cambridge University Press 1989).
5 Ruth Leger Sivard, *World Military and Social Expenditures, 1989* (Washington, DC: World Priorities Inc. 1989)
6 United States Committee for Refugees, *World Refugee Survey – 1989* (Washington, DC 1990)
7 John Winthrop, as quoted by Louis Auchincloss, *The Winthrop Covenant* (Boston: Houghton Mifflin 1976)
8 Euripides, *Medea*, 1.650 (c. 431 BC)
9 Essam El-Hinnawi, *Environmental Refugees* (Nairobi: United Nations Environment Programme 1985)
10 A. Wijkman and L. Timberlake, *Natural Disasters: Acts of God or Acts of Man* (London: Earthscan, International Institute for Environment and Development 1985)
11 J.L. Jacobson, 'Abandoning Homelands,' in L.R. Brown, ed., *State of the World, 1989* (New York and London: W.W. Norton 1989), 59–76
12 This is of a total of seventy thousand deaths overall in the past decade. See Anthony Lewis, *New York Times*, 23 April 1990.
13 H.J. Leonard, 'Managing Central America's Renewable Resources,' *International Environmental Affairs* 1 (1990), 38–56
14 E.B. Burns, 'The Modernization of Underdevelopment: El Salvador, 1855–1931,' *The Journal of Developing Areas* 18 (1984), 293–316
15 G. Foy and H. Daly, 'Allocation, Distribution and Scale as Determinants of Environmental Degradation,' World Bank Environment Department Working Paper No. 19, Washington, DC, and T.P. Anderson, *The War of the Dispossessed; Honduras and El Salvador* (Lincoln: University of Nebraska Press 1981)
16 As quoted in Foy and Daly, 13
17 Leonard, 'Managing Central America's Renewable Resources'
18 Foy and Daly, 17
19 S. Lamb, 'Boomerang of Fortune,' *Refugees* 45 (1987), 9
20 Wijkman and Timberlake, *Natural Disasters*, 11
21 Ibid
22 Hon. Monique Landry to House of Commons Standing Committee on External

Affairs and International Trade, 10 April 1990, Ottawa

23 United States Committee for Refugees, *World Refugee Survey – 1989*, 3
24 Independent Commission on International Humanitarian Issues, *Street Children: A Growing Urban Tragedy* (London: Weidenfeld and Nicolson 1986), 16
25 Michael Harrington, *The Other America* (New York: Penguin 1971)
26 Employment and Immigration, Canada, *Immigration Statistics: 1987*, and preliminary statistics for 1988, 1989, and January–July 1990
27 A.H. Richmond, 'The Income of Caribbean Immigrants in Canada,' in S.S. Halli, F. Travato, L. Dreidger, eds, *Ethnic Demography: Canadian Immigrant, Racial and Cultural Variations* (Ottawa: Carleton University Press 1990)
28 T.R. Balakrishnan, 'Immigration and the Changing Ethnic Mosaic,' 23

CHAPTER VI

1 General Curtis E. LeMay, *Mission with LeMay* (New York: Doubleday 1965)
2 Hannah Arendt, *On Revolution* (London: Penguin 1963), 15
3 Father Mathew Fox, *The Coming of the Cosmic Christ: The Healing of Mother Earth and the Birth of a Global Renaissance* (San Francisco: Harper Row 1988)
4 Obituary, *New York Times*, 17 February 1988, D27
5 See Commission on Integrated Long-Term Strategy, Regional Conflict Working Group, *Commitment to Freedom: Security Assistance as U.S. Policy Instrument in the Third World* (Washington, DC: U.S. Government Printing Office 1988)
6 Thomas Jefferson, 'To the Republican Citizens of Washington County, Maryland,' 31 March 1809
7 Thucydides, *The Peloponnesian Wars*
8 Shakespeare, *Henry the Fifth*, IV, iii
9 Dale Wasserman and Joe Darian, 'The Man of La Mancha,' in Otis L. Guernsey Jr., ed., *Best Plays of 1965–1966* (New York: Dodd Mead and Co. 1966), 213–14
10 *The Challenge of Peace: God's Promise and Our Response – A Pastoral Letter on War and Peace by the National Conference of Catholic Bishops, 3 May 1983* (Washington, DC: United States Catholic Conference 1983), 51
11 Barbara W. Tuchman, *A Distant Mirror: The Calamitous 14th Century* (New York: Random House 1978)
12 *Common Security*, The Report of the Independent Commission on Disarmament and Security Issues under the Chairmanship of Olof Palme (London: Pan Books 1982), 85
13 Ibid, 95
14 Ibid, 76
15 Dwight D. Eisenhower, Farewell Television Address, 17 January 1961
16 Dr George Keyworth, Dinner Address, *R & D and the New National Agenda, Colloquium Proceedings* (Washington: AAAS, June 1981)
17 ACDA, *World Military Expenditures and Arms Transfers, 1987* (Washington, DC 1988)
18 See M. Brzoska and T. Ohlson, eds, *Arms Production in the Third World* (London: Taylor and Francis 1986).

19 Overseas Development Council, 'U.S. Foreign Aid in a Changing World,' *Policy Focus*, 1990, No. 2 (Washington, DC)

20 Brzoska and Ohlson, *Arms Production in the Third World*

21 Ruth Leger Sivard, *World Military and Social Expenditures 1987–88* (Washington, DC: World Priorities 1988)

22 Shakespeare, *Measure for Measure*, IV, ii, 22

23 Theodore H. Whyte, *Breach of Faith: The Fall of Richard Nixon* (New York: Atheneum Press 1975)

24 Winston Churchill: 'I cannot forecast to you the action of Russia. It is a riddle wrapped in a mystery inside an enigma.' Radio broadcast, 1 October 1939

25 George F. Kennan, *The Nuclear Delusion: Soviet-American Relations in the Atomic Age* (New York: Pantheon 1983)

26 'Shun security,' attributed to Thales of Miletus, c. 6th century, BC

27 James Russell Lowell, *Literary Essays* (Salem, NH: Ayer Co. Pubs., Inc. 1972)

28 Karl von Clausewitz, 1780–1831, author of *On War*, who advocated that war was a political act ('diplomacy by other means')

29 *New York Times*, 3 August 1990, A13

30 Hans J. Morgenthau, *Politics among Nations* (New York: Alfred A. Knopf 1948), 32

31 Ibid, 26–7

32 *Globe and Mail*, 20 November 1990, A1

33 Prime Minister's Office, Ottawa

34 S.Y. Chu, J.W. Buchler, and R.L. Berkelman, 'Impact of the Human Immunodeficiency Virus Epidemic on Mortality in Women of Reproductive Age, United States,' *Journal of the American Medical Association*, 11 July 1990, 228

35 *New York Times*, 25 June 1990, A15

36 Barbard Ward, *Spaceship Earth* (New York: Columbia University Press 1966)

37 Bill Moyers, Presidential Inauguration, Middlebury College, Middlebury, Vermont, November 1975

CHAPTER VII

1 Al Purdy: '... then the rare arrival of something entirely beyond us, beyond this repeated daily dying, the singing moment'

2 Peter F. Drucker, *The Age of Discontinuity* (New York: Harper and Row 1968)

3 J. Bronowski, *The Ascent of Man* (Boston: Little Brown 1973), 62

4 Harold Eeman, *Prelude to Diplomacy: My Early Years, 1893–1919* (London: Robert Hale 1983)

5 Abraham Lincoln, Independence Day Address, 4 July 1861

6 *New York Times*, 15 September 1990, A5

7 Pope Paul VI, *Encyclical Letter of His Holiness Pope Paul VI on the Development of People: Populorem progressio* (Boston: St. Paul Editions 1967)

8 Brandt Commission, *North–South: A Programme for Survival*, The Report of the Independent Commission on International Development Issues under the Chairmanship of Willy Brandt (London: Pan Books 1980), 8

9 François-René de Chateaubriand, *Mémoires d'outre-tombe*, vol. VI (Paris: Garner 1924), 451
10 Cicero, *Pro Milone*, IV, II
11 'Be not forgetful to entertain strangers: for thereby some have entertained angels unawares' (Hebrews 13:1)

Index